The Best TOEFL Junior®

저자

Michael A. Putlack

- MA in History, Tufts University, Medford, MA, USA
- Expert test developer of TOEFL, TOEIC, and TEPS
- Main author of the Darakwon *Decoding the TOEFL® iBT* series, *TOEFL® MAP* series, and *How to Master Skills for the TOEFL® iBT* series

Stephen Poirier

- Candidate for PhD in History, University of Western Ontario, Canada
- Certificate of Professional Technical Writing, Carleton University, Canada
- Co-author of the Darakwon *Decoding the TOEFL® iBT* series, *TOEFL® MAP* series, and *How to Master Skills for the TOEFL® iBT* series

Tony Covello

- BA in Political Science, Beloit College, Beloit, WI, USA
- MA in TEFL, International Graduate School of English, Seoul, Korea
- Assistant Professor at Catholic University of Korea, Bucheon, Korea
- Doctoral student majoring in Higher Education Leadership and Management at Luiss Business School, Rome, Italy

The Best TOEFL Junior® LC Intermediate

지은이 Michael A. Putlack, Stephen Poirier, Tony Covello
펴낸이 정규도
펴낸곳 (주)다락원

초판 1쇄 발행 2026년 1월 20일

편집장 허윤영
편집 김민주, 유나래, 김은혜
디자인 하태호, 정규옥

다락원 경기도 파주시 문발로 211
내용문의: (02)736-2031 내선 524
구입문의: (02)736-2031 내선 250~252
Fax: (02)732-2037
출판등록 1977년 9월 16일 제406-2008-000007호

ISBN 978-89-277-0240-5 63740

http://www.darakwon.co.kr

• 다락원 홈페이지를 방문하시면 상세한 출판정보와 함께 동영상 강좌, MP3자료 등 다양한 어학 정보를 얻으실 수 있습니다.

The Best TOEFL Junior®

LC

Intermediate

DARAKWON

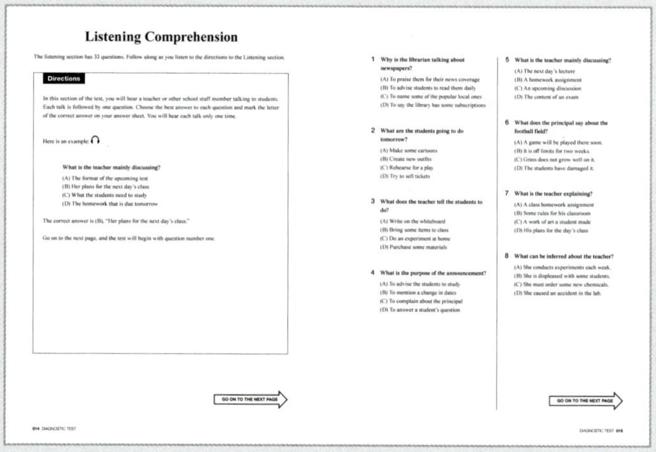

DIAGNOSTIC TEST

본격적인 학습을 시작하기 전에 DIAGNOSTIC TEST를 풀어 보면서 자신의 실력이 어느 정도인지 확인할 수 있습니다. DIAGNOSTIC TEST는 실제 TOEFL Junior Listening Comprehension과 같은 형식과 순서로 제시되며, 문제 수는 실제 시험의 3/4 정도 분량입니다.

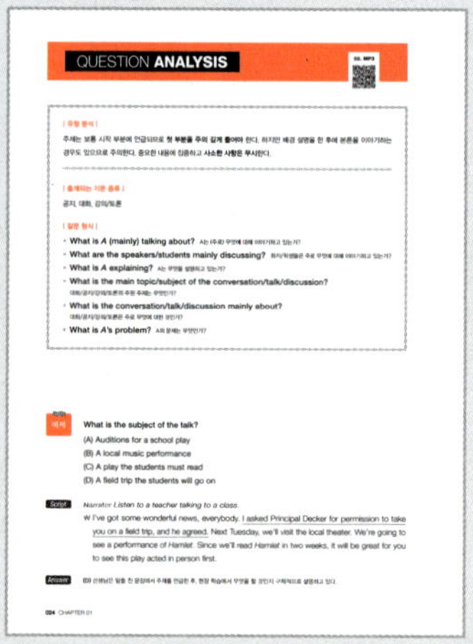

QUESTION ANALYSIS

각 CHAPTER에서 집중적으로 다루는 문제 유형에 대한 분석입니다. 해당 문제 유형이 묻는 것, 공략법, 출제되는 지문의 종류, 질문 형식이 소개되어 있습니다. 또한 예제가 스크립트, 정답, 해설과 함께 제공되어 실제로 어떤 문제가 출제되는지 파악할 수 있습니다.

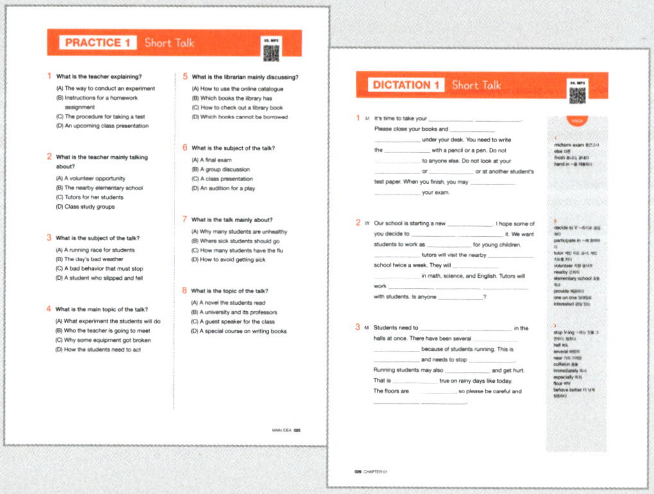

PRACTICE 1: Short Talk
DICTATION 1: Short Talk

PRACTICE 1에서는 공지(Short Talk) 지문에 대한 문제를 8문제 풀어 보고, 이어지는 DICTATION 1에서 해당 지문을 다시 들으며 빈칸을 채워 봅니다. 지문에 등장하는 단어가 오른쪽에 정리되어 있어 단어 학습을 함께 할 수 있습니다.

*CHAPTER 06~07에서는 공지(Short Talk) 지문이 출제되지 않아 PRACTICE/DICTATION 1이 대화(Conversation) 지문으로 구성됩니다.

PRACTICE 2: Conversation
DICTATION 2: Conversation

PRACTICE 2에서는 대화(Conversation) 지문에 대한 문제를 7~8문제 풀어 보고, 이어지는 DICTATION 2에서 해당 지문을 다시 들으며 빈칸을 채워 봅니다. 지문에 등장하는 단어가 오른쪽에 정리되어 있어 단어 학습을 함께 할 수 있습니다.

*CHAPTER 06~07에서는 PRACTICE/DICTATION 2가 강의/토론(Lecture/Discussion) 지문으로 구성됩니다.

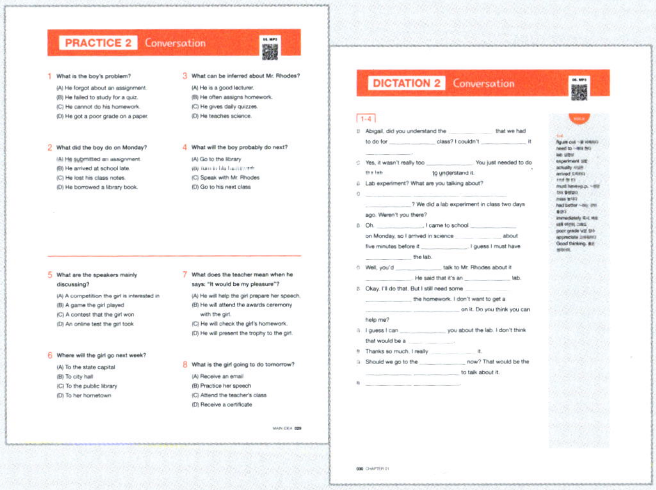

PRACTICE 3: Lecture/Discussion
DICTATION 3: Lecture/Discussion

PRACTICE 3에서는 강의/토론(Lecture/Discussion) 지문에 대한 문제를 8~9문제 풀어 보고, 이어지는 DICTATION 3에서 해당 지문을 다시 들으며 빈칸을 채워 봅니다. 지문에 등장하는 단어가 오른쪽에 정리되어 있어 단어 학습을 함께 할 수 있습니다.

*CHAPTER 06~07에는 PRACTICE/DICTATION 3이 없습니다.

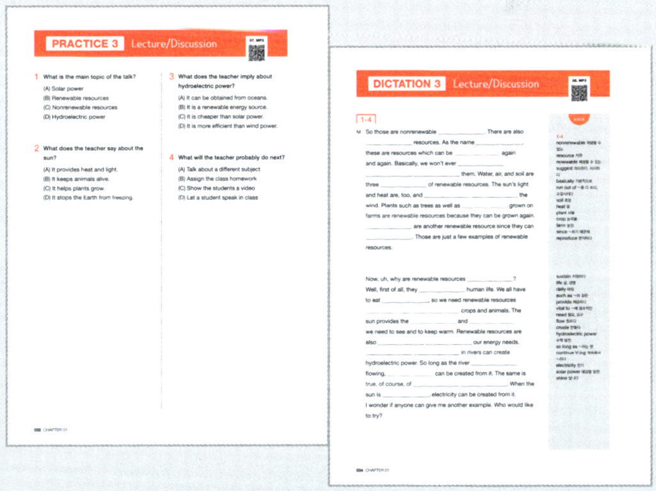

PRACTICE TEST

각 CHAPTER의 마지막에는 실전 TOEFL Junior 시험과 유사한 형식으로 구성된 PRACTICE TEST가 제공되어, CHAPTER에서 학습한 내용을 점검할 수 있습니다. PRACTICE TEST는 공지, 대화, 강의/토론 지문이 골고루 출제되며 총 12~13문제로 구성됩니다.

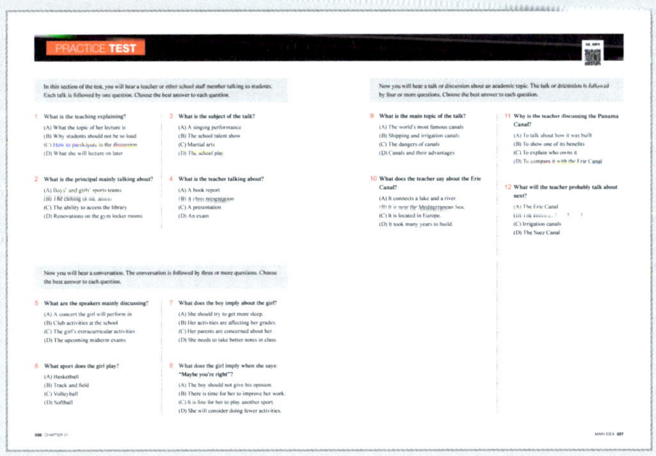

CONTENTS

TOEFL Junior® 시험 소개

1. TOEFL Junior®란?

TOEFL Junior®는 ETS(Educational Testing Service)에서 개발한 영어 능력 평가 시험으로, 중학생 및 고등학생 초반 수준의 학습자를 대상으로 한다. 이 시험은 청소년 학습자의 실제 영어 사용 능력을 객관적으로 측정하기 위해 고안되었으며, 학업 환경과 일상생활에서의 영어 이해력을 종합적으로 평가한다.

TOEFL Junior®는 영어권 학교 진학을 준비하거나 영어 실력을 진단하고 싶은 학생들에게 적합한 시험으로, 전 세계 여러 국제학교, 영어 특성화 중·고등학교, 사립 교육기관 등에서 영어 성취도 평가 및 입학 전형 자료로 활용되고 있다. ETS에서 직접 개발·관리하는 시험이기 때문에 공정성과 신뢰도가 높으며, CEFR(Common European Framework of Reference for Languages, 유럽공통언어기준) 수준과도 연계되어 있어 국제적 영어 능력 수준 비교가 가능하다.

2. TOEFL Junior® 시험 종류 및 운영 방식

한국에서 응시할 수 있는 TOEFL Junior®는 현재 4가지 시험 형태로 운영된다. TOEFL YSS Korea가 국내 공식 주관 기관으로, TOEFL Junior® Standard Test는 일 년에 4회 정기 시험을 실시한다(PBT 기준). 시험을 응시할 수 있는 별도의 연령 제한은 없다. TOEFL YSS Korea 홈페이지(https://www.toeflyss.or.kr)에서 시험 접수가 가능하다.

종류	방식	문항 수	시험 시간
TOEFL Junior® Standard	지필 시험(PBT)	126문항	1시간 55분
TOEFL Junior® Speaking	디지털 방식(IBT)	4문항	18분
TOEFL Junior® Writing	디지털 방식(IBT)	5문항	40분
TOEFL Junior® Digital	디지털 방식(IBT)	126문항	1시간 55분

TOEFL Junior® Standard Test

TOEFL Junior® Standard Test는 3개의 파트로 구성된다.

파트	영역	문항 수	시험 시간	출제되는 내용
PART 1	Listening Comprehension (청해)	42문항	40분	학교 공지 사항, 학교 생활 관련 대화, 강의 및 토론
PART 2	Language Form and Meaning (언어 형태와 의미)	42문항	25분	문법, 문장 구조, 어휘의 의미
PART 3	Reading Comprehension (독해)	42문항	50분	짧은 기사, 이메일, 교과서 발췌문 등
합계		126문항	1시간 55분	

- 시험 형식: 모두 객관식 4지선다형
- 점수 범위: 각 영역 200~300점, 총점 600~900점
- 결과 제공: 총점, 전체 레벨(1~5레벨), 영역별 점수, 영역별 CEFR 수준(A2~B2), Reading에는 Lexile® 지수 포함

전체 레벨	총점	전반적인 수행 능력	CEFR 기준
5 Superior	865~900	복잡한 문어 및 구어 자료에 대한 이해를 일관되게 보이며, 복잡한 언어 구조와 어휘에 대한 지식을 활용할 수 있다.	모든 영역에서 B2 수준
4 Accomplished	785~860	복잡한 문어 및 구어 자료에 대한 이해를 자주 보이며, 복잡한 언어 구조와 어휘 지식을 활용할 수 있다.	모든 영역에서 B1 수준
3 Expanding	730~780	일부 복잡한 문어 및 구어 자료에 대한 이해를 보이며, 기본 수준의 자료는 대부분 이해한다. 기본적인 언어 구조와 어휘 지식을 활용한다.	대부분의 영역에서 B1 수준이지만, 때때로 A2 수준
2 Progressing	625~725	기본적인 문어 및 구어 자료에 대한 이해를 때때로 보이며, 기초적인 언어 구조와 어휘 지식을 활용한다.	대부분의 영역에서 A2 수준이지만, LC와 RC에서는 때때로 A1 수준
1 Emerging	600~620	매우 기초적인 문어 및 구어 자료 일부를 이해할 수 있으며, 기본적인 언어 구조와 어휘 지식을 활용하지만, 이러한 언어 기술과 이해 능력을 더욱 발전시켜야 한다.	LC와 RC는 대부분 A1 수준, LFM은 대부분 A2 수준

TOEFL Junior® Speaking Test

TOEFL Junior® Speaking Test는 4개의 문항으로 구성되며, 총 시험 시간은 18분 정도이다.

문항	평가 항목	평가 내용	시간
Task 1	Read Aloud	짧은 지문을 눈으로 읽고 나서 지문을 소리 내어 읽기	준비 시간: 1분 말하기 시간: 1분
Task 2	Picture Narration	6개의 그림을 보고 그림이 나타내는 이야기를 설명하기	준비 시간: 1분 말하기 시간: 1분
Task 3	Non-academic Listen-Speak	학교 생활과 관련된 내용을 듣고 들은 내용을 말하기	준비 시간: 45초, 말하기 시간: 1분
Task 4	Academic Listen-Speak	아카데믹한 내용을 듣고 들은 내용을 말하기	준비 시간: 45초 말하기 시간: 1분

- 점수 범위: 1~16점
- 결과 제공: 점수, 레벨(1~4레벨), CEFR 수준, 세부 평가 항목별 피드백 포함

TOEFL Junior® Writing Test

TOEFL Junior® Writing Test는 4개의 문제 유형에 5문항으로 구성되며, 총 시험 시간은 40분 정도이다.

문제 유형	평가 항목	문항 수	시험 형식	평가 내용	시간
Task 1	Edit	2세트	4지선다형	아카데믹한 내용의 단락을 읽고, 빈칸에 들어갈 말을 4개의 옵션 중에서 선택	2분 30초
Task 2	E-mail	1문항	답안 작성	학교 생활과 관련된 이메일을 읽고, 그에 대한 답장을 작성	7분
Task 3	Opinion	1문항	답안 작성	질문이나 진술을 읽고, 그에 대한 자신의 의견을 작성(100~150단어)	10분
Task 4	Listen-Write	1문항	답안 작성	그림과 함께 제시되는 아카데믹한 내용을 듣고, 들은 내용을 작성	10분

- 점수 범위: 1~16점
- 결과 제공: 점수, 레벨(1~4레벨), CEFR 수준, 세부 평가 항목별 피드백 포함

3. TOEFL Primary®, TOEFL iBT®와 비교

TOEFL Primary®는 초등학생에게 권장되는 시험으로, TOEFL Junior®와 구성과 방식은 비슷하면서 쉬운 문제로 구성되어 있다. Reading & Listening 시험이 2단계로 나누어져 있고(Step 1, Step 2), Speaking과 Writing 시험이 별도로 운영된다.

TOEFL iBT®는 성인을 대상으로 한 시험으로, 한 번의 시험에서 Reading, Listening, Speaking, Writing 4개 영역을 모두 평가한다. TOEFL Junior는 TOEFL iBT의 준비 단계로 적합하며, 학습자가 국제 표준 영어 시험의 형식에 익숙해지는 데 도움을 준다.

구분	TOEFL Primary®	TOEFL Junior®	TOEFL iBT®
대상	초등학생	중학생~고등학생 초반	대학생 및 성인
난이도	CEFR A1~B1 수준	CEFR A2~B2 수준	CEFR B1~C2 수준
영역	Reading, Listening (Speaking, Writing 별도)	Listening, Language Form & Meaning, Reading (Speaking, Writing 별도)	Reading, Listening, Speaking, Writing
응시 목적	학습 진단 및 수준 평가	학습 진단 및 수준 평가	대학 입학 및 공인영어성적 인증
총점	Step 1: 101~109 Step 2: 104~115 Speaking: 1~27 Writing: 1~17	Standard: 600~900점 Speaking: 1~16점 Writing: 1~16점	0~120점

TOEFL Junior Listening Comprehension 개요

1. 개요

Listening Comprehension Section은 TOEFL Junior Standard test의 첫 번째 영역으로, 학교 생활이나 일상생활에서 들을 수 있는 내용을 얼마나 잘 이해하는지 평가한다. 시험 시간은 40분이며, 문항 수는 총 42문항으로 모두 객관식 4지선다형으로 구성된다. 모든 지문과 질문은 한 번만 들려 주며, 질문은 시험지에 인쇄되어 있다.

2. 시험 구성

Listening Comprehension Section은 3개의 파트로 구성되어 있다.

파트	지문 종류	주요 내용	지문당 문항 수
Part 1	Short Talk (공지)	학교 생활과 관련된 공지 사항 예) 과제 설명, 수업 준비물 안내, 행사 일정 공지, 학생들의 잘못된 행동에 대한 지적 등	1문항
Part 2	Conversation (대화)	학교 생활과 관련된 두 학생 사이의 대화 또는 학생과 교직원 사이의 대화 예) 학생이 겪고 있는 문제 상황, 동아리 활동, 학교 생활 관련 조언, 부탁 등	3~4문항
Part 3	Lecture/ Discussion (강의/토론)	학교 강의 내용, 수업 중 토론, 라디오 교양 프로그램 일부 등 아카데믹한 내용 예) 과학, 역사, 예술, 지리 등 중학 교과 내용	4~5문항

3. 문제 유형

Listening Comprehension Section의 문제 유형은 총 7가지이다.

문제 유형	설명	예시 질문
Main Idea	주제를 묻는 문제	What is the main topic of the conversation?
Detail	중요한 세부 사항을 묻는 문제	What time does the meeting start?
Inference	직접 언급되지 않은 내용을 유추하는 문제	What can be inferred about the student's opinion on the project?
Prediction	지문 내용을 바탕으로 화자가 할 행동을 예측하는 문제	What will the boy probably do next?
Speaker's Purpose	어떤 것을 언급한 목적이나 의도를 묻는 문제	Why does the teacher mention the experiment?
Rhetorical Device	수사적 기법을 사용한 표현을 묻는 문제	Why does the speaker say 'time is money'?
Prosody	화자의 감정이나 의도를 파악하는 문제	How does the speaker feel about the announcement?

4. 평가 방식 및 점수

Listening Comprehension Section의 점수는 200~300점 범위로 환산되어 제공된다. 점수는 정답의 개수에 따라 자동 환산되며, 오답에 대한 감점은 없다.

성적표에는 다음과 같은 세부 정보가 제공된다:

- Listening Comprehension Section점수
- CEFR 등급(A2~B2)
- 강점 및 약점 분석

점수 범위	응시자의 능력에 대한 설	CEFR
290~300	• 학문적이거나 비학문적인 긴 구어 텍스트에서 명시적이든 암시적이든 주요 내용을 이해할 수 있다. • 학문적·비학문적 긴 구어 텍스트에서 중요한 세부 사항을 파악할 수 있다. • 화자의 억양(intonation)이나 강세(stress)를 바탕으로 추론할 수 있다. • 길고 복잡한 말 속에 사용된 관용적 표현(idiomatic language)을 대체로 이해할 수 있다. • 화자가 정보를 비교, 근거 제시, 주장 강화 등 어떤 목적으로 사용하는지를 이해할 수 있다.	B2
245~285	• 언어가 단순하고 문맥이 명확한 학문적·비학문적 긴 구어 텍스트에서 명시적으로 제시된 주요 내용을 이해할 수 있다. • 같은 조건의 텍스트에서 중요한 세부 사항을 파악할 수 있다. • 언어가 단순하고 문맥이 명확한 짧은 구어 텍스트에서 추론할 수 있다. • 비교적 복잡한 말에서 사용되는 일부 일반적인 관용 표현을 이해할 수 있다. • 문맥이 익숙할 경우, 화자가 정보를 비교하거나 주장에 근거를 제시하는 방식을 이해할 수 있다.	B1
210~240	• 명시적으로 제시된 내용이라면 짧은 교실 안내방송의 주요 내용을 이해할 수 있다. • 짧은 발표나 대화에서 명시적이고 반복된 세부 정보를 이해할 수 있다. • 언어가 단순하고 문맥이 명확할 경우, 구어 정보의 직설적 바꾸어 말하기(paraphrase)를 이해할 수 있다. • 짧은 담화에서, 언어가 단순하고 문맥이 명확할 경우 화자의 의도를 파악할 수 있다.	A2
210 미만	다음과 같은 능력 개발 필요: • 안내 방송, 짧은 발표, 단순한 대화의 주요 내용과 세부 사항 이해하기 • 언어가 단순하고 문맥이 명확할 때 짧은 담화에서 화자의 의도 파악하기 • 언어가 단순하고 문맥이 명확할 때 구어 정보를 바꾸어 표현(paraphrase)하기	A2 미만

DIAGNOSTIC TEST

01. MP3

Listening Comprehension

The listening section has 33 questions. Follow along as you listen to the directions to the Listening section.

Directions

In this section of the test, you will hear a teacher or other school staff member talking to students. Each talk is followed by one question. Choose the best answer to each question and mark the letter of the correct answer on your answer sheet. You will hear each talk only one time.

Here is an example:

What is the teacher mainly discussing?

(A) The format of the upcoming test
(B) Her plans for the next day's class
(C) What the students need to study
(D) The homework that is due tomorrow

The correct answer is (B), "Her plans for the next day's class."

Go on to the next page, and the test will begin with question number one.

GO ON TO THE NEXT PAGE

1 **Why is the librarian talking about newspapers?**

(A) To praise them for their news coverage
(B) To advise students to read them daily
(C) To name some of the popular local ones
(D) To say the library has some subscriptions

2 **What are the students going to do tomorrow?**

(A) Make some cartoons
(B) Create new outfits
(C) Rehearse for a play
(D) Try to sell tickets

3 **What does the teacher tell the students to do?**

(A) Write on the whiteboard
(B) Bring some items to class
(C) Do an experiment at home
(D) Purchase some materials

4 **What is the purpose of the announcement?**

(A) To advise the students to study
(B) To mention a change in dates
(C) To complain about the principal
(D) To answer a student's question

5 **What is the teacher mainly discussing?**

(A) The next day's lecture
(B) A homework assignment
(C) An upcoming discussion
(D) The content of an exam

6 **What does the principal say about the football field?**

(A) A game will be played there soon.
(B) It is off limits for two weeks.
(C) Grass does not grow well on it.
(D) The students have damaged it.

7 **What is the teacher explaining?**

(A) A class homework assignment
(B) Some rules for his classroom
(C) A work of art a student made
(D) His plans for the day's class

8 **What can be inferred about the teacher?**

(A) She conducts experiments each week.
(B) She is displeased with some students.
(C) She must order some new chemicals.
(D) She caused an accident in the lab.

GO ON TO THE NEXT PAGE

Now you will hear some conversations. Each conversation is followed by three or more questions. Choose the best answer to each question and mark the letter of the correct answer on your answer sheet. You will hear each conversation only one time.

9 **What are the speakers mainly discussing?**

(A) Their upcoming presentations
(B) The hobbies they have
(C) Their valuable possessions
(D) The skills they have acquired

10 **What can be inferred about the boy's father?**

(A) He collects coins with the boy.
(B) He went to Rome a few times in the past.
(C) He no longer travels abroad for work.
(D) He helps the boy acquire ancient coins.

11 **What does the boy say about ancient Roman coins?**

(A) He usually buys them online.
(B) They are hard to find.
(C) His father gave him some.
(D) Some of them can be cheap.

12 **Why does the girl talk about still lifes?**

(A) To offer to teach the boy to make them
(B) To talk about a painting she just made
(C) To describe her favorite painting style
(D) To say she will learn to make them soon

GO ON TO THE NEXT PAGE

13 **What are the speakers mainly talking about?**

(A) An assignment that the boy will do
(B) The boy's recent class performance
(C) A way for the boy to get bonus points
(D) The most recent paper the boy wrote

14 **What can be inferred about the teacher?**

(A) She teaches the boy history.
(B) She is unhappy with the boy.
(C) She dislikes the boy's topic.
(D) She has to go to class now.

15 **What is the boy going to do tomorrow?**

(A) Submit his final report
(B) Join a study group for the class
(C) Write an essay in the class
(D) Give the teacher a new topic

16 **What is the boy concerned about?**

(A) Not finding enough information
(B) His partner doing a poor job
(C) Being too nervous to speak
(D) His parents not helping him

GO ON TO THE NEXT PAGE

17 **What is the subject of the conversation?**

(A) A group the teacher is going to lead
(B) The girl's performance in math class
(C) A contest the girl went to
(D) The best way for the girl to improve

18 **How does the girl probably feel when she says: "I didn't think the school had a math team"?**

(A) She feels disappointed.
(B) She feels surprised.
(C) She feels pleased.
(D) She feels unhappy.

19 **Why does the teacher think the girl will do well?**

(A) She enjoys competing with others.
(B) She can memorize many answers.
(C) She can solve problems quickly.
(D) She likes performing in public.

20 **What will the girl probably do tomorrow?**

(A) Practice with her teammates
(B) Attend her first competition
(C) Work one on one with the teacher
(D) Study with a math tutor

GO ON TO THE NEXT PAGE

Now you will hear some talks and discussions about academic topics. Each talk or discussion is followed by four or more questions. Choose the best answer to each question and mark the letter of the correct answer on your answer sheet. You will hear each talk or discussion only one time.

21 What is the man mainly discussing?

(A) Some famous airplanes
(B) The principles of flight
(C) Important parts of airplanes
(D) Air resistance and its effects

22 Why does the man mention the *Wright Flyer*?

(A) To say how much it weighed
(B) To note when it flew first
(C) To call it a famous airliner
(D) To point out who invented it

23 Why is the man discussing lift?

(A) To compare it with thrust
(B) To note its relationship with engines
(C) To say how it moves a plane forward
(D) To say how a plane's wings affect it

24 According to the man, what creates thrust?

(A) A plane's wings
(B) A plane's propellers
(C) A plane's tail
(D) A plane's weight

25 What is drag similar to?

(A) Gravity
(B) Thrust
(C) Air resistance
(D) Lift

GO ON TO THE NEXT PAGE

26 What is the main topic of the discussion?

(A) *Moby-Dick*
(B) *The Call of the Wild*
(C) The life of Jack London
(D) Writers of the 1800s

27 What does the boy say about *The Call of the Wild*?

(A) It was the best book he has ever read.
(B) It has realistic descriptions.
(C) It was as good as *Moby-Dick*.
(D) It was full of action and adventure.

28 What can be inferred about Herman Melville?

(A) He influenced the writing of Jack London.
(B) He was the most famous writer of the 1800s.
(C) He wrote a book based on his time on whaling ships.
(D) He was influenced by his time reporting on wars.

29 What will the teacher probably talk about next?

(A) The plot of *Moby-Dick*
(B) A different book by Jack London
(C) The events in *The Call of the Wild*
(D) Another theme of *The Call of the Wild*

GO ON TO THE NEXT PAGE

30 What is the subject of the talk?

(A) Some accomplishments of Captain Cook
(B) The early life of Captain Cook
(C) Captain Cook's third expedition
(D) The reason people remember Captain Cook

31 Why does the teacher mention the Age of Exploration?

(A) To say Captain Cook lived after it
(B) To name some great explorers from it
(C) To call it a great period of time
(D) To discuss some places discovered during it

32 Why is the teacher discussing scurvy?

(A) To compare it with another problem
(B) To explain how Captain Cook stopped it
(C) To talk about how it was once treated
(D) To discuss how many sailors it killed

33 Where did Captain Cook go first on his first expedition?

(A) New Zealand
(B) Tahiti
(C) Malaysia
(D) Australia

STOP

CHAPTER 01

MAIN IDEA

지문의 주제를 묻는 문제 유형이다. 지문이 전체적으로 무엇에 관한 것인지 파악하는 능력을 평가한다. 대화나 강의에서 거의 항상 첫 번째 문제로 출제되므로 매우 중요한 문제 유형이다.

QUESTION **ANALYSIS**

02. MP3

| 유형 분석 |

주제는 보통 시작 부분에 언급되므로 **첫 부분을 주의 깊게 들어야** 한다. 하지만 배경 설명을 한 후에 본론을 이야기하는 경우도 있으므로 주의한다. 중요한 내용에 집중하고 **사소한 사항은 무시**한다.

| 출제되는 지문 종류 |

공지, 대화, 강의/토론

| 질문 형식 |

- **What is *A* (mainly) talking about?** A는 (주로) 무엇에 대해 이야기하고 있는가?
- **What are the speakers/students mainly discussing?** 화자/학생들은 주로 무엇에 대해 이야기하고 있는가?
- **What is *A* explaining?** A는 무엇을 설명하고 있는가?
- **What is the main topic/subject of the conversation/talk/discussion?** 대화/공지/강의/토론의 주된 주제는 무엇인가?
- **What is the conversation/talk/discussion mainly about?** 대화/공지/강의/토론은 주로 무엇에 대한 것인가?
- **What is *A*'s problem?** A의 문제는 무엇인가?

예제

What is the subject of the talk?

(A) Auditions for a school play
(B) A local music performance
(C) A play the students must read
(D) A field trip the students will go on

Script

Narrator *Listen to a teacher talking to a class.*

W I've got some wonderful news, everybody. I asked Principal Decker for permission to take you on a field trip, and he agreed. Next Tuesday, we'll visit the local theater. We're going to see a performance of *Hamlet*. Since we'll read *Hamlet* in two weeks, it will be great for you to see this play acted in person first.

Answer

(D) 선생님은 밑줄 친 문장에서 주제를 언급한 후, 현장 학습에서 무엇을 할 것인지 구체적으로 설명하고 있다.

PRACTICE 1 Short Talk

03. MP3

1 What is the teacher explaining?

(A) The way to conduct an experiment
(B) Instructions for a homework assignment
(C) The procedure for taking a test
(D) An upcoming class presentation

2 What is the teacher mainly talking about?

(A) A volunteer opportunity
(B) The nearby elementary school
(C) Tutors for her students
(D) Class study groups

3 What is the subject of the talk?

(A) A running race for students
(B) The day's bad weather
(C) A bad behavior that must stop
(D) A student who slipped and fell

4 What is the main topic of the talk?

(A) What experiment the students will do
(B) Who the teacher is going to meet
(C) Why some equipment got broken
(D) How the students need to act

5 What is the librarian mainly discussing?

(A) How to use the online catalogue
(B) Which books the library has
(C) How to check out a library book
(D) Which books cannot be borrowed

6 What is the subject of the talk?

(A) A final exam
(B) A group discussion
(C) A class presentation
(D) An audition for a play

7 What is the talk mainly about?

(A) Why many students are unhealthy
(B) Where sick students should go
(C) How many students have the flu
(D) How to avoid getting sick

8 What is the topic of the talk?

(A) A novel the students read
(B) A university and its professors
(C) A guest speaker for the class
(D) A special course on writing books

DICTATION 1 Short Talk

04. MP3

1 M It's time to take your ______ ______.
Please close your books and ______ ______ under your desk. You need to write the ______ with a pencil or a pen. Do not ______ to anyone else. Do not look at your ______ or ______ or at another student's test paper. When you finish, you may ______ ______ your exam.

2 W Our school is starting a new ______. I hope some of you decide to ______ ______ it. We want students to work as ______ for young children. ______ tutors will visit the nearby ______ school twice a week. They will ______ ______ in math, science, and English. Tutors will work ______ ______ ______ with students. Is anyone ______?

3 M Students need to ______ ______ in the halls at once. There have been several ______ ______ because of students running. This is ______ and needs to stop ______.
Running students may also ______ and get hurt.
That is ______ true on rainy days like today.
The floors are ______, so please be careful and ______ ______.

voca

1
midterm exam 중간고사
else 다른
finish 끝나다, 끝내다
hand in ~을 제출하다

2
decide to V ~하기로 결심하다
participate in ~에 참여하다
tutor 개인 지도 교사; 개인 지도를 하다
volunteer 자원 봉사자
nearby 근처의
elementary school 초등학교
provide 제공하다
one on one 일대일로
interested 관심 있는

3
stop V-ing ~하는 것을 그만두다, 멈추다
hall 복도
several 여럿의
near 거의 가까운
collision 충돌
immediately 즉시
especially 특히
floor 바닥
behave better 더 낫게 행동하다

4 W Everyone, please ________ ________. I need to leave the ________ for a few minutes to speak with the ________. While I'm ________, do not use any of the ________ ________. Some of this equipment is very ________. It's also ________ and can break easily. Please wait until I ________ to start your ________.

5 M In ________ to find a book here, use the ________ ________. Searching for a book is very ________. If you know the ________, type it in. If you know the ________, you can ________ the author's name. If you aren't looking for a ________ book, type the ________ you want. Then, you'll get a list of ________ books.

6 W For your ________ ________, you are all going to give class ________. You'll work with a partner on this ________. You must first choose a ________. It should be ________ something we studied this year. Then, ________ a presentation about that topic. Your presentation should be ten minutes ________. If you need any ________, please ask me.

voca

4
Listen up. 잘 들으세요.
be gone 부재 중이다
lab 실험실
equipment 장치, 장비
expensive 비싼
fragile 약한
experiment 실험

5
in order to V ~하기 위해
catalogue 카탈로그, 목록
search for ~을 찾다
title (책·영화 등의) 제목
type in 타자로 입력하다
author 저자
specific 구체적인
subject 주제
possible 가능한

6
final 기말의, 최종의
project 프로젝트, 과제
presentation 발표
partner 파트너, 짝
assignment 과제
assistance 도움

7 M This has been a ______________ semester, so everyone is tired. Please make sure to get ______________ ______________. That will help you avoid ______________ ______________ ______________ a cold or the flu. Your body needs rest in order to ______________ ______________. Don't stay up late. Instead, go to bed early and ______________ ______________ ______________ eight hours of sleep a night.

8 W I have some ______________ ______________, everyone. Tomorrow, we're going to have a ______________ ______________. Her name is Elizabeth Wilson, and she's a professor of English at the ______________ ______________. She's also a famous novelist. Some of you ______________ ______________ ______________ her books. She's going to speak about writing to us tomorrow. I hope you all ______________ ______________.

voca

7
semester 학기
make sure 꼭 ~하도록 하다
rest 휴식
avoid V-ing ~하는 것을 피하다
come down with ~에 걸리다
stay up 깨어 있다

8
guest speaker 초청 강연자
professor 교수
local 지역의
novelist 소설가

PRACTICE 2 Conversation

05. MP3

1 What is the boy's problem?

(A) He forgot about an assignment.
(B) He failed to study for a quiz.
(C) He cannot do his homework.
(D) He got a poor grade on a paper.

2 What did the boy do on Monday?

(A) He submitted an assignment.
(B) He arrived at school late.
(C) He lost his class notes.
(D) He borrowed a library book.

3 What can be inferred about Mr. Rhodes?

(A) He is a good lecturer.
(B) He often assigns homework.
(C) He gives daily quizzes.
(D) He teaches science.

4 What will the boy probably do next?

(A) Go to the library
(B) Turn in his homework
(C) Speak with Mr. Rhodes
(D) Go to his next class

---

5 What are the speakers mainly discussing?

(A) A competition the girl is interested in
(B) A game the girl played
(C) A contest that the girl won
(D) An online test the girl took

6 Where will the girl go next week?

(A) To the state capital
(B) To city hall
(C) To the public library
(D) To her hometown

7 What does the teacher mean when he says: "It would be my pleasure"?

(A) He will help the girl prepare her speech.
(B) He will attend the awards ceremony with the girl.
(C) He will check the girl's homework.
(D) He will present the trophy to the girl.

8 What is the girl going to do tomorrow?

(A) Receive an email
(B) Practice her speech
(C) Attend the teacher's class
(D) Receive a certificate

DICTATION 2 Conversation

06. MP3

1-4

B Abigail, did you understand the ______________ that we had to do for ______________ class? I couldn't ______________ it ______________.

G Yes, it wasn't really too ______________. You just needed to do the lab ______________ to understand it.

B Lab experiment? What are you talking about?

G ______________ ______________ ______________ ______________? We did a lab experiment in class two days ago. Weren't you there?

B Oh. ______________, I came to school ______________ on Monday, so I arrived in science ______________ about five minutes before it ______________. I guess I must have ______________ the lab.

G Well, you'd ______________ talk to Mr. Rhodes about it ______________. He said that it's an ______________ lab.

B Okay. I'll do that. But I still need some ______________ ______________ the homework. I don't want to get a ______________ ______________ on it. Do you think you can help me?

G I guess I can ______________ you about the lab. I don't think that would be a ______________.

B Thanks so much. I really ______________ it.

G Should we go to the ______________ now? That would be the ______________ ______________ to talk about it.

B ______________ ______________.

voca

1-4

figure out ~을 이해하다
need to ~해야 한다
lab 실험실
experiment 실험
actually 사실은
arrived 도착하다
end 끝나다
must have+p.p. ~했던 것이 틀림없다
miss 놓치다
had better ~하는 것이 좋겠다
immediately 즉시, 바로
still 여전히, 그래도
poor grade 낮은 점수
appreciate 고마워하다
Good thinking. 좋은 생각이야.

5-8

G Mr. Gardner, I'm so glad I just ________ ________ ________. I have some great ________.

M You do? What is it, Tiffany?

G Do you ________ that online speech contest I ________ two months ago? You helped me with it.

M Sure. Did you get the ________?

G Yes, sir. And, well . . . I came in ________ ________ in the entire city. I can't believe it.

M ________, Tiffany. You worked really ________ on your speech and the presentation, so you ________ it.

G Thanks so much. There's an ________ ________ I have to attend at city hall next week. I'll ________ a trophy and a certificate there. Oh, there's something else.

M Yeah? What is it?

G Because I ________ the city contest, I now ________ ________ participate in the state speech contest. That's going to ________ ________ in the state capital one month from now. It won't be an ________ event this time. So I was ________ . . . Can you ________ me ________ my speech?

M Of course. It would be my ________. What are you ________ to talk about?

G I'll ________ ________ the topic tomorrow. I'm supposed to get an email from the event ________ then. I'll let you know as soon as I can.

voca

5-8
run into ~와 마주치다
remember 기억하다
speech 말하기, 연설
contest 대회
enter ~에 참가하다
result 결과
come in first place 1등을 하다
entire 전체의
Congratulations. 축하해.
presentation 발표
deserve ~을 받을 자격이 있다
awards ceremony 시상식
attend 참석하다
city hall 시청
receive 받다
trophy 트로피
certificate 증명서, 상장
qualify to V ~할 자격이 되다
participate in ~에 참가하다
state (미국의) 주
state capital 주도
wonder 궁금해하다
be supposed to V ~하기로 되어 있다
find out ~을 알아내다
event organizer 행사 주최자

PRACTICE 3 Lecture/Discussion

07. MP3

1 What is the main topic of the talk?

(A) Solar power
(B) Renewable resources
(C) Nonrenewable resources
(D) Hydroelectric power

2 What does the teacher say about the sun?

(A) It provides heat and light.
(B) It keeps animals alive.
(C) It helps plants grow.
(D) It stops the Earth from freezing.

3 What does the teacher imply about hydroelectric power?

(A) It can be obtained from oceans.
(B) It is a renewable energy source.
(C) It is cheaper than solar power.
(D) It is more efficient than wind power.

4 What will the teacher probably do next?

(A) Talk about a different subject
(B) Assign the class homework
(C) Show the students a video
(D) Let a student speak in class

5 **What are the speakers mainly discussing?**

(A) How people vote
(B) When people vote
(C) Why people vote
(D) Where people vote

6 **What is one reason that people vote?**

(A) To declare war on other countries
(B) To determine their leaders
(C) To show the importance of democracy
(D) To support lower taxes

7 **What does the teacher suggest about the boy?**

(A) He gave a good answer to her question.
(B) He is almost old enough to vote.
(C) He is very interested in local politics.
(D) He should pay more attention in class.

8 **What does the boy say about the election for mayor?**

(A) It is going to happen next week.
(B) More than half of residents voted.
(C) The candidate that he liked won.
(D) A small number of votes decided it.

DICTATION 3 Lecture/Discussion

08. MP3

1-4

M So those are nonrenewable ________. There are also ________ resources. As the name ________, these are resources which can be ________ again and again. Basically, we won't ever ________ ________ ________ them. Water, air, and soil are three ________ of renewable resources. The sun's light and heat are, too, and ________ ________ the wind. Plants such as trees as well as ________ grown on farms are renewable resources because they can be grown again. ________ are another renewable resource since they can ________. Those are just a few examples of renewable resources.

Now, uh, why are renewable resources ________? Well, first of all, they ________ human life. We all have to eat ________, so we need renewable resources ________ ________ crops and animals. The sun provides the ________ and ________ we need to see and to keep warm. Renewable resources are also ________ ________ our energy needs. ________ ________ in rivers can create hydroelectric power. So long as the river ________ flowing, ________ can be created from it. The same is true, of course, of ________ ________. When the sun is ________, electricity can be created from it. I wonder if anyone can give me another example. Who would like to try?

voca

1-4

nonrenewable 재생할 수 없는
resource 자원
renewable 재생할 수 있는
suggest 의미하다, 시사하다
basically 기본적으로
run out of ~을 다 쓰다, 고갈시키다
soil 토양
heat 열
plant 식물
crop 농작물
farm 농장
since ~하기 때문에
reproduce 번식하다

sustain 지탱하다
life 삶, 생명
daily 매일
such as ~와 같은
provide 제공하다
vital to ~에 필수적인
need 필요, 요구
flow 흐르다
create 만들다
hydroelectric power 수력 발전
so long as ~하는 한
continue V-ing 계속해서 ~하다
electricity 전기
solar power 태양열 발전
shine 빛나다

5-8

W We live in a ________ republic, so adults eighteen years of age or older can ________. There are any number of ________ we can vote in. There are national, state, and ________ elections. I know you're all ________ young ________ vote yet. But can you tell me ________ we vote?

B Voting lets us ________ ________ ________ the political process. When we vote, we get to ________ a ________ in who our leaders are. Our leaders make important ________, and these decisions ________ our lives. For instance, they ________ laws, taxes, and foreign policy. If the people we vote for win, then we should see ________ that we prefer.

W I see you have done the ________, Allen. Good job. I know some of you think voting is ________. But do you remember the election for ________ of this city last month? What ________?

B It was a really ________ election. The winner of the election only had five more ________ than his opponent. So people's votes really were important ________ ________ ________.

W That's right. So, uh, basically, if only six more ________ of his opponent had voted, we would have a ________ mayor. Six people isn't very ________ if you think about it.

voca

5-8

constitutional 헌법에 입각한, 입헌의
republic 공화국
adult 성인
vote 투표하다; 득표수
national 국가의, 전국의
state (미국의) 주

political 정치적인, 정치의
process 과정
have a say in ~에 대해 의견을 내다
decision 결정
affect ~에 영향을 주다
determine 결정하다
law 법, 법률
tax 세금
foreign policy 외교 정책
result 결과

useless 쓸모없는
mayor 시장
happen 일어나다

close 접전의
opponent 상대편, 경쟁자
case 경우, 사례

supporter 지지자

PRACTICE TEST

In this section of the test, you will hear a teacher or other school staff member talking to students. Each talk is followed by one question. Choose the best answer to each question.

1 **What is the teaching explaining?**

(A) What the topic of her lecture is
(B) Why students should not be so loud
(C) How to participate in the discussion
(D) What she will lecture on later

2 **What is the principal mainly talking about?**

(A) Boys' and girls' sports teams
(B) The closing of the school
(C) The ability to access the library
(D) Renovations on the gym locker rooms

3 **What is the subject of the talk?**

(A) A singing performance
(B) The school talent show
(C) Martial arts
(D) The school play

4 **What is the teacher talking about?**

(A) A book report
(B) A class presentation
(C) A presentation
(D) An exam

Now you will hear a conversation. The conversation is followed by three or more questions. Choose the best answer to each question.

5 **What are the speakers mainly discussing?**

(A) A concert the girl will perform in
(B) Club activities at the school
(C) The girl's extracurricular activities
(D) The upcoming midterm exams

6 **What sport does the girl play?**

(A) Basketball
(B) Track and field
(C) Volleyball
(D) Softball

7 **What does the boy imply about the girl?**

(A) She should try to get more sleep.
(B) Her activities are affecting her grades.
(C) Her parents are concerned about her.
(D) She needs to take better notes in class.

8 **What does the girl imply when she says: "Maybe you're right"?**

(A) The boy should not give his opinion.
(B) There is time for her to improve her work.
(C) It is fine for her to play another sport.
(D) She will consider doing fewer activities.

09. MP3

Now you will hear a talk or discussion about an academic topic. The talk or discussion is followed by four or more questions. Choose the best answer to each question.

9 **What is the main topic of the talk?**

(A) The world's most famous canals
(B) Shipping and irrigation canals
(C) The dangers of canals
(D) Canals and their advantages

10 **What does the teacher say about the Erie Canal?**

(A) It connects a lake and a river.
(B) It is near the Mediterranean Sea.
(C) It is located in Europe.
(D) It took many years to build.

11 **Why is the teacher discussing the Panama Canal?**

(A) To talk about how it was built
(B) To show one of its benefits
(C) To explain who owns it
(D) To compare it with the Erie Canal

12 **What will the teacher probably talk about next?**

(A) The Erie Canal
(B) The construction of canals
(C) Irrigation canals
(D) The Suez Canal

CHAPTER 02

DETAIL

세부 사항 문제는 지문에 언급된 사실과 정보를 묻는 문제 유형이다. 공지에서는 자주 출제되지 않지만, 대화나 강의/토론에서는 반드시 지문당 1문제 이상 출제되며 2문제 이상 출제되는 경우도 있으므로 매우 중요한 문제 유형이다.

QUESTION **ANALYSIS**

10. MP3

| 유형 분석 |

세부 사항 문제는 **사소한 내용보다는 중요한 내용**을 물어볼 때가 많다. **듣기 전에 문제를 먼저 읽어 보고** 어떤 내용을 들어야 할지 생각한다. 들으면서 내용을 이해해도 세부 사항은 금방 잊어버릴 수 있으므로 **필기**를 하는 것이 좋다.

| 출제되는 지문 종류 |

공지, 대화, 강의/토론

| 질문 형식 |

- **According to *A*, what is *B*?** A에 따르면 B는 무엇인가?
- **What does *A* say about *B*?** B에 대해 A는 뭐라고 말하는가?
- **What B does *A* mention?** A는 어떤 B를 언급하는가?
- **Why does *A* think that . . . ?** A는 왜 ~라고 생각하는가?
- **What is one reason . . . ?** ~한 한 가지 이유는 무엇인가?

예제

What was the boy's presentation about?

(A) Conditions in his hometown

(B) Cleaning up local beaches

(C) Preventing beach erosion

(D) The town council

Script

Narrator *Listen to a conversation between a student and a teacher.*

W Carl, that was an outstanding presentation you gave on the environment today. I was really impressed.

B Thank you. I'm very passionate about the environment.

W I could tell that. You have a lot of knowledge about beaches and how they're being eroded. I liked your suggestions on how to stop that process.

B I just wish people would do more to protect our beaches.

Answer (C) 밑줄 친 부분에 남학생의 발표 주제가 언급되어 있다.

PRACTICE 1 Short Talk

11. MP3

1 What does the teacher tell sick students to do?

(A) Visit the hospital
(B) Go to see the school nurse
(C) Stay home from school
(D) Drink a lot of water

2 What does the school principal say about the cafeteria food?

(A) The quality of the food is poor now.
(B) It will become more costly next week.
(C) The helpings are not enough for students.
(D) It will change every day of the week.

3 According to the teacher, what should the students do?

(A) Prepare a presentation on the human body
(B) Write a report on human bones
(C) Draw a picture of an arm and a hand
(D) Fill in some names on a worksheet

4 Why does the school coach think that the students should congratulate Stephanie Watson?

(A) She became the captain of the volleyball team.
(B) She led the basketball team to victory.
(C) She is the state long jump champion.
(D) She came in first in a running race.

5 What does the teacher say about the students?

(A) They are going to take a test next.
(B) They should work harder in class.
(C) They need to check one another's homework.
(D) They have to turn in an assignment.

6 What does the teacher say the students must do on the test?

(A) Spell and define words
(B) Remember important dates
(C) Analyze some poetry
(D) Understand scientific theories

7 What feature of the program does the teacher mention?

(A) University students will teach classes.
(B) It takes place during winter.
(C) Students will live in a dormitory.
(D) It lasts for six weeks.

8 According to the school principal, what kind of event is the fundraiser?

(A) A bake sale
(B) A fun run
(C) A school raffle
(D) A silent auction

DICTATION 1 Short Talk

12. MP3

1 W I know many people are ______________ nowadays, and that includes students here at school. If you don't ______________ ______________, please visit the school nurse. She can give you some ______________ and let you lie down ______________ one of your parents comes to pick you up. ______________ ______________ ______________ your schoolwork for now. Just try to ______________ ______________.

2 W Your attention, please. Starting on Monday, the lunch menu will ______________ some ______________. We'll have more nutritious food with a ______________ ______________ meat, fruits, and vegetables. However, the price of a meal is going to ______________ ______________ fifty cents. I think you're really going to love the new cafeteria food. Please ______________ your parents ______________ this change.

3 M I'd like to do some ______________ ______________ now. At the start of class, I gave everybody a handout. It's a ______________ of the ______________ in a human hand and arm. Right now, please find a ______________. With your partner, you ______________ ______________ label all of the bones by writing their ______________ names in the blanks. You have ten minutes.

voca

1
nowadays 요즘
include 포함하다
nurse 보건 교사
medicine 약
lie down 눕다
pick up ~을 데리러 오다
schoolwork 학업

2
attention 주의
undergo 겪다
nutritious 영양가 있는
with a focus on ~에 초점을 맞추어
price 가격
meal 식사
increase 올라가다
cafeteria 구내식당
inform A about B A에게 B에 대해 알리다

3
group work 조별 활동
handout 유인물
bone 뼈
human 인간의
partner 짝
label 이름을 쓰다
blank 빈칸

4 W I want to ________ Stephanie Watson ________ her performance at the track meet this past weekend. She ________ ________ ________ ________ in the 100-meter dash, so she is the new state champion. She ________ came in second in the 200-meter dash and ________ ________ in the long jump. Please be sure to ________ Stephanie when you see her today.

5 M Everyone, please ________ ________ your math notebooks and open them to the page ________ your ________ on it. Then, give your notebook to the person ________ ________ you. We're going to ________ ________ last night's homework now. Each person needs to check ________ student's homework. Please be sure to mark ________ correct ________ incorrect answers.

6 M Please ________ ________ that you have a vocabulary test ________ ________ tomorrow morning. You must be able to ________ all twenty of the words that we learned in class on Monday. You should also know ________ ________ of speech they are and ________ their definitions are. The test will ________ ________ fifty points.

voca

4
commend 칭찬하다
performance 성과
track meet 육상 경기
past 지난
dash 단거리 달리기
state (미국의) 주
place 위치하다
long jump 멀리뛰기
congratulate 축하하다

5
beside ~ 옆에
go over ~을 검토하다
mark 표시하다
both A and B A와 B 둘 다
correct 맞는
incorrect 틀린

6
vocabulary 어휘
spell 철자를 쓰다
part of speech 품사
definition 정의
worth ~의 가치가 있는
point 점수

7 W I'd like to inform you of an _______________ _______________ happening this summer. The local university is _______________ a special summer program for middle school and high school students. Students will live in a dormitory _______________ _______________ for four weeks and _______________ _______________ with professors at the school. If you're interested, I can give you an _______________ form.

8 M Next Saturday, April 14, we are having a special _______________ in the school auditorium. It will be a _______________ _______________. There are tons of great _______________ which will be available to bid on. You can see each of them on our _______________ _______________. Please inform your parents about this fun event. All money _______________ will be _______________ to improve the school.

voca

7
inform A of B A에게 B를 알리다
opportunity 기회
local 지역의
host 주최하다
dormitory 기숙사
campus 교정
interested 관심 있는
application form 지원서

8
fundraiser 모금 행사
auditorium 강당
silent auction 입찰식 경매
tons of 엄청나게 많은
item 물품
available 이용 가능한
bid on ~에 입찰하다
event 행사
improve 향상시키다

PRACTICE 2 Conversation

13. MP3

1 What are the speakers mainly discussing?

(A) Their concerns about their final exams
(B) The activities they will do during vacation
(C) The grades they got in their classes
(D) Their favorite subjects at school

2 What does the boy say about his plans for winter vacation?

(A) He hopes to stay home every day.
(B) He is going to visit his relatives.
(C) He will go skiing with his family.
(D) He is taking a family trip abroad.

3 What can be inferred about the girl?

(A) She expects A's in all of her classes.
(B) She has not begun studying yet.
(C) She will study together with the boy.
(D) She does not like Mr. Owens.

4 Why does the boy mention science?

(A) To state that he is getting an A in it
(B) To claim that it is his best subject
(C) To point out that Mr. Owens teaches it
(D) To express his concern about that class

---

5 What are the speakers mainly talking about?

(A) Their plans for a holiday
(B) Presents for their family members
(C) The sizes of their families
(D) The trips they recently took

6 What does the girl imply when she says: "We have school on that day"?

(A) The boy is leaving too early.
(B) The boy will travel very far.
(C) She does not want to go to school.
(D) There is a test on that day.

7 What does the boy say about his relatives?

(A) He visits them every year.
(B) They sometimes travel to his home.
(C) He often communicates with them.
(D) He has not seen some of them in a long time.

8 What does the girl imply about her home?

(A) It is located near the boy's home.
(B) It is not big enough to hold many people.
(C) It recently underwent some repairs.
(D) It can hold more than fifty people.

DICTATION 2 Conversation

14. MP3

1-4

B I'm so ______ we have final exams next week. I'm really ______ ______ ______ winter vacation. My family is planning to ______ ______ for a few days as soon as the last test finishes.

G That ______ ______ a wonderful plan. But don't think too much about your skiing trip. ______ ______, our tests are not going to be easy.

B You can ______ ______ ______. Have you started studying yet? I ______ ______ the first couple of chapters in our science book last night.

G You're ______ ______ me. I was planning to begin reviewing my notes tonight.

B Which test are you the ______ ______ about?

G History for sure. It's my best subject. I seem to have a ______ ______ remembering names, dates, and places.

B Yeah, Mr. Owens loves you, so I'm sure you'll do well in his class.

G ______ ______ ______?

B My best subject is math, so I don't really need to ______ ______ for it. But I'm having trouble in science this year, so I have to ______ a lot for that test. I'm just glad science is the ______ ______ we have to take.

G Yeah, I'll have to study hard for that test ______ ______ to make sure I can get an A on it.

voca

1-4
final exam 기말고사
look forward to ~을 기대하다
plan to V ~할 계획이다
as soon as ~하자마자
after all 어쨌든, 결국
You can say that again. 네 말이 맞아.
a couple of 두어 개의
chapter (책의) 장, 챕터
ahead of ~보다 앞선
review 복습하다, 검토하다
confident 자신 있는
for sure 확실히, 분명히
subject 과목
knack 요령, 재능
date 날짜
trouble 문제, 곤란
make sure 반드시 ~하도록 하다

5-8

G Hey, Jimmy. What are you doing for the Thanksgiving ______________?

B My family is flying out to ______________ my grandparents. We're going to ______________ on Wednesday morning.

G We have school on that day.

B Yeah, my parents already ______________ the school ______________ what we're doing. We're having a family ______________, so about fifty relatives should be at my grandparents' ______________. I haven't seen a few of them in several years.

G It sounds like you're going to have ______________ ______________ ______________.

B I sure hope so. What about you, Tina? Are you doing anything ______________?

G We're not going anywhere because we have some family members ______________ ______________ our house. My dad's brother and his family are coming, ______________ ______________ ______________ my mom's brother and his family.

B That's going to be a ______________ ______________.

G Yeah, it will be pretty crowded, but they're ______________ ______________ for three days. So I think everything will be okay. I'm just ______________ ______________ all of the cooking we're going to have to do.

B Yeah, I'm not sure how we're going to ______________ fifty people. I'm kind of curious how that's going to ______________ ______________.

G Let me know about it when you ______________ ______________.

B Sure.

voca

5-8

Thanksgiving 추수감사절
holiday 휴일, 방학
fly out 비행기로 떠나다
already 이미, 벌써
reunion 모임
relatives 친척들
several 여러
loads of 아주 많은
crowded 붐비는, 사람이 많은
pretty 꽤, 매우
feed 먹이다, 식사를 제공하다
work out (일이) 풀리다
curious 궁금한

PRACTICE 3 Lecture/Discussion

15. MP3

1 **What is the topic of the talk?**

(A) Clouds and their formation
(B) Clouds and weather conditions
(C) Clouds and rain production
(D) Clouds and their altitudes

2 **Why does the teacher suggest that the students look in their books?**

(A) To look at a fact sheet about clouds
(B) To see a picture of thunderclouds
(C) To look at an article about clouds
(D) To see the many names of clouds

3 **What can be inferred about middle-level clouds?**

(A) They usually result in rain.
(B) They include altocumulus clouds.
(C) They can be higher than 20,000 feet.
(D) They bring cool weather.

4 **According to the teacher, what is a stratocumulus cloud?**

(A) A puffy gray cloud
(B) A thin, wispy cloud
(C) A flat, sheetlike cloud
(D) A flat white cloud

5 What are the speakers mainly discussing?

(A) The Louisiana Purchase
(B) The Lewis and Clark Expedition
(C) Native American tribes
(D) The Louisiana Territory

6 Why does the teacher mention President Thomas Jefferson?

(A) To call him a great president of the United States
(B) To point out he was an American Founding Father
(C) To credit him with buying the Louisiana Territory
(D) To prove that he was friends with Louis and Clark

7 According to the girl, what kind of route were Lewis and Clark looking for?

(A) A water route to the Pacific Ocean
(B) A land route over the Rocky Mountains
(C) A land route to California
(D) A water route to France

8 What does the teacher suggest about some native American tribes?

(A) They sold horses to the explorers.
(B) They traded food with the explorers.
(C) They gave gifts to the explorers.
(D) They were hostile to the explorers.

DICTATION 3 Lecture/Discussion

16. MP3

1-4

M The three main types of ________ are cumulus, stratus, and cirrus. Cumulus clouds are white and look fluffy ________ stratus clouds resemble flat sheets ________ in the air. As for cirrus clouds, they're ________ and have a wispy look. Now, uh, you're probably ________ ________ there are more than three names for clouds. ________ a ________ at page 145 in your books, and you'll see names like altocumulus and cirrostratus. You see, the ________ of a cloud is important when determining its name.

There are low-level clouds, middle-level clouds, and high-level clouds. Low-level clouds ________ at an altitude 6,500 feet above the ________ or lower. The word "stratus" is often used for these clouds. Middle-level clouds are ________ 6,500 ________ 20,000 feet above the ground and have the word "alto" in their names. ________, high-level clouds form above 20,000 feet and ________ ________ "cirro" or "cirrus" in their names.

Let's start with low-level clouds first. Stratus clouds are ________ clouds which are ________ and usually ________. They also typically ________ most of the sky but only ________ a small amount of rain. Stratocumulus clouds, ________ ________ ________ ________, are low and puffy gray-colored clouds. They sometimes ________ ________ rain but may also transform into clouds that

voca

1-4
cumulus 적운
stratus 층운
cirrus 권운
fluffy 솜털 같은, 푹신한
resemble 닮다
as for ~으로 말하자면, ~에 대해서는
wispy 가늘게 흩어진, 성긴
aware ~을 알고 있는
altitude 고도, 높이
determine 결정하다, 규정하다

level 층, 높이
form 형성되다

typically 대체로
cover 덮다, 뒤덮다
drop 떨어뜨리다, 내리다
amount 양
stratocumulus 층적운
on the other hand 한편
puffy 뭉게뭉게 피어 오른
result in ~을 가져오다
transform into ~으로 변하다

_______________ thunderstorms. The cloud cover we have outside now is _______________ _______________ stratocumulus clouds by the way.

5-8

M President Thomas Jefferson _______________ the Louisiana Territory _______________ France in 1803. The Louisiana Territory was land _______________ of the Mississippi River and essentially covered the _______________ section of what is the United States today. The following year, he _______________ the Lewis and Clark Expedition _______________. Who can tell me _______________? Tabitha?

G There were _______________ _______________ the expedition was sent out, but three were of great _______________. First, this was mostly unexplored land, so one _______________ of the expedition was to _______________ the land for future settlers. Secondly, Lewis and Clark wanted to find a _______________—uh, preferably by water—all the way to the Pacific Ocean.

M You are _______________ _______________ both of those. And what about the third important reason?

G Well, there were many _______________ American _______________ living on the land. Lewis and Clark were asked to _______________ _______________ _______________ them and to establish peaceful relations. They brought _______________ _______________ for the tribes to show that they wanted peace, not war.

M Right again. _______________ of the tribes the explorers met on the way were _______________, and some even helped the _______________ during its journey.

voca

produce 만들어 내다
thunderstorm 뇌우

5-8
purchase 구입하다
territory 영토, 지역
essentially 본질적으로, 사실상
section 구획, 부분
following 그 다음의
expedition 원정대, 탐험대

of importance 중요한
unexplored 탐험되지 않은, 미지의
task 일, 과업, 임무
map 지도화하다, 표시하다
settler 정착민
route 길, 경로
preferably 되도록이면
Pacific Ocean 태평양

native 원주민의, 토착의
tribe 부족, 십난
contact 접촉, 연락
establish 확립하다
peaceful 평화로운
relation 관계

explorer 탐험가
peaceful 평화적인
journey 여행, 여정

PRACTICE TEST

In this section of the test, you will hear a teacher or other school staff member talking to students. Each talk is followed by one question. Choose the best answer to each question.

1 **What does the teacher say about the students?**

(A) Most of them should take better notes.
(B) They need to study hard for the test.
(C) They are not answering his questions.
(D) Most of them are not doing any reading.

2 **What does the principal say about the volleyball team?**

(A) They won the last game that they played.
(B) They are the state champions.
(C) They have a chance to become champions.
(D) They have tryouts later today.

3 **What does the teacher say about the upcoming test?**

(A) It is the students' final exam.
(B) It will include information from five chapters.
(C) It will not cover information on the handouts.
(D) It will be worth 100 points.

4 **What does the nurse say students who feel like fainting should do?**

(A) Sit down in the shade
(B) Go to the nurse's office
(C) Drink some fluids
(D) Find a cold place

Now you will hear a conversation. The conversation is followed by three or more questions. Choose the best answer to each question.

5 **What is the main topic of the conversation?**

(A) A field trip the girl went on
(B) The girl and her father's weekend plans
(C) The girl's desire to go on a trip
(D) A family picnic at Lake Mitchell

6 **What activity does the girl mention?**

(A) Fishing
(B) Waterskiing
(C) Snowboarding
(D) Ice skating

7 **What does the girl want her father to do?**

(A) Drive her to her friend's house
(B) Sign her school permission slip
(C) Speak with Sandy's parents
(D) Pick her up from school later

8 **What will the girl probably do next?**

(A) Send an email
(B) Go to school
(C) Catch the bus
(D) Make a telephone call

17. MP3

Now you will hear a talk or discussion about an academic topic. The talk or discussion is followed by four or more questions. Choose the best answer to each question.

9 What is the subject of the talk?

(A) Baroque characteristics and composers
(B) The music of Johann Sebastian Bach
(C) The works of George Frideric Handel
(D) The most famous Baroque composers

10 What does the teacher say about Handel?

(A) He was good friends with Bach.
(B) He wrote the work *The Faerie Queene*.
(C) He is a composer that she really likes.
(D) He did not write polyphonic music.

11 Why does the teacher mention Antonio Vivaldi?

(A) To name his most famous work
(B) To compare him with Purcell
(C) To say he was a Baroque composer
(D) To call his music too loud

12 What can be inferred about Bach?

(A) He composed music with Henry Purcell.
(B) Most of his compositions are church music.
(C) He wrote music with flourishes and trills.
(D) He made both monophonic and polyphonic music.

13 What feature of Baroque music does the teacher mention?

(A) It made people feel various emotions.
(B) There were frequent pauses in the music.
(C) It relied upon the piano and the violin.
(D) It featured many symphonies and operas.

CHAPTER 03

INFERENCE

추론 문제는 지문 내용을 바탕으로 추측하거나 추론할 수 있는 사항을 묻는 문제 유형이다. 세부 사항 문제에 비해 난이도가 높기 때문에 고득점을 받기 위해 반드시 공략해야 하는 문제 유형이다.

QUESTION **ANALYSIS**

18. MP3

| 유형 분석 |

추론 문제의 정답은 지문 내에 직접적으로 언급되지 않고, **간접적으로 암시**되거나 **둘 이상의 정보를 연결**해서 추론해야 한다. 그러므로 말의 **숨은 의미**를 파악할 수 있어야 하고, 따로 언급된 정보를 연결지어 생각하는 능력이 요구된다.

| 출제되는 지문 종류 |

공지, 대화, 강의/토론

| 질문 형식 |

- **What does *A* imply about *B*?** A는 B에 대해 무엇을 암시하는가?
- **What can be inferred about *B*?** B에 대해 무엇을 추론할 수 있는가?
- **What is probably true about *B*?** B에 대해 아마도 사실인 것은 무엇인가?
- **What does *A* suggest about *B*?** A는 B에 대해 무엇을 넌지시 드러내는가?

예제 What is probably true about deserts?

(A) They are located far from oceans.
(B) They have temperatures that vary.
(C) They have conditions ideal for life.
(D) They are slowly increasing in size.

Script Narrator *Listen to a talk in a science class.*

M Around seventy percent of the Earth's surface is covered by water. The rest, of course, is land. Of that land, approximately twenty percent of it is desert. All of the Earth's continents—even Antarctica—have deserts. Ah, before I go any further, I should define what a desert is. It's simply an area of land—hot or cold—that receives very little or no precipitation on a yearly basis. Scientists differ on what the amount of precipitation is. Some say it's only twenty centimeters of rain. I, however, say that fifty or fewer centimeters a year qualifies as a desert.

Answer (B) 밑줄 친 부분 중 사막이 "hot or cold"할 수 있다는 말에서 사막의 기온이 변동한다는 것을 추론할 수 있다.

PRACTICE 1 Short Talk

19. MP3

1 What can be inferred about the students?

(A) They do not have ID numbers yet.
(B) They are not using the computers correctly.
(C) They are new students at the school.
(D) They are good at using computers.

2 What is probably true about the teacher?

(A) He often gives the students handouts.
(B) He assigns homework every week.
(C) He expects the students to take notes.
(D) He responds to email from students.

3 What does the teacher suggest about the students?

(A) They should study during the holiday.
(B) They must submit a report next week.
(C) Many of them will travel this weekend.
(D) They are expected at school on Monday.

4 What can be inferred about the teacher?

(A) He is disappointed with the students' performance.
(B) He is concerned about the environment.
(C) He grades the students' papers with a pen.
(D) He plans to return the students' papers this week.

5 What is probably true about the coach?

(A) She is happy with the team's performance.
(B) She believes the team is going to lose.
(C) She thinks the team needs to shoot better.
(D) She wants number ten to play harder.

6 What can be inferred about the librarian?

(A) He will donate some of his own books.
(B) He has already ordered new books.
(C) He will hold a fundraiser for the library.
(D) He has to throw away many books.

7 What is probably true about the students?

(A) They have to pay for food with cash tomorrow.
(B) They must prepare their own lunches tomorrow.
(C) They cannot eat in the cafeteria tomorrow.
(D) They must find a new way to get snacks tomorrow.

8 What can be inferred about the teacher?

(A) He expects many students to see the play.
(B) He is the director of the student play.
(C) He has a role in the school play tonight.
(D) He teaches several performers in the play.

DICTATION 1 Short Talk

20. MP3

1 W It's ______ ______ create a username. All students here need ______ to log on to and to use school computers ______ they graduate. First, look at the ______ of the screen. Click on "New User" right now. A new screen will ______. Please type your name and student ______ ______ into the correct boxes and then ______ the enter button.

2 M Before you leave, I have an announcement ______ ______. If you are absent, it is your responsibility to ______ ______ what you missed in class. This includes any ______ ______. You can check the class website, ask a ______, or even email me. Absence is not an ______ ______ not doing assignments. Does everyone understand?

3 W We have a long weekend ______ ______, so I know everyone is happy. However, we will have our ______ ______ on Tuesday. Even though Monday is a holiday, I still ______ you ______ be prepared for the test. There's nothing I can do about the test ______, so please don't ask. Just come here ______ ______ the test, and you'll do well.

voca

1
create 만들다, 생성하다
username 사용자 이름
log on 로그인하다
graduate 졸업하다
appear 나타나다
type 입력하다

2
announcement 공지
absent 결석한
responsibility 책임
find out ~을 알아내다
miss 놓치다
include 포함하다
assignment 과제
classmate 같은 반 친구
absence 결석
excuse 변명, 핑계

3
however 그러나, 하지만
midterm exam 중간고사
holiday 공휴일, 휴일
still 여전히, 그래도
expect A to V A가 ~하기를 기대하다

4 M I ______________ ______________ want you to print your reports and then submit them to me ______________ ______________. Instead, I would prefer that you ______________ them to me before the due date. It's ______________ for me to read your reports and to make ______________ to them on the computer. Plus, we should ______________ ______________ ______________ to reduce paper usage to help save forests.

5 W You're doing wonderfully now. We're ten ______________ ______________, but we still have an entire ______________ of basketball to play. Just keep ______________ the ball and taking open ______________ when you have them. We need to ______________ number ten on their team. She's ______________ a lot, so we're going to double-team her ______________ ______________ she gets the ball.

6 M As you all know, the library ______________ water damage during the ______________ this past weekend. A large percentage of our ______________ has been ruined, so those books are ______________ now. We need more books ______________ ______________, but we don't have enough money to ______________ many. Please consider ______________ any unwanted books at home to the library.

voca

4
no longer 더 이상 ~ 않다
submit 제출하다
in person 직접
prefer 선호하다
due date 마감일
correction 수정
do one's part ~의 몫을 하다, 힘쓰다
reduce 줄이다
usage 사용

5
wonderfully 훌륭하게
entire 전체의
pass 넘기다, 패스하다
open shot 수비의 방해를 받지 않는 슛
score 점수를 내다
double-team 더블팀을 하다(두 명이 수비하다)
every time ~할 때마다

6
suffer 당하다, 겪다
damage 손상, 피해
storm 폭풍
percentage 비율
collection 소장 도서
ruin 파괴하다, 망치다
unreadable 읽을 수 없는
at once 즉시, 당장
purchase 구입하다
consider V-ing ~할 것을 고려하다
donate 기부하다
unwanted 필요 없는

7 W Your attention, please. Tomorrow, you will ______ ______ ______ ______ use any of the vending machines to buy drinks and snacks in the cafeteria or ______ ______ in the school. All of the machines are being ______. So one company will remove them in the morning, and a ______ ______ will install new machines in the afternoon. Please make ______ arrangements.

8 M Let me remind you that the ______ ______ is being held tonight at 8:00. I ______ everybody ______ attend to support our student actors. The students have ______ ______ rehearsing for the past two months. I know they're going to ______ ______ a great show. Be sure to ______ the performers ______ ______ if you see them today.

voca

7
attention 주의
vending machine 자동 판매기, 자판기
cafeteria 구내식당
replace 교체하다
remove 제거하다
install 설치하다
alternative 대안의
arrangement 준비, 마련

8
remind 상기시키다
play 연극
urge 촉구하다, 권하다
attend 참석하다
support 응원하다
actor 배우
rehearse 연습하다
put on (공연을) 무대에 올리다
performer 공연자

PRACTICE 2 Conversation

21. MP3

1 What is the girl's problem?

(A) One of her classes is not hard enough.
(B) She cannot understand some material.
(C) She cannot fit a class into her schedule.
(D) One of her teachers dislikes her.

2 What can be inferred about the girl?

(A) She just moved to a new school.
(B) She is talented at math.
(C) She likes speaking up in class.
(D) She usually does her homework.

3 What does the student want to do?

(A) Write a report for extra credit
(B) Go on a school field trip
(C) Take more classes than usual
(D) Change one of her classes

4 What does the student imply when she says: "I've never spoken to her before"?

(A) She does not speak in Ms. Weston's class.
(B) She heard that Ms. Weston is unfriendly.
(C) She cannot find Ms. Weston's office.
(D) She wants an introduction to Ms. Weston.

---

5 What are the students mainly discussing?

(A) Their dinner plans
(B) Mr. Sorenson's class
(C) Their weekend activities
(D) A movie they watched

6 What does the girl mean when she says: "Don't waste your time on it"?

(A) Some food tasted bad.
(B) A movie was not good.
(C) A class is not fun.
(D) A book is very boring.

7 What did the boy do with his family?

(A) He celebrated a birthday.
(B) He watched a movie.
(C) He went to the beach.
(D) He cooked dinner at home.

8 What can be inferred about Mr. Sorenson?

(A) He is the school's history teacher.
(B) He is going to give the students a test.
(C) He saw the boy at the shopping center last weekend.
(D) He gets upset when students are late for his class.

DICTATION 2 Conversation

22. MP3

1-4

M Hello, Katie. Ms. Kingwood said you've been ______________ ______________ me all day. What can I do for you?

G Good afternoon, sir. I need to talk about my math class.

M ______________ ______________, please . . . Which math class are you enrolled in, and who's your ______________?

G I'm taking Algebra 1 with Mr. Jefferson. I'm in his class in third ______________.

M Ah, that's right. So . . . what's wrong with his class? Are you ______________ ______________ understanding the material?

G On the contrary, the class is too ______________. I mean, uh, I haven't ______________ a single question in the three weeks I've been taking it. I also ______________ ______________ the book. I already know how to do everything we'll be ______________ this year.

M I see. So you'd like to take a ______________ class. Is that correct?

G Yes, sir. I'd love to take Ms. Weston's ______________ algebra class. She teaches it during third period, so it ______________ ______________ with my schedule. But I was told I need to get her ______________ as well as yours to take the class. And, uh . . . I've never ______________ to her before.

M Ah, sure. Why don't we go and ______________ a ______________ with her now? She's on ______________, so she should be in her office.

G Thank you, sir.

voca

1-4

remind 상기시키다, 기억나게 하다
enroll 등록하다
instructor 교사, 강사
algebra 대수학
period 교시
material 내용
on the contrary 반대로
miss 놓치다, 틀리다
advanced 고급의
fit 들어맞다
perfectly 완벽하게
permission 허락, 승인
on break 쉬는 중인
office 사무실

5-8

B Wendy, were you at the ________ ________ on Sunday evening? I thought I saw you there.

G Yeah, I went there with a ________ ________ my friends. Where did you see me?

B You were ________ the movie theater around, uh, seven.

G David, Cathy, and I were ________ ________ go in to watch a movie. We saw that new ________ movie everyone is talking about.

B Cool. How was it?

G Don't ________ your ________ ________ it.

B Oh . . . That's too bad. I was thinking of seeing it later this week.

G What were you doing at the mall? You ________ ________ ________ ________ and said hi to us.

B I couldn't. I was with my parents and my grandmother. It was my mother's ________, so we had dinner at the new Italian restaurant on the third floor. It was ________ good. You ought to ________ ________ ________ if you can.

G Thanks for the ________. I'll let my parents know ________ ________ ________. They were discussing going out to eat tonight.

B Sounds good. ________, the bell is about to ring. I'd better ________ ________ my class. You know how Mr. Sorenson gets when students ________ after the bell.

G You don't have to remind me. See you at lunch.

voca

5-8

about to V 막 ~하려고 하는
waste 낭비하다
should have+p.p. ~했어야 했다
come over 가까이 오다
say hi 인사하다
amazingly 굉장히
ought to ~해야 하다
check out 가 보다
tip 조언, 정보
discuss V-ing ~할 것을 의논하다
anyway 어쨌든
arrive 도착하다

PRACTICE 3 Lecture/Discussion

23. MP3

1 What is the purpose of the talk?

(A) To focus on whale hunting methods
(B) To discuss individual whale species
(C) To describe two types of whales
(D) To talk about endangered whales

2 What can be inferred about baleen whales?

(A) Large fish are not in their diets.
(B) They prefer to live in warm water.
(C) Most of them are average sized.
(D) They can dive deep in the ocean.

3 Why does the man mention dolphins?

(A) To describe the pods they travel in
(B) To say that they are toothed whales
(C) To mention the type of food they eat
(D) To talk about their hunting methods

4 What will the man probably talk about next?

(A) Food that killer whales eat
(B) Places baleen whales live
(C) Toothed whale pods
(D) Porpoises and dolphins

5 **What is the subject of the discussion?**

(A) Henry Ford
(B) Worker specialization
(C) The Ford Motor Company
(D) The assembly line

6 **What does the boy imply about Henry Ford?**

(A) He built more cars than any other person.
(B) He improved specialization with the assembly line.
(C) He made cars popular with regular Americans.
(D) He was the inventor of the assembly line.

7 **According to the teacher, how fast could one Model T be made?**

(A) One hour
(B) One and a half hours
(C) Two hours
(D) Two and a half hours

8 **Why does the boy talk about specialization?**

(A) To name one effect of the assembly line
(B) To show how it helped prices decline
(C) To argue that it decreased quality
(D) To point out how it made wages increase

DICTATION 3 Lecture/Discussion

24. MP3

1-4

M There are ________ ________ eighty species of whales, including blue whales, sperm whales, killer whales, and narwhals. Whales can be found ________ in all of the world's oceans. Some species are ________ the largest animals ever to live on the Earth. For instance, the largest blue whale ever ________ was 111 feet long. Some blue whales can ________ up to 200 tons, too.

Whales are ________ into two separate types: baleen whales and toothed whales. There are fourteen species of baleen whales, ________ ________ blue whales, humpback whales, and fin whales. Baleen whales ________ to be larger than toothed whales. Despite their ________ sizes, baleen whales mostly eat krill, a small shrimp-like crustacean. Baleen are plates ________ of keratin found in the mouths of baleen whales. Basically, when they feed, baleen whales open their mouths and ________ ________ large amounts of water. When they expel the water, their baleen ________ ________ krill, zooplankton, and various small fish, which they eat.

Toothed whales are all of ________ ________ whales. Among them are sperm whales, killer whales, dolphins, and porpoises. They are social animals and often live in ________ called pods. Toothed whales actively hunt fish and marine ________ in the oceans. However, the types of creatures they pursue ________. For instance, sperm whales dive deep to hunt ________ ________. What about killer whales?

voca

1-4

species 종
including ~을 포함하여
blue whale 흰긴수염고래
sperm whale 향유고래
killer whale 흰줄박이물돼지
narwhal 일각고래
for instance 예를 들어
record 기록하다
weigh 무게가 ~이다
up to ~까지

divide 나누다, 분류하다
separate 별개의
baleen 수염 고래의 여과판
toothed 이빨이 있는
humpback 혹등
fin 지느러미
tend to V ~하는 경향이 있다
despite ~에도 불구하고
enormous 거대한
krill 크릴
crustacean 갑각류
plate 판
keratin 케라틴
basically 기본적으로
take in ~을 받아들이다
expel 내뿜다
filter out ~을 여과하다
zooplankton 동물성 플랑크톤

porpoise 참돌고래
social 사회적인
actively 활발히
marine 해양의
creature 생물
pursue 추적하다
differ 다르다

5-8

W Many people believe Henry Ford invented the ____________ ____________. They are mistaken, but Ford did make great use of it by ____________ the Model T, a type of car, on it. We're going to talk more about the assembly line later, but I'd like to ____________ ____________ what you know about it. Who can tell me what some of its ____________ are? Jeff, your hand is up.

B It makes the production process ____________ ____________ ____________ because each worker specializes in just one or two tasks. Before the assembly line, a single person ____________ ____________ ____________ every step of the manufacturing process. This was a very slow ____________ of making things. But when Ford's workers began ____________ ____________ specific tasks, they could produce cars or other objects quickly.

W Correct, Jeff. By 1913, ____________ ____________ the assembly line, the Ford Motor Company was able to make a single Model T in around ninety-three minutes. ____________ ____________. A single car made in an hour and a half. That ____________ ____________ ____________ unthinkable merely ten or twenty years earlier.

B I also want to say that the assembly line ____________ ____________ the quality of manufactured goods. Because workers were so ____________ at their tasks, they did those tasks well. So ____________ became standardized.

W A very good point. Who can tell me what some ____________ of this standardization of parts were?

voca

5-8
invent 발명하다
assembly line 조립 라인
mistaken 잘못 생각하는
make use of ~을 이용하다
manufacture 제조하다
advantage 장점, 이점

production 생산
process 과정
specializes in ~을 전문으로 하다
task 업무, 작업
involve 관여하게 하다
step 단계
specific 특정한
produce 생산하다
object 물건, 제품

thanks to ~ 덕분에
imagine 상상하다
would have+p.p. ~했을 것이다
unthinkable 생각할 수 없는
merely 단지, 겨우

improve 개선하다, 향상시키다
quality 품질
goods 상품, 제품
part 부품
standardize 표준화하다

results 결과
standardization 표준화

PRACTICE **TEST**

In this section of the test, you will hear a teacher or other school staff member talking to students. Each talk is followed by one question. Choose the best answer to each question.

1 **What does the teacher imply about the birthday parties?**

(A) They have always been allowed.
(B) They may last for up to one hour.
(C) They should happen after classes end.
(D) They may be held at different times.

2 **What can be inferred about the nurse?**

(A) He has touched poison ivy before.
(B) He walks in the forest every day.
(C) He has a rash from poison ivy now.
(D) He has medicine to treat poison ivy.

3 **What is probably true about the teacher?**

(A) She dislikes interruptions in class.
(B) She wants her students to take notes.
(C) She allows students to ask questions.
(D) She ignores students talking in class.

4 **What can be inferred about Mr. Wilson?**

(A) He teaches history at the school.
(B) He started at the school this summer.
(C) He is familiar with musical instruments.
(D) He will hold band practice every day.

Now you will hear a conversation. The conversation is followed by three or more questions. Choose the best answer to each question.

5 **What is the main topic of the conversation?**

(A) Where the family is having dinner
(B) What the boy needs to do next
(C) What the mother needs to cook
(D) How the boy should act tonight

6 **What does the mother say about Mr. Rogers?**

(A) He is hosting a dinner at his house.
(B) He has met her before in the past.
(C) He will arrive at five o'clock.
(D) He is visiting their home tonight.

7 **What does the mother imply about the boy?**

(A) He can be forgetful at times.
(B) He seldom cleans his room.
(C) He just arrived home from school.
(D) He should help her cook dinner.

8 **What will the boy probably do next?**

(A) Visit the supermarket
(B) Help make dinner
(C) Clean up his living room
(D) Set the table

25. MP3

Now you will hear a talk or discussion about an academic topic. The talk or discussion is followed by four or more questions. Choose the best answer to each question.

9 What is the teacher mainly talking about?

(A) The remains of Hadrian's Wall
(B) The effectiveness of Hadrian's Wall
(C) The construction of Hadrian's Wall
(D) The battles at Hadrian's Wall

10 What does the teacher say about Hadrian's Wall?

(A) It took twenty years to construct.
(B) It had walls up to twenty feet high.
(C) It was guarded by 600 soldiers.
(D) It required 10,000 soldiers to build it.

11 Why does the teacher mention the forts on Hadrian's Wall?

(A) To state that some are still standing
(B) To describe how tall they were
(C) To explain how the Romans built them
(D) To say how many soldiers they held

12 What can be inferred about the teacher?

(A) He has visited Hadrian's Wall in person.
(B) He thinks Hadrian's Wall was not effective.
(C) He finds Roman construction impressive.
(D) He believes Hadrian's Wall was built quickly.

CHAPTER 04

PREDICTION

예측 문제는 지문 내용을 바탕으로 화자가 어떤 행동을 할 것인지, 또는 무엇에 대해 이야기할 것인지를 추측하는 문제 유형이다. 난이도는 높지 않은 편이므로 지문을 집중해서 듣는다면 쉽게 정답을 찾을 수 있다.

QUESTION **ANALYSIS**

26. MP3

| 유형 분석 |

추측 문제의 경우, **공지에서는 지문의 초반부 또는 마지막**에, **대화나 강의/토론에서는 후반부**에서 단서가 제시되는 경우가 많다. 대화에서는 화자가 할 일이 여러 가지가 언급되는 경우가 있으므로, **'언제'** 어떤 행동을 할 것인지도 유의해서 들어야 한다.

| 출제되는 지문 종류 |

공지, 대화, 강의/토론

| 질문 형식 |

- **What will *A* probably do next?** A는 다음에 아마도 무엇을 할 것인가?
- **What is *A* going to do after school today?** A는 오늘 방과 후에 무엇을 할 것인가?
- **What will *A* probably talk about next?** A는 다음에 아마도 무엇에 대해 이야기할 것인가?

예제

What are the students going to do tomorrow?

(A) Listen to a lecture on trees

(B) Watch a movie in class

(C) Display their leaf collections

(D) Spend some time outside

Script

Narrator *Listen to a science teacher talking to a class.*

M You need to learn to identify different types of trees. So in tomorrow's class, we'll go into the forest by the school. Be sure to bring your tree identification books to school. We'll look at the leaves and bark of different trees and try to identify them. It's going to be both educational and lots of fun.

Answer

(D) 밑줄 친 부분에서 학생들이 내일 할 일이 언급된다. 학생들은 학교 밖의 숲에서 나무의 종류를 배울 것이다.

PRACTICE 1 Short Talk

27. MP3

1 What will the students probably do next?

(A) Go to another classroom
(B) Have lunch in the cafeteria
(C) Clean up the classroom
(D) Give the teacher some cash

2 What will the teacher probably do next?

(A) Discuss a documentary
(B) Give the students a paper
(C) Talk about coral reefs
(D) Have the students take a test

3 What is the principal going to do on Saturday?

(A) Have a staff meeting
(B) Celebrate a birthday
(C) Host a school picnic
(D) Plant some trees

4 What will the teacher probably talk about next?

(A) Class project topics
(B) Her recent lecture
(C) Tonight's homework
(D) A class field trip

5 What is the teacher going to do on the weekend?

(A) Join a marching band
(B) Enjoy a movie at the theater
(C) Watch a parade
(D) Relax at her home

6 What will the teacher probably do next?

(A) Explain how to take notes
(B) Go over the previous lesson
(C) Let the students leave
(D) Teach history to his class

7 What is the team going to do after school tomorrow?

(A) Play a game
(B) Lift weights
(C) Have practice
(D) Take the day off

8 What is the teacher going to do after class?

(A) Have a review session
(B) Talk about tutoring
(C) Conduct a lab experiment
(D) Visit some younger students

DICTATION 1 Short Talk

28. MP3

1 W The ______ ______ ______ will ring in a moment. Before we go, I should tell you about the new ______ ______ at the cafeteria. You can ______ them from the machines by the door. Then, ______ the ______ by handing her your card. Cash is ______ ______ an acceptable payment method in the cafeteria. ______ ______?

2 M I want to show you a documentary about ______ ______ today. However, first, I need to give you a ______. It has important information about coral reefs, including ______ they can be ______ and what kinds of animals ______ in them. Please be sure ______ ______ ______ it because you will be tested on this information.

3 M Good morning, everybody. Arbor Day is this Saturday, and we're going to celebrate it the ______ ______ ______ ______. That means we'll be planting some trees on the ______ ______. If you want to come and help, please ______ the ______ that your teachers will show you right now.

voca

1
in a moment 잠시 후에
cash 현금
cafeteria 구내식당
machine 기계
cashier 계산원
no longer 더 이상 ~ 않다
acceptable 허용되는
payment 지불
method 방법

2
documentary 다큐멘터리
coral reef 산호초
handout 유인물
information 정보
including ~을 포함해

3
Arbor Day 식목일
celebrate 기념하다
plant 심다
sign 서명하다

4 W Some of you have ______ ______ our class project, so I'd like to talk about it. First, your class project is ______ ______ November 22. That's six weeks ______ ______, so you have plenty of time to ______ ______ it. Now, what about the ______? Well, you can choose from a ______ of them. Let me give you some ______.

5 W This weekend, our very own school marching band will be ______ ______ the city's Foundation Day parade. The parade starts at City Hall at 9:00 AM. It will ______ ______ around ninety minutes. I'm going to be attending the parade to ______ ______ our students. I hope ______ ______ go there, too.

6 M Some of you are ______ ______ ______ in class. You absolutely must ______ ______ the important things I say in your notebooks. ______ ______, the information I write on the board is ______ ______ this class, so write it down. All right. ______ ______ ______ get started on today's class? We're ______ the American Revolution today.

voca

4
inquire 문의하다
project 과제
due 마감인
plenty of 많은
a variety of 다양한
example 예시

5
participate in ~에 참가하다
foundation 건립
parade 퍼레이드
city hall 시청
last 계속되다
attend 참석하다
cheer for ~을 응원하다

6
take notes 필기하다
absolutely 반드시
write down 받아 적다
in addition 게다가, 또한
crucial 매우 중요한
get started 시작하다
discuss 토의하다
American Revolution 미국 독립혁명

7 W Congratulations on ______________ the game tonight. You played an amazing game and ______________ ______________ ______________. I know you're tired, so we're going to have an ______________ ______________ after school tomorrow. We're only going to ______________ ______________ around thirty minutes. Now, ______________ ______________ ______________, go home, and get some rest. Great game, everybody.

8 M Some of the younger students at our school are ______________ ______________ ______________ science. They need tutoring, so I ______________ ______________ any of you are interested in ______________. If you have an A or a B in this class, you're ______________ ______________ ______________ younger kids. I'd like you to ______________ ______________ ______________ and talk to me if you'd like to help.

voca

7
Congratulations on ~을 축하합니다
amazing 놀라운
deserve to V ~할 만하다

8
have trouble V-ing ~하는 데 어려움이 있다
tutor 개인 지도를 하다
wonder if ~인지 궁금하다
interested in ~에 관심이 있는
qualified to V ~할 자격이 있는

PRACTICE 2 Conversation

29. MP3

1 What are the speakers mainly discussing?

(A) Their performances in class
(B) A track meet they went to
(C) The school's sports teams
(D) An activity they might do

2 Why are the students discussing their parents?

(A) To state why they have to play a sport
(B) To complain about their parents
(C) To thank their parents for helping them
(D) To say their parents go jogging with them

3 What activity does the girl mention the boy should do?

(A) Long-distance running
(B) Sprinting
(C) The long jump
(D) The discus

4 What will the students probably do next?

(A) Speak with the principal
(B) Look for Coach Wilson
(C) Go to the track and run
(D) Finish eating lunch

---

5 What is the conversation mainly about?

(A) The boy's recent test score
(B) The boy's class presentation
(C) The boy's specific problems at home
(D) The boy's performance in class

6 What problem does the boy mention?

(A) He does not understand the material.
(B) He has a problem at his home.
(C) He does not have time to study.
(D) He has some financial issues.

7 What can be inferred about the boy?

(A) He is frequently absent from school.
(B) He is uncomfortable talking to the teacher.
(C) He is getting a low grade in every class.
(D) He has not studied with the teacher before.

8 What will the boy probably do next?

(A) Go to the cafeteria
(B) Borrow a book from the teacher
(C) Meet with the counselor
(D) Fill out a form

DICTATION 2 Conversation

30. MP3

1-4

G My parents ________ ________ ________ I should play a sport at school this spring.

B ________ ________ ________, but I don't enjoy team sports. ________, I can't play golf or tennis.

G I feel the ________ ________ ________ you. I guess that means I have to ________ ________ ________ the track and field team.

B I didn't even know that our school had ________.

G Yeah, we do, but there ________ ________ ________ on the team. Basically, any student who tries out for the team will ________ ________.

B That's not bad. What are you ________ ________ doing?

G I'm not a good sprinter, and I really ________ ________ long-distance running. I think I should try to do ________ the 400-meter run ________ the 800-meter run.

B Those sound okay. I don't know what I would do though. I ________ run fast ________ ________.

G But you're pretty strong. You could ________ the discus or the shot put. Those require ________, and you don't have to do any ________.

B What a great idea. ________ ________ ________ try to find Coach Wilson right now?

G Okay. Let's do it. We ________ have about fifteen minutes ________ lunch is over.

voca

1-4
keep V-ing 계속 ~하다
plus 게다가
try out 선발 시험을 보다
track and field 육상
basically 기본적으로
make it 팀에 들어가다
sprinter 단거리 주자
stand 참다
long-distance 장거리
either A or B A 아니면 B
not ~ at all 전혀 ~ 않다
pretty 꽤, 상당히
discus 원반
shot put 포환
require 필요로 하다
strength 힘

5-8

W Ken, would you ________ ________ for a moment, please? I'd like to ________ a ________ with you.

B ________ ________, Ms. Hampton.

W Have a seat here, Ken . . . I want to talk to you about your ________ this semester.

B It hasn't been very good, ________ ________?

W No, it hasn't. And I'm ________ ________ ________. After all, you got an A in my history class ________ ________ last year. You also spoke in class regularly and showed a real ________ ________ history. I haven't seen any of that this year.

B I'm sorry, Ms. Hampton. I just . . . I just haven't been ________ ________ these days. So, uh, I haven't really studied ________ ________ ________ I should.

W Well, that ________ your poor performance on the test. But ________ ________ your lack of interest during class? What's ________ ________?

B Well . . . I'm kind of having some problems at home. I don't want to talk about them ________ ________ ________ ________ though. But things are not very good.

W I'm so sorry to hear that. You know, we have a ________ at this school. You can talk to him if you have problems.

B Yeah . . . That ________ ________ ________.

W Let's go then. Mr. Jackson's office is ________ ________ ________ from mine.

voca

5-8

have a word with ~와 말하다
have a seat 앉다
performance 성적, 수행
semester 학기
curious 궁금한
regularly 정기적으로
affinity 애정, 친밀감
explain 설명하다
poor 나쁜
lack 부족, 결어
interest 흥미, 관심
mind 꺼리다
though 하지만
counselor 상담사
office 사무실

PRACTICE 3 Lecture/Discussion

31. MP3

1 **What is the teacher mainly discussing?**

(A) The Mediterranean region
(B) The Bronze Age
(C) The Mycenaean civilization
(D) The Iron Age

2 **According to the teacher, what is bronze?**

(A) A combination of carbon and copper
(B) A combination of tin and copper
(C) A combination of iron and tin
(D) A combination of carbon and iron

3 **What can be inferred about steel?**

(A) It was first created in modern times.
(B) It appeared in the Bronze Age.
(C) It is stronger than bronze.
(D) It contains some copper.

4 **What will the teacher probably talk about next?**

(A) Some types of tools made from iron
(B) Reasons why some civilizations fell
(C) Stories involving the Trojan War
(D) Differences between the Bronze and Iron ages

5 **What are the speakers mainly discussing?**

(A) How to dissect animals
(B) Arguments against dissecting animals
(C) The costs of dissecting animals
(D) Why students dissect animals

6 **What does the girl say about dissecting animals?**

(A) It is too expensive for some schools.
(B) Most students are interested in it.
(C) Many schools have stopped doing it.
(D) It is effective hands-on learning.

7 **Why does the teacher mention computer programs?**

(A) To explain how to utilize them
(B) To suggest them as a teaching method
(C) To argue that they are better than dissection
(D) To point out how cheap they have become

8 **What is probably true about the girl?**

(A) She is getting a good grade in biology.
(B) She supports dissecting animals.
(C) She wants to become a veterinarian.
(D) She dissected a fish last year.

9 **What will the teacher probably do next?**

(A) Ask the girl a question
(B) Let another student talk
(C) Show a picture to the students
(D) Lecture on a new topic

DICTATION 3 Lecture/Discussion

32. MP3

1-4

W The Iron Age started ______________ 1200 and 600 B.C. That's a very broad ______________ of time. The reason is that like the Bronze Age, which came ______________ it, the Iron Age didn't start at the same time ______________. It took time for the knowledge of ______________ ______________ work with iron to spread. The first places the Iron Age began were in the Mediterranean ______________ and the Middle East. Later, it ______________ to other places in Europe, Asia, and northern Africa.

What's ______________ is that iron isn't as strong or ______________ as bronze. Bronze, by the way, is an alloy made of copper and tin. So if bronze is ______________ ______________ iron, why is the Iron Age considered a more ______________ time than the Bronze Age . . . ? The answer is that during the Iron Age, people ______________ ______________ make steel by adding carbon to iron. This ______________ people ______________ develop tools superior to those made of bronze, especially weapons, which were strong and ______________ ______________.

You should also know that when the Bronze Age ended and the Iron Age began, many civilizations ______________. The Mycenaean civilization in Greece was ______________. The Hittite Empire in the modern-day country of Turkey was ______________. The city of Troy, famous in stories about the Trojan War, was ______________ as well. Let's look at the ______________ ______________ they collapsed now.

voca

1-4
Iron Age 철기 시대
period 기간
Bronze Age 청동기 시대
at the same time 동시에
knowledge 지식
spread 퍼지다, 확산되다
Mediterranean 지중해의
region 지역
Middle East 중동
northern 북부의

durable 내구성이 있는
bronze 청동
alloy 합금
copper 구리
tin 주석
superior to ~보다 우수한
consider A B A를 B라고 생각하다
advanced 발전된
steel 강철
add 첨가하다
carbon 탄소
allow A to V A가 ~할 수 있게 하다
develop 발전시키다
long lasting 오래가는

civilization 문명
collapse 붕괴하다
Mycenaean 미케네의
Hittite 히타이트족
empire 제국
modern-day 현대의
Trojan War 트로이 전쟁
destroy 파괴하다

5-9

M ________ the 1920s, American schoolchildren have been regularly ________ animals in their science classes. ________ ________ twelve million animals are believed to be dissected ________ ________. Can anyone tell me why we ________ ________ animals in science class?

G It's a kind of ________ learning that is ideal for biology. ________ ________ just looking at pictures and diagrams, students can see the ________ of various animals ________ ________. This kind of activity can interest students ________ don't particularly ________ lectures and learning from books. It can also ________ students to decide to ________ ________ in biology or zoology.

M Correct, Stephanie. Now, uh, ________ ________, there are computer programs which ________ ________ alternatives to animal dissection. These were ________ because some people complained about animal dissection being ________.

G I kind of understand that ________, but what about veterinarians? They have to ________ ________ ________ look at the insides of animals if they want to ________ on them or just understand ________ animals' bodies ________. And, uh, it's not like we're dissecting dogs or other ________ ________. Last year, we dissected frogs, grasshoppers, and earthworms. ________ aren't animals that anyone ________ ________.

M That's the argument ________ ________ ________ dissection. Does anyone want to provide a ________ to her argument?

voca

5-9
schoolchild (어린) 학생
regularly 정기적으로
dissect 해부하다
up to ~까지
million 백만(의)
cut up ~을 조각내다

hands-on 직접 해 보는
ideal 이상적인
biology 생물학
diagram 도표
interest ~의 관심을 끌다
particularly 특히
inspire A to V A가 ~하도록 영감을 주다
pursue 추구하다
career 직업, 진로
zoology 동물학

act 기능하다
alternative 대안
dissection 해부
complain 비난하다
inhumane 비인도적인

argument 주장, 논거
veterinarian 수의사
operate 수술하다
work 작동하다, 기능하다
similar 비슷한
grasshopper 메뚜기
earthworm 지렁이

in favor of ~에 찬성하는
provide 제공하다
counterpoint 반론

PRACTICE **TEST**

In this section of the test, you will hear a teacher or other school staff member talking to students. Each talk is followed by one question. Choose the best answer to each question.

1 **What will the teacher probably do next?**

(A) Write on the board
(B) Go over a story
(C) Read from the book
(D) Leave the classroom

2 **What will the students probably do next?**

(A) Complete a survey
(B) Ask some questions
(C) Leave the classroom
(D) Turn in their reports

3 **What will the students probably do next?**

(A) Learn a new song
(B) Sign up for a special event
(C) Vote on the winner of the contest
(D) Watch a singing competition

4 **What is the teacher going to do next?**

(A) Collect the students' homework
(B) Give the students a test
(C) Explain the definitions of words
(D) Continue giving her lecture

Now you will hear a conversation. The conversation is followed by three or more questions. Choose the best answer to each question.

5 **What is the student's problem?**

(A) She lost a personal item.
(B) She forgot to bring a book.
(C) She does not have her jacket.
(D) She cannot find her bag.

6 **According to the girl, what is special about the ring?**

(A) It cost a lot of money.
(B) It has a large diamond.
(C) It belonged to a relative.
(D) It was a birthday present.

7 **What can be inferred about Mr. Mandell?**

(A) He found the missing ring.
(B) He knows the student's name.
(C) He has spoken to the student before.
(D) He is responsible for lost items.

8 **What will the student probably do next?**

(A) Go to her next class
(B) Write a thank-you note
(C) Try to find Ian Kennedy
(D) Leave school for the day

33. MP3

Now you will hear a talk or discussion about an academic topic. The talk or discussion is followed by four or more questions. Choose the best answer to each question.

9 **What is the topic of the talk?**

(A) The world's greatest myths
(B) Myths and their purposes
(C) The heroes of various myths
(D) Myths from ancient times

10 **Why is the teacher discussing Helios?**

(A) To talk about a myth explaining a natural event
(B) To give the reason people thought earthquakes happen
(C) To describe why people still enjoy reading myths
(D) To say what happened to the island of Atlantis

11 **What is one reason people created myths in the past?**

(A) To make the actions of some people famous
(B) To entertain others with stories
(C) To describe how the world was created
(D) To change their cultural beliefs

12 **What will the students probably do next?**

(A) Watch a video the teacher will show
(B) Read a story in their books
(C) Answer the teacher's question
(D) Write a short essay in class

CHAPTER 05

SPEAKER'S PURPOSE

화자의 목적 문제는 화자가 어떤 말을 하는 목적 또는 의도를 묻는 문제 유형이다. 공지와 강의/토론에서 주로 출제되나 대화에서도 간혹 출제된다.

QUESTION **ANALYSIS**

34. MP3

| 유형 분석 |

화자의 목적 문제는 지문 전체의 목적을 묻는 경우가 있고, 일부 내용에 대해 말하는 목적에 대해 묻는 경우가 있다. **지문 전체의 목적을 물을 때**는 주제(Main Idea) 문제와 마찬가지로 **첫 부분**을 주의 깊게 듣는다. **일부 내용에 대해 물을 때**는 **문제를 먼저 읽어 보고, 해당되는 부분**을 주의해서 듣는다.

| 출제되는 지문 종류 |

공지, 대화, 강의/토론

| 질문 형식 |

- **What is the purpose of the talk/announcement?** 담화/공지의 목적은 무엇인가?
- **Why does *A* suggest that . . . ?** A는 왜 ~할 것을 제안하는가?
- **Why is *A* discussing *B*?** A는 왜 B에 대해 논의하는가?
- **Why is *A* talking about *B*?** A는 왜 B에 대해 이야기하는가?

예제

What is the purpose of the talk?

(A) To give an assignment

(B) To make an introduction

(C) To ask a student's name

(D) To talk about the class material

Script

Narrator *Listen to a teacher speaking to a class.*

W Good morning, everyone. As you probably already know, Mr. Arnold is sick and won't return for the rest of the semester. I'm going to be your teacher for the next few weeks. My name is Ms. Kennedy. I hope to learn all of your names soon. Would someone tell me which page we're on, please?

Answer

(B) 밑줄 친 부분에서 선생님은 학생들에게 자기소개를 하고 있음을 알 수 있다.

PRACTICE 1 Short Talk

35. MP3

1 What is the purpose of the announcement?

(A) To advise the students to do their reading
(B) To tell the students to open their books
(C) To find out who left the classroom last
(D) To ask which student lost a book

2 What is the purpose of the announcement?

(A) To encourage the students to study hard
(B) To discuss an upcoming open house
(C) To invite parents to a sporting event
(D) To tell the students to ask more questions

3 What is the purpose of the announcement?

(A) To tell the students to avoid the flowers
(B) To ask for help planting flowers
(C) To point out where some flowers are
(D) To find out which flowers the students prefer

4 Why is the librarian discussing lost books?

(A) To discuss the cost of the replacement fee
(B) To warn the students to care for books better
(C) To insist that the students apologize for them
(D) To advise the students to speak to him about them

5 What is the purpose of the talk?

(A) To talk about some published reports
(B) To request the papers the students wrote
(C) To assign the students some homework
(D) To ask for some help from the students

6 What is the purpose of the talk?

(A) To describe some class activities
(B) To tell the students to try harder
(C) To excuse the students from an activity
(D) To convince the students to play a sport

7 What is the purpose of the announcement?

(A) To tell the students to go home
(B) To state that an exam is over
(C) To assign some homework
(D) To collect some essays

8 What is the purpose of the talk?

(A) To say what will happen during practice
(B) To warn the team about an opponent
(C) To congratulate the team on winning a tournament
(D) To describe the coach's newest strategy

DICTATION 1 Short Talk

36. MP3

1 M Yesterday, after everyone ______________ the classroom, I ______________ a textbook on the floor. ______________, the book didn't have a name ______________ in it. So I don't know who it ______________ ______________. Did any of you ______________ your science book yesterday? If you did, I've got it ______________ ______________.

2 W This is a ______________ ______________ the open house we're having tomorrow night. Your parents are ______________ ______________ ______________. It begins at seven and should ______________ ______________ eight thirty. Your parents can ______________ ______________ and your other teachers. They can ______________ ______________ and learn what you do here. It's a very ______________ ______________, so I hope they come.

3 W This is an important ______________. Please do not walk on the ______________ beside the sidewalk. Ms. Powers planted flowers last week, and they're ______________ ______________ ______________. But some students have been ______________ in the flowerbeds and ______________ the flowers. Please ______________ that. We're trying to ______________ our school ______________, so we'd like those flowers to ______________.

voca

1
textbook 교과서
floor 바닥
unfortunately 안타깝게도
belong to ~의 것이다

2
reminder 상기시키는 것, 알림
open house 학부모 초청 행사
invite 초대하다
attend 참석하다
educational 교육적인
event 행사

3
announcement 공지
flowerbed 화단
beside ~ 옆에
sidewalk 인도

4 M Sometimes students ______________ books and then ______________ them. If that ______________ ______________ you, please come and talk to me. We ______________ ______________ ______________ ______________ get a replacement copy easily. But it might be ______________ ______________ other times. And you'll have to pay a ______________ ______________. But you really need to tell me about it ______________ ______________ ______________. All right?

5 W Before we ______________ ______________, I believe everyone has homework for me. You all need to ______________ ______________ your five-page papers. Everyone, please ______________ your papers ______________ the front of the class. Stacy, ______________ ______________ ______________ collect them and give them to me? I'm really ______________ ______________ ______________ ______________ them.

6 M Most of you are not very ______________, so we need to ______________ ______________ stretches today. You should all be able to ______________ your ______________ without bending your ______________. We're going to ______________ that today and also do some other ______________. So let's get to it. We have a ______________ ______________ today.

voca

4
happen 일어나다
replacement 교체, 대체
copy (책) 한 부
other times 다른 경우에는
fee 요금

5
turn in ~을 제출하다
paper 과제, 리포트, 보고서
pass 전달하다
front 앞쪽
collect 수집하다
look forward to V-ing ~하는 것을 기대하다

6
flexible 유연한
stretch 스트레칭
without V-ing ~하지 않고
bend 구부리다

7 W Okay, everybody. The test is now ______________.
Please put your pens and pencils on the desk. I'm going to ______________ ______________ the classroom to ______________ your test papers. Please give them to me when I ______________ ______________. We have about ten minutes ______________ ______________ ______________, so why don't you ______________ ______________ ______________ before we finish?

8 M We've got a big tournament ______________ ______________ in two weeks. You guys are ______________ ______________ these days, but we can ______________ ______________. Let's try working a bit ______________ in practice starting today. I've got some new ______________ which I believe can help us. We'll ______________ them today. Two weeks is ______________ ______________ to master them.

voca

7
collect 모으다
test paper 시험지
pass by 지나가다

8
tournament 토너먼트, 대회
come up 다가오다
strategy 전략
master 숙달하다

PRACTICE 2 Conversation

37. MP3

1 What is the purpose of the conversation?

(A) To praise a teacher at school
(B) To complain about final exams
(C) To discuss news about a teacher
(D) To talk about a fellow classmate

2 Why is Mr. Kendrick leaving the school?

(A) He is retiring from teaching.
(B) He is changing professions.
(C) He is not happy at the school.
(D) He is moving to another city.

3 When do the students decide to have the party?

(A) Before school begins
(B) During lunchtime
(C) After school finishes
(D) On the last day of exams

4 What can be inferred about the students?

(A) They do not like Mr. Kendrick's class.
(B) They have planned parties in the past.
(C) They will talk again later in the day.
(D) They always leave school at 3:00.

5 What is the boy's problem?

(A) He forgot to do an assignment.
(B) He wakes up late each day.
(C) He is getting poor grades now.
(D) He is often late for school.

6 What does the boy say about his parents?

(A) They sometimes drive him to school.
(B) They pick him up from school each day.
(C) They go to work before he gets up.
(D) They do not help him with his homework.

7 Why is the boy talking about cycling?

(A) To reject the teacher's suggestion
(B) To note how much he enjoys it
(C) To say he does not have a bicycle
(D) To express an interest in doing it

8 What will the boy probably do next?

(A) Turn in his report to the teacher
(B) Give the teacher his address
(C) Go to the school cafeteria
(D) Get ready to take an exam

DICTATION 2 Conversation

38. MP3

1-4

G George, did you hear the ______________ ______________ Mr. Kendrick? He's going to ______________ ______________ the school at the end of the semester.

B He's ______________? Isn't he a bit too young for that?

G No, he's not ______________ ______________ ______________. Apparently, he's going to start a new job in his hometown. He wants to ______________ ______________ ______________ to help take care of his parents.

B He's a ______________ teacher. I'm going to ______________ him, but I'm glad he can ______________ ______________ his parents.

G Yeah, you're right about that.

B Hey. We ______________ ______________ have a going-away party for him. ______________ ______________ ______________ ______________?

G That's a wonderful idea. When should we do it?

B We can't have it during the ______________ ______________, so how about on the ______________ ______________ of classes? We could do it ______________ during lunch ______________ at the end of school.

G Lunch would be better ______________ some students have to leave school ______________ at 3:00.

B Sure. That works. Oh, this needs to be a ______________ ______________. We can't let him find out.

G I'll talk to Jennifer. She's great at ______________ ______________ and can also keep a secret. I'll ______________ ______________ ______________ what she says later today.

voca

1-4
semester 학기
retire 은퇴하다
give up V-ing ~하는 것을 그만두다
apparently 듣자 하니
take care of ~을 돌보다
ought to ~해야 한다
going-away party 송별 파티
wonderful 멋진, 훌륭한
period 기간
either A or B A 아니면 B
immediately 즉시
work 가능하다
surprise party 깜짝 파티
find out 알아내다
plan 계획하다
event 행사
keep a secret 비밀을 지키다

5-8

B Here's my ________________, Ms. Campbell. I'm sorry I was ________________ and couldn't ________________ it ________________ at the beginning of class.

W Thanks for the paper, Eric. I'm ________________ ________________ ________________ reading it.

B Great. I need to ________________ ________________ my next class now.

W Hold on a minute.

B Yes?

W Eric, you've been late for school ________________ ________________ this week. What's going on?

B I have to ________________ ________________ school every morning. It ________________ me around ________________ an ________________ to get here. It's kind of a long walk. Sorry.

W Can't your parents ________________ you ________________ school?

B That's not possible. ________________ ________________ ________________ start their jobs early in the morning, so they ________________ ________________ ________________ home by the time I wake up.

W I see. Then how about ________________ a ________________ to school? That would be a lot faster, ________________ ________________?

B Er . . . I'm not really good at cycling. The ________________ ________________ I was on a bike, I crashed and hurt myself.

W Why don't you let me know your ________________? I'll see if someone else here ________________ ________________ you. Then, I'll talk to that student's parents and ________________ them ________________ they would drive you to school in the morning.

B Thank you, Ms. Campbell. I ________________ ________________ that very much.

voca

5-8

report 보고서, 리포트
turn in ~을 제출하다
beginning 시작
paper 보고서, 리포트
look forward to V-ing ~하는 것을 기대하다
take 데려다주다
possible 가능한
by the time ~할 때쯤에는
wake up 일어나다
cycle 자전거를 타다
crash 충돌하다
address 주소
see if ~인지 알아보다
appreciate 감사하다

PRACTICE 3 Lecture/Discussion

39. MP3

1 **What is the purpose of the talk?**

(A) To compare Shakespeare and Marlowe
(B) To describe some events in the Elizabethan Era
(C) To discuss the life and works of Marlowe
(D) To talk about the story in *Tamburlaine the Great*

2 **Why does the teacher mention Edmund Spenser?**

(A) To name his most famous written work
(B) To call him the greatest writer of the Elizabethan Era
(C) To argue that he wrote better works than Shakespeare
(D) To say that he lived during England's golden age

3 **What does the teacher mean when he says: "But what works he wrote"?**

(A) He prefers Marlowe's works to Shakespeare's.
(B) Marlowe's plays were impressive.
(C) The students need to answer his question.
(D) He will discuss Marlowe's plays next.

4 **What does the teacher say about *Doctor Faustus*?**

(A) It was the first play that Marlowe wrote.
(B) People still perform it today.
(C) It includes a very famous line.
(D) Performers prefer it to *Tamburlaine the Great*.

5 **What will the students probably do next?**

(A) Read one of Marlowe's plays
(B) Learn about Shakespeare
(C) Perform part of *Tamburlaine the Great*
(D) See a video on the Elizabethan Age

6 **What does the teacher say about inventions?**

(A) They help humans do work.
(B) They can make people rich.
(C) They are hard to come up with.
(D) They are made by few people.

7 **Why is the boy discussing the wheel?**

(A) To compare it with another invention
(B) To say who invented it first
(C) To say when it was invented
(D) To call it the most important invention

8 **What is probably true about the microscope?**

(A) It is mainly used by biologists.
(B) It was invented within the last 500 years.
(C) It led to the invention of the computer.
(D) It is the teacher's favorite invention.

9 **What will the teacher probably do next?**

(A) Ask the boy another question
(B) Give the class her opinion
(C) Listen to a student's response
(D) Conduct a survey of the students

DICTATION 3 Lecture/Discussion

40. MP3

1-5

M The Elizabethan Era in England ______________ ______________ 1558 ______________ 1603. This was when Queen Elizabeth I ______________. It's considered a ______________ ______________ for England, particularly with regard to ______________. William Shakespeare is the ______________ writer from this time. Edmund Spenser, ______________ we talked about in our last class, also wrote during this era. ______________ ______________ is playwright Christopher Marlowe.

Marlowe lived from 1564 to 1593. It's ______________ ______________ we don't speak of him as Shakespeare's ______________—or even his better—because he ______________ so ______________. He therefore has a much smaller ______________ of ______________ than Shakespeare. But what works he wrote. He ______________ *Tamburlaine the Great*, a play in two parts. It is a ______________ ______________ Timur, a warlord from Central Asia. This was Marlowe's first ______________ to be ______________ regularly in London.

______________ his other plays, *Doctor Faustus* is the best known. It ______________ the tale of a man who makes a ______________ ______________ the devil and what happens ______________. It features a famous ______________ about Helen of Troy. It goes, "Was this the face that launched a thousand ships and ______________ the topless towers of Ilium?" ______________, Marlowe died in mysterious conditions before ______________ thirty. Now, uh, let's take a ______________ at *Doctor Faustus*. Open your books to page 194, please.

voca

1-5
era 시대
last 지속되다
reign 통치하다
golden era 황금기
particularly 특히
with regard to ~와 관련해서
literature 문학
best-known 가장 유명한
playwright 극작가

likely 아마
equal 동등한 (존재)
body 모음
work 작품
pen 쓰다
play 희곡, 연극
drama 드라마
warlord 군주
Central Asia 중앙아시아
perform 공연하다
regularly 정기적으로

tale 이야기
deal 거래
devil 악마
happen 발생하다
afterward 이후에
feature ~을 특징으로 하다
line 대사
launch 시작하다
topless 지붕이 없는
sadly 슬프게도
mysterious 신비로운
condition 상황
turn (나이가) ~이 되다

6-9

W ________ ________, there have been countless inventions. These inventions have ________ ________ ________ for people and enabled us to do ________ ________ of activities. Most people today would say that ________, the Internet, or ________ are the most important inventions. But I ________ ________ you. Excluding those three things, ________ ________ ________ ________ the most important invention in history is?

B That's ________ ________ ________. It's definitely the wheel. ________ ________ the wheel, transportation became easier. People could make pottery ________ ________ the potter's wheel. Farming became easier and more ________ as well.

W Chad makes a ________ ________, everybody. The wheel was ________ around 3500 B.C. in Mesopotamia. It had a tremendous effect ________ ________ on ancient times ________ ________ on modern times. But what, Chad, do you ________ the most important invention in the ________ 500 years is?

B Hmm . . . I'd go with the ________. It enabled biologists to see tiny things ________ ________ cells, bacteria, and viruses. Thanks to the microscope, humans have ________ great ________ in the fields of biology, botany, and medicine. Pretty much every ________ in those fields has ________ ________ thanks to the microscope.

W A very ________ answer. How about you, Hilda? What's your ________?

voca

6-9
throughout history 역사를 통틀어
countless 셀 수 없이 많은
invention 발명품
enable A to V A가 ~할 수 있게 하다
all sorts of 온갖 종류의
excluding ~을 제외하고

definitely 당연히, 분명히
transportation 교통, 이동
pottery 도자기
farming 농업
productive 생산적인

invent 발명하다
tremendous 엄청난
effect 영향
ancient 고대의
modern 현대의
past 과거의

microscope 현미경
biologist 생물학자
tiny 아주 작은
cell 세포
advance 발전
biology 생물학
botany 식물학
medicine 의학
discovery 발견

insightful 통찰력 있는
opinion 의견

PRACTICE **TEST**

In this section of the test, you will hear a teacher or other school staff member talking to students. Each talk is followed by one question. Choose the best answer to each question.

1 What is the purpose of the talk?

(A) To advise students to take good notes
(B) To ask students to stop bothering others
(C) To prohibit students from using laptops
(D) To tell students to turn off all electronic devices

2 Why is the coach discussing Robert?

(A) To describe his current condition
(B) To call him a valuable team member
(C) To say that he missed the game
(D) To mention he will visit Robert's home

3 What is the purpose of the talk?

(A) To give a reading assignment
(B) To discuss how some work will be graded
(C) To explain a story the students read
(D) To describe how to write a paper

4 What is the purpose of the announcement?

(A) To recommend alternative food choices
(B) To discuss options for lunch
(C) To warn students about food vendors
(D) To talk about the updated cafeteria menu

Now you will hear a conversation. The conversation is followed by three or more questions. Choose the best answer to each question.

5 What are the speakers mainly discussing?

(A) Books the girl has borrowed
(B) The library's lack of material
(C) The girl's upcoming art paper
(D) A missing item the girl needs

6 Why is the book the student wants unavailable?

(A) Someone else has borrowed it.
(B) A teacher is using it now.
(C) It was lost by another student.
(D) The book suffered some damage.

7 Why is the librarian discussing the public library?

(A) To recommend its collection of art books
(B) To claim that he knows the librarian there
(C) To state that it stays open late every night
(D) To provide a solution to the student's problem

8 What will the librarian probably do next?

(A) Locate a book
(B) Check out a book
(C) Make a telephone call
(D) Find some reference material

41. MP3

Now you will hear a talk or discussion about an academic topic. The talk or discussion is followed by four or more questions. Choose the best answer to each question.

9 **What is the main topic of the talk?**

(A) The lives of cockroaches
(B) Dangerous diseases
(C) The life cycles of pests
(D) One kind of pest

10 **According to the teacher, where do most cockroach species live?**

(A) In people's homes
(B) In urban areas
(C) In the wild
(D) In hot places

11 **Why is the teacher discussing various diseases?**

(A) To mention problems many pests spread
(B) To warn the students about them
(C) To note that cockroaches cannot catch them
(D) To say that cockroaches spread them

12 **What will the teacher probably talk about next?**

(A) How to kill cockroaches
(B) Where to find cockroaches
(C) When cockroaches are active
(D) Why people dislike cockroaches

CHAPTER 06

RHETORICAL DEVICE

수사학적 장치 문제는 어떤 내용이 지문에서 왜 언급되었는지 묻는 문제 유형으로, 주로 대화나 강의/토론에서 출제된다. 화자의 의도를 파악해야 하고, 지문 내용이 유기적으로 연결되는 것을 이해할 수 있어야 하므로 다소 어려운 문제 유형이다.

QUESTION **ANALYSIS**

42. MP3

| 유형 분석 |

수사학적 장치 문제에서 묻는 대상은 지문에서 짧고 간단히 언급되는 것도 있고, 자세히 설명되는 것도 있다. **짧게 언급되는 경우**에는 **해당 부분에만 주의**를 기울이면 되지만, 강의에서 자세히 설명하는 **주제일 경우**에는 **요지를 이해하고 요약할 수 있는 능력**도 필요하다.

| 출제되는 지문 종류 |

대화, 강의/토론

| 질문 형식 |

- **Why does *A* mention *B*?** A는 왜 B를 언급하는가?
- **Why does *A* talk about *B*?** A는 왜 B에 대해 이야기하는가?

예제

Why does the boy talk about the great migration in Africa?

(A) To explain why some animals go on it

(B) To state which countries it happens in

(C) To describe the path the animals take

(D) To name the animals involved in it

Script

Narrator *Listen to part of a discussion in a science class.*

W Many animals live in the same place all year long, but other animals migrate. So they move to another place during part of the year and then return to their original location some time later. Why do you think that some animals migrate?

B The most obvious answer is that they migrate to places where they can acquire food and shelter. Birds fly south in winter to go to warm places that have plenty of food. In the Serengeti in Africa each year, a great migration takes place involving millions of animals. They're escaping drought conditions to go to plains where they can obtain plenty of food.

W That's a perfect example.

Answer

(A) 밑줄 친 부분에서 남학생은 아프리카의 대이동에 대해 말하고 있다. 그 앞에서는 동물들이 이동하는 이유가 먹이와 주거지를 확보할 수 있는 곳으로 가기 위해서라고 말했다. 따라서 남학생은 동물들이 아프리카의 대이동을 떠나는 이유를 설명하기 위해 그것을 언급하고 있다.

PRACTICE 1 Conversation

43. MP3

1 What is the girl's problem?

(A) She cannot locate a book that she needs.
(B) She does not have a public library card.
(C) She lacks enough time to finish her paper.
(D) She cannot get access to some documents.

2 What is the girl planning to write about?

(A) Relationships between people in the past
(B) A battle that took place near the town
(C) The early settlers who built the town
(D) A fort that was constructed at a nearby place

3 Why does the teacher mention Ms. Reynolds?

(A) To ask the girl's opinion of her
(B) To call her a good librarian
(C) To indicate that he knows her
(D) To say she knows a lot about the town

4 What is the girl going to do after school today?

(A) Visit the town library
(B) Meet her study group
(C) Write a paper at home
(D) Check out some books

5 What is the boy's problem?

(A) He has not made any friends yet.
(B) His teachers do not like him.
(C) He did not make the football team.
(D) He is doing poorly in his classes.

6 How long has the boy been at the school?

(A) A few days
(B) One week
(C) Two weeks
(D) One month

7 **Why does the mother mention the boy's father's job?**

(A) To say why he comes home late daily
(B) To explain why they moved to a new city
(C) To state that he makes more money now
(D) To describe his duties at his job

8 **What does the mother mean when she says: "I had a similar experience as you"?**

(A) She tried hard and made some friends.
(B) She went to live with her grandparents.
(C) She failed a couple of classes in her youth.
(D) She had trouble at her new school.

---

9 **What are the speakers mainly discussing?**

(A) Their inability to keep up in their classes
(B) The amount of homework they have
(C) The number of classes they are taking
(D) The difficulty they have on their tests

10 **What does the boy imply when he says: "I've already put that book in my bag"?**

(A) He has to study for a Spanish test tonight.
(B) He is going to read a book for English class.
(C) He needs to return a book to the library.
(D) He has not done his math homework yet.

11 **Why does the boy talk about his book report?**

(A) To state he will work on it at home today
(B) To say he has not read the book yet
(C) To complain about how long it must be
(D) To ask the girl what he should write about

12 **What can be inferred about the students?**

(A) They are going to their next class.
(B) They are willing to study more now.
(C) They want to have a meeting with a teacher.
(D) They will not finish an assignment on time.

DICTATION 1 Conversation

44. MP3

1-4

G Mr. Watkins, I ________________ ________________ ________________ to you about my term paper, please.

M Of course, Cindy. Is there a ________________ with it?

G Yes, sir. There is. I'm ________________ ________________ ________________ enough sources for it.

M You are writing about the early ________________ in this town, aren't you?

G Uh, no. That's not me. I think that's Thomas. I was ________________ ________________ write about the relationships ________________ the early settlers ________________ the Native Americans living here.

M Ah, that's right. I believe the town library has a lot of ________________ ________________. You need to take a look at them.

G That's the problem. I spoke to the ________________, but she wouldn't ________________ me ________________ the archives. She said I'm not ________________ ________________. I think I may need a new topic.

M I see. Well, I ________________ ________________ you not change subjects.

G But how am I ________________ to get the information I need to write about it?

M After school today, I'll visit the library and ________________ ________________ Ms. Reynolds. I've known her for a long time. I can probably ________________ her ________________ let you into the archives.

G Wow. That's great. ________________ ________________ ________________ ________________ I went there with you? I'd like to start doing my ________________ today.

M Of course not. Let's go there ________________ ________________ ________________ school finishes.

voca

1-4

term paper 기말 과제
have trouble V-ing ~하는 데 어려움을 겪다
source 자료
settler 정착민
plan to V ~할 계획이다
relationship 관계
Native American 아메리카 원주민
original 원본의
document 문서
take a look at ~을 한번 보다
librarian 사서
archive 기록 보관소
subject 주제
be supposed to V ~해야 하다
probably 아마도
convince A to B A가 ~하도록 설득하다
research 연구, 자료 조사

5-8

W How was your day at school today, Martin?

B The ______________ ______________ ______________.

W I'm sorry to hear that. What ______________ today?

B I just don't like this school. It's not ______________ ______________ my old school. The students aren't particularly ______________ either. I've been there for two weeks now and ______________ ______________ a single friend ______________.

W Are you trying to talk to any of the students?

B Yes, I am. But ______________ ______________ ______________ want to talk to me. Can't I go back to my old school?

W I'm sorry, Martin, but that's ______________ ______________ ______________. We had to move to this city for your father's ______________ ______________. Your old school is too far away ______________ ______________ ______________ ______________ back there to study.

B Yeah, but ______________ ______________ I was happy there.

W I understand ______________ ______________ it can be to change schools in the middle of the ______________. I had to do the same thing ______________ when I was your age.

B Really? ______________ ______________ ______________ ______________?

W I had a similar experience as you. But I didn't ______________ ______________ and ______________ ______________ to make friends. Eventually, I ______________ ______________ like my new school.

B Okay. I get it. I won't give up.

voca

5-8
usual 평소의
happen 일어나다
particularly 특별히
friendly 친근한
possible 가능한
at least 적어도
in the middle of ~의 중간에
semester 학기
once (과거의) 한때
similar 비슷한
experience 경험
give up 포기하다
keep V-ing 계속 ~하다
try to V ~하려고 노력하다
make friends 친구를 사귀다
eventually 결국
come to V ~하게 되다

9-12

G Can you believe ________ ________ ________ we have?

B I know. It's horrible, and this is only the first week of school. How bad ________ ________ ________ it is going to be a couple of months from now?

G ________ a lot ________.

B You can say that again. ________ ________ do we have homework in again?

G English, history, science, math, and Spanish. At least I ________ ________ my math homework, so I don't have to take my book home.

B ________ ________. I've already put that book in my bag.

G Don't worry. If you ________ ________ in class, you should be able to solve the problems pretty quickly.

B That's ________ ________ ________. How much of your book report have you written?

G I ________ ________ ________ on it. We've got to finish it by tomorrow, don't we?

B That's correct. I'm going to start writing it ________ ________ ________ I arrive home. I guess we're going to have to study ________ ________ ________ ________ this year.

G You're probably right. Anyway, I imagine we'll ________ ________ ________ the heavier workload in a couple of weeks.

B Yeah. We're older now, so we're ________ ________ ________ ________. Good luck finishing up your assignments. See you tomorrow.

voca

9-12
horrible 끔찍한
a couple of 두어 개의
probably 아마도
a lot 많이
worse 더 나쁜
You can say that again. 맞는 말이야.
Spanish 스페인어
already 벌써, 이미
pay attention 주의를 기울이다
solve 풀다
pretty 꽤
quickly 빨리
book report 독후감
as soon as ~하자마자
arrive 도착하나
imagine 상상하다
workload 작업량, 공부량
be expected to V ~하도록 기대받다
Good luck V-ing ~하는 데 행운을 빌어
assignment 과제

PRACTICE 2 Lecture/Discussion

45. MP3

1 **What is the teacher mainly discussing?**

(A) The way acid rain gets created
(B) The places affected by acid rain
(C) The causes and effects of acid rain
(D) Acid rain and how to prevent it

2 **What can be inferred about the Midwest?**

(A) Its acid rain situation has improved.
(B) It has a large number of factories.
(C) Acid rain has destroyed its farmland.
(D) Few of its lakes have any fish today.

3 **Why does the teacher mention fossil fuels?**

(A) To name the most common ones
(B) To explain how people use them
(C) To describe some chemicals in them
(D) To blame them for acid rain

4 **According to the teacher, what can acid rain harm?**

(A) Rivers
(B) Oceans
(C) Buildings
(D) People

5 **What is the main topic of the discussion?**

(A) The Egyptian pyramids in ancient times
(B) The difficulties of building a pyramid
(C) The importance of the pyramids
(D) The history of the Great Pyramid of Giza

6 **What does the teacher say about the stone blocks in the Great Pyramid of Giza?**

(A) They were moved without animals.
(B) They were dug up close to the pyramids.
(C) They were transported across the sea.
(D) They were cut to precise measurements.

7 **Why is the boy discussing quarries?**

(A) To explain what their purpose was
(B) To mention moving stone blocks from them
(C) To respond to the teacher's question
(D) To say that no quarries were in Egypt

8 **Why does the teacher mention the Nile River?**

(A) To state that it floods every year
(B) To discuss its importance to the Egyptians
(C) To say the Great Pyramid of Giza is close to it
(D) To note that stones were transported on it

9 **What is the teacher mainly talking about?**

(A) Some of the outer planets in the solar system
(B) A mission to interstellar space by some probes
(C) The accomplishments of the *Voyager* probes
(D) Specific discoveries the *Voyager* probes made

10 **What does the teacher mean when she says: "Both probes exceeded the wildest dreams of their creators"?**

(A) The probes will visit more planets soon.
(B) The probes did more than was planned.
(C) The probes flew close to moons and planets.
(D) The probes are still sending information.

11 **What did *Voyager 1* do on its mission?**

(A) Explored the atmosphere of Titan
(B) Did a flyby of the planet Uranus
(C) Searched for alien life on Europa
(D) Took closeup pictures of Neptune

12 **What does the teacher say about the *Voyager* probes' computers?**

(A) They are no longer working properly.
(B) They can access the Internet.
(C) They stopped transmitting information.
(D) They are fairly simple ones.

13 **Why does the teacher talk about *Voyager 1*'s thrusters?**

(A) To explain how the probe moves around
(B) To say they are operational now
(C) To claim they are out of fuel
(D) To mention that they no longer work

DICTATION 2 Lecture/Discussion

46. MP3

1-4

M A couple of ________ ago, acid rain was a ________ ________ in some places, especially in the Midwest. It's ________ so bad ________, but some places still suffer from it. Acid rain, ________ ________ you don't know, is rain which is highly acidic. ________ a ________ ________, it is created when pollutants such as sulfur and nitrous oxide ________ ________ water in clouds. They then fall to the ground ________ ________. These pollutants can be released by ________ when they erupt. However, most experts believe the burning of fossil fuels ________ ________ most acid rain. This means that ________, factories, and power plants are primarily ________ ________ acid rain.

Acid rain has a number of ________ ________. It can damage lakes and ponds ________ much ________ all life in them dies. It's so sad to see beautiful lakes with ________ ________ ________ in them. It can also harm the ________ it falls on. This makes farming the land difficult or ________ ________. Acid rain further damages trees and ________ them to harm. It even damages buildings and ________ that it falls on by ________ the stone they are made of. That ________ ________, doesn't it? Fortunately, there are ways to ________ acid rain and to restore the places that it ________.

voca

1-4
decade 십 년
acid rain 산성비
suffer from ~으로 고통받다
acidic 산성의
as a general rule 일반적으로
pollutant 오염 물질
sulfur 황
nitrous oxide 질소 산화물
combine with ~와 결합하다
release 방출하다
erupt 폭발하다
expert 전문가
fossil fuel 화석 연료
account for ~을 차지하다
vehicle 차량
power plant 발전소
primarily 가장, 일차적으로
responsible for ~의 원인이 되는

a number of 많은
negative 부정적인
effect 영향
damage 손상시키다
absolutely 완전히
harm 해를 끼치다; 피해
soil 토양
further 나아가서
expose 노출시키다
erode 침식하다
horrible 끔찍한
fortunately 다행히
eliminate 제거하다
restore 복원하다
affect 영향을 미치다

5-8

W The Great Pyramid of Giza was constructed ______________ ______________ 4,500 years ago. It was an enormous ______________ which took approximately twenty years to ______________. Here's a picture of it . . . Now, I want you to think for a moment. ______________ ______________ ______________, what kinds of difficulties would the builders of that pyramid have ______________?

B I think the biggest problem would have been ______________ the stones ______________ ______________. I remember reading that some of those stones ______________ around 2.5 tons. How did the Egyptians ______________ ______________ lift those stones and move them into place?

W Yes, that ______________ ______________ ______________ an enormous problem. Many historians believe they constructed ______________ to get the stone blocks up to ______________ ______________. Still, without horses or other ______________ ______________, it must have been a very slow process to move the stones up.

B I just ______________ ______________ something. How did they move the blocks ______________ the quarries ______________ the pyramid? I mean, uh, I just see ______________ in that picture. I don't think the rocks came from the ______________ ______________. So where did they come from, and ______________ did they get there?

W The stones were ______________ ______________ by ship down the Nile River. But that also must have been very ______________ ______________ ______________.

voca

5-8
construct 건설하다
enormous 거대한
undertaking 일, 프로젝트
approximately 대략
complete 완성하다
builder 건축자
face 직면하다

in place 제자리에
remember V-ing ~한 것을 기억하다
weigh 무게가 나가다
manage to V ~해 내다
lift 들어 올리다

historian 역사학자
ramp 경사로
block 블록, 덩어리
level 높이
still 그래도, 하지만
pack animal 짐을 나르는 동물
process 과정

think of ~을 떠올리다
quarry 채석장
rock 바위
local 가까운
area 지역

likely 아마도
transport 운반된
by ship 배로

9-13

W In 1977, NASA, the American space _______________, launched two space probes: *Voyager 1* and *Voyager 2*. Their primary _______________ was to explore the outer planets of the solar system and then to _______________ the solar system. Both probes exceeded the _______________ dreams of their creators.

Voyager 1 _______________ around two weeks after *Voyager 2*. It _______________ _______________ both Jupiter and Saturn on its _______________ _______________ _______________ the solar system. NASA then had to _______________ _______________ doing a flyby of Titan, a moon of Saturn, or Pluto, a dwarf planet. Titan was selected _______________ _______________ _______________ examine its atmosphere. _______________ _______________ *Voyager 2*, it flew by all four _______________ _______________: Jupiter, Saturn, Uranus, and Neptune. It is the only probe to _______________ _______________ Uranus and Neptune. The two probes explored the _______________ of the planets, their atmospheres, their _______________, and many other aspects of the planets.

The probes then _______________ out of the solar system. Even today, NASA remains in _______________ with both probes. Their computer systems are primitive by _______________ _______________. Yet they can still send information back to the Earth. In addition, NASA is still _______________ _______________ fixing problems with the probes. In 2025, it _______________ to activate some of *Voyager 1*'s thrusters. They had been _______________ since 2004. This will help the probe as it continues its _______________ into interstellar space.

voca

9-13
agency 기관
launch 발사하다, 발사되다
space probe 우주 탐사선
primary 주요한
mission 임무
explore 탐험하다
outer planet 외행성
solar system 태양계
depart 떠나다
exceed 능가하다
creator 창조자

pass by ~을 지나가다
flyby 근접 통과
Titan 타이탄
moon 위성
Pluto 명왕성
dwarf planet 왜성
select 선택하다
in order to V ~하기 위해
examine 조사하다
atmosphere 대기
as for ~로 말하자면
Uranus 천왕성
Neptune 해왕성
ring 고리
aspect 측면

head 향하다
remain in contact with ~와 연락을 유지하다
primitive 원시적인
by modern standards 현대적인 기준으로
yet 그러나
capable of V-ing ~할 수 있는
activate 활성화하다
thruster 추진기
inactive 비활성의
journey 여행
interstellar 성간의

PRACTICE **TEST**

Now you will hear two conversations. Each conversation is followed by three or more questions. Choose the best answer to each question.

1 What is the girl's problem?

(A) She missed a class due to sickness.
(B) She forgot to submit an assignment.
(C) She does not have some class notes.
(D) She was absent on the day of a test.

2 Why does the girl talk about lab experiments?

(A) To ask what she can learn from them
(B) To complain about doing them
(C) To express that she likes them
(D) To find out how to do them

3 What is probably true about the girl?

(A) She is an athlete.
(B) She studies hard.
(C) She has low grades.
(D) She still feels sick.

4 What does the teacher imply when he says: "I'll see you here at noon then"?

(A) He is willing to have lunch with the girl.
(B) The girl should turn in a paper then.
(C) He agrees with the girl's suggestion.
(D) The girl does not have much free time.

5 What is the speakers' problem?

(A) They forgot to bring their lunch money.
(B) They dislike the food in the cafeteria.
(C) They did not eat a snack this morning.
(D) They ordered the wrong food for lunch.

6 Why does the boy mention the principal?

(A) To complain about some of her actions
(B) To mention a meeting he had with her
(C) To ask why she is not taking any action
(D) To state that she cannot provide any help

7 What is the boy going to do tomorrow?

(A) Eat his lunch in the cafeteria
(B) Carry enough money to buy a snack
(C) Bring his lunch from home
(D) Have a meeting with the principal

8 What does the girl imply when she says: "It's the same with me"?

(A) She will talk to the principal with the boy.
(B) She feels hungry in the afternoon.
(C) She is willing to assist the boy.
(D) She is just as upset as the boy.

47. MP3

Now you will hear a talk or discussion about an academic topic. The talk or discussion is followed by four or more questions. Choose the best answer to each question.

9 What is the purpose of the talk?

(A) To say how the Mariana Trench formed
(B) To describe the Challenger Deep
(C) To talk about some deep-sea creatures
(D) To discuss the world's most inhospitable places

10 Why does the teacher mention Mount Everest?

(A) To describe conditions there
(B) To say few animals live there
(C) To make a comparison
(D) To discuss its features

11 What does the teacher say about the bottom of the Mariana Trench?

(A) It is too dark to see anything.
(B) It contains an active volcano.
(C) It has lots of large fish.
(D) No humans have ever been there.

12 What is probably true about the teacher?

(A) He enjoys spending time at the ocean.
(B) He has climbed Mount Everest before.
(C) He knows how to pilot a submersible.
(D) He would like to visit the Mariana Trench.

CHAPTER 07

PROSODY

어조 문제는 화자가 한 말에 담겨 있는 의미나 암시, 감정 등을 이해할 수 있는 능력을 평가하는 문제 유형으로, 대화나 강의/토론에서 출제된다. 숨겨진 의미와 맥락(context)을 이해할 수 있어야 하므로 다소 어려운 문제 유형이다.

QUESTION **ANALYSIS**

48. MP3

| 유형 분석 |

어조 문제는 지문에서 언급된 문장을 인용하면서 **화자가 의미하는 것** 또는 **화자의 감정**을 묻는다. 인용하는 문장이 어디에서 나왔는지 기억나지 않을 수도 있으므로, **미리 문제를 읽어 두었다가** 인용하는 부분이 나올 때 주의해서 듣는 것이 좋다.어조 문제를 공략하기 위해서는 **내용의 흐름**을 잘 파악해야 하며, 화자의 **억양이나 말투**에도 주의를 기울여야 한다.

| 출제되는 지문 종류 |

대화, 강의/토론

| 질문 형식 |

- **What does *A* imply when he/she says: ". . ."?** A가 ~라고 할 때 무엇을 암시하는가?
- **What does *A* mean when he/she says: ". . ."?** A가 ~라고 할 때 무엇을 의미하는가?
- **How does *A* probably feel when he/she says: ". . ."?** A가 ~라고 할 때 아마도 어떻게 느낄까?

예제 **What does the teacher imply when she says: "So don't ever let people tell you you're too young to do something"?**

(A) Young people can accomplish great things.
(B) The students in her class are still very young.
(C) Youth is something people should enjoy.
(D) It is hard for young people to act by themselves.

Script Narrator *Listen to a teacher talking in a social studies class.*

W Louis Braille was blind yet still learned to read at a special school. Tacks were hammered in the shapes of letters and numbers into wood. He would feel them and thus learned to spell words. Later, a French military captain told the students at his school about night writing. He believed it could be used by the blind to read. Louis considered that idea too simple, so he devised his own system. He used six dots in a grid position to represent letters, numbers, and other symbols. The dots were raised, so blind people could feel the letters to read them. This ingenious system gave blind people the ability to read and was called Braille. And guess what . . . He created Braille when he was only fifteen. So don't ever let people tell you you're too young to do something. If you have an idea, go for it. You might just change the world.

Answer (A) 선생님은 브라유가 겨우 15살이었을 때 점자를 고안했다는 것을 언급하면서 밑줄 친 문장을 말한다. 따라서 선생님은 어린 사람들도 위대한 일을 성취할 수 있다는 것을 암시한다.

PRACTICE 1 Conversation

49. MP3

1 What is the main topic of the conversation?

(A) The girl's parents and their help
(B) The girl's improved performance
(C) The girl's midterm exams
(D) The girl's need to study harder

2 What does the counselor suggest about the girl's teachers?

(A) They will return her exams soon.
(B) They wish she would study harder.
(C) They think she might be cheating.
(D) They like the papers she writes.

3 What does the counselor imply when he says: "That's not what he said"?

(A) The girl is a good basketball player.
(B) The girl's math score is improving.
(C) The girl's father is impressed with her.
(D) The girl is a good all-around student.

4 What is the girl going to do after school today?

(A) Practice a presentation
(B) Speak with a coach
(C) Review her exams
(D) Go straight home

---

5 What are the speakers mainly discussing?

(A) An academic competition
(B) A homework assignment
(C) A surprise party
(D) A group presentation

6 Why was the boy absent from school yesterday?

(A) He was very sick.
(B) He was at a contest.
(C) He was on vacation.
(D) He was at a sporting event.

7 What is probably true about Ms. Marsh?

(A) She is David's sister.
(B) She is organizing the event.
(C) She is a school teacher.
(D) She is the girl's mother.

8 How does the boy probably feel when he says: "You all have thought of everything"?

(A) He is unhappy.
(B) He is proud.
(C) He is surprised.
(D) He is impressed.

9 **What are the speakers mainly talking about?**

(A) The girl's dinosaur fossils
(B) A dig they went on in the past
(C) An outing the teacher has planned
(D) An opportunity for bonus points

10 **What does the girl mean when she says: "That makes sense"?**

(A) The event will help many students.
(B) She is glad the teacher has equipment.
(C) It is fine with her to help pay.
(D) Going on a one-day trip is smart.

11 **According to the teacher, where will the group go?**

(A) To a river
(B) To a cave
(C) To a field
(D) To a museum

12 **Why does the girl mention her parents?**

(A) To note that they are out of town now
(B) To state they must give her permission
(C) To point out that they will let her go
(D) To say they already have weekend plans

DICTATION 1 Conversation

50. MP3

1-4

M Good afternoon, Julie. ________ ________ ________ to my office. Have a seat, please.

G Thank you, sir.

M I know you're busy, so I won't ________ ________ ________ ________ with small talk. I'd like to talk about your ________.

G My grades? I . . . I thought I was ________ ________ this semester.

M You're actually do ________ ________ fine. Your teachers showed me your ________ ________ grades, and you got all A's on them. ________ ________.

G Oh, wow. I had ________ ________. No teachers have given them back yet.

M ________ them tomorrow. You know, two years ago, you were a C and B student. Last year, you ________ ________ B's. This year, you are ________ ________ show steady improvement. ________.

G Thanks. My mom and dad have been helping me study after school every night. They ________ the ________.

M Well, I think you have had quite a lot ________ ________ ________ ________, too. Now, uh, one more thing . . . Coach Brady ________ ________ ________ about you. He has seen you in P.E. class and wants you to ________ ________ ________ the basketball team.

G Really? I don't think I'm that good.

M That's ________ ________ ________ ________. Why don't you have a talk with him after school today?

G Okay. I ________ I can do that.

voca

1-4
office 사무실
have a seat 앉다
grades 성적
semester 학기
midterm 중간고사
expect 예상하다
continue to V 계속해서 ~하다
steady 꾸준한
improvement 향상
Congratulations. 축하해.
deserve 받을 만하다
credit 공로
quite 상당히
P.E. 체육
try out 선발 시험을 보다
suppose 추측하다

5-8

G Jason, you're going to the ____ ____ after school today, right?

B Birthday party?

G Yeah, the ____ ____ for David. Melissa told us about it in class yesterday. ____ ____?

B I wasn't at school yesterday. I was at an academic competition ____ ____ ____, so I had no idea there's a party ____ today.

G Well, she invited everyone in the class. So ____ ____ you weren't there, you can still go.

B When and where is it?

G It's ____ ____ ____. Everyone is going to David's house, which is right ____ the ____ from school.

B Oh, wait. I don't have a present for him. What should I do?

G David won't ____ ____ at his house until around 3:30. Ms. Marsh ____ us she would ____ to him about his class presentation after school and ____ him ____ for us. So you'll have time to ____ ____ a store really quickly to purchase him something.

B Wow. You all have ____ ____ ____. This sounds like a fun time. You can ____ ____ ____.

G Wonderful. Just be sure ____ ____ ____ anything to him. We don't want to ____ the surprise.

B I won't say a word. ____ ____ ____ I would mess this kind of thing up.

voca

5-8
surprise party 깜짝 파티
academic 학문의
competition 경쟁, 대회
invite 초대하다
show up 나타나다
promise 약속하다
presentation 발표
drop by ~에 잠깐 들르다
purchase 사다
ruin 망치다
there is no way ~할 리 없다
mess up ~을 망치다

9-12

M Carrie, I'm going to be ________ a small group of students ________ ________ next weekend. I know you're ________ ________ dinosaurs. Would you like to go?

G ________. When are you going?

M We'll be leaving early on Saturday morning and ________ ________ on Saturday night.

G It's not an ________ trip? I thought you usually did that.

M Everyone who's going said they aren't interested in ________. Plus, it's supposed to rain on Sunday, so we'll just make this a ________ ________.

G That makes sense. Where will you be ________ ________ fossils?

M We're driving out to the river about an hour from school. There's a ________ ________ lots of fossils are already exposed, so we ________ ________ ________ ________ dig much.

G It sounds like a lot of fun. But I need to ________ my parents ________ permission before I can go.

M That's totally understandable. Can you ________ ________ ________ by tomorrow morning?

G Of course. I'll ________ ________ ________ when they get home. I'll email you their response ________ ________.

M Thanks a lot. Oh, you won't need to ________ any digging ________. I have enough for everybody.

G That's good to know. Thanks. I really hope they ________ ________ ________ ________.

voca

9-12
fossil 화석
hunting 사냥, 채집
dinosaur 공룡
totally 완전히
overnight 하룻밤 자고 오는
be supposed to V ~하기로 되어 있다
make sense 말이 되다
dig 파다, 캐다
expose 드러내다, 노출하다
permission 허락
understandable 이해할 수 있는
response 답변
equipment 장비
permit A to V A가 ~하도록 허락하다

PRACTICE 2 Lecture/Discussion

51. MP3

1 **What is the subject of the talk?**

(A) The construction of Roman roads
(B) The routes of Roman roads
(C) The uses of Roman roads
(D) The most famous Roman roads

2 **Why does the teacher mention the Appian Way?**

(A) To call it the first Roman road
(B) To say where it started and ended
(C) To name it as a famous road
(D) To give the Latin word for "road"

3 **What does the teacher imply when she says: "It seems impossible, doesn't it?"**

(A) The Romans rarely built roads poorly.
(B) Nobody can build roads like the Romans today.
(C) She thinks the Romans built too many roads.
(D) It is amazing that Roman roads exist today.

4 **According to the teacher, what does the *rudus* contain?**

(A) Sand or compacted dry soil
(B) Large stones or bricks
(C) Gravel and mortar
(D) Fine gravel and crushed stones

5 **How were the stones in the *pavimentum* arranged?**

(A) They were completely flat.
(B) They were slightly raised.
(C) They were angled upward.
(D) They were tilted from the center.

6 **What are the speakers mainly talking about?**

(A) Why the Great Depression lasted so long

(B) The government's effect on the Great Depression

(C) Who suffered during the Great Depression

(D) Causes and effects of the Great Depression

7 **What does the girl say about the Great Depression?**

(A) It started during World War II.

(B) People believe a stock market crash caused it.

(C) It only happened in the United States.

(D) Most Americans lost their jobs during it.

8 **What can be inferred from the discussion about the New Deal?**

(A) It gave many people new jobs.

(B) It made the depression worse.

(C) It started around the year 1929.

(D) It was created by the president.

9 **What does the teacher imply when he says: "However, you're getting a bit ahead of the discussion"?**

(A) The girl knows more than other students.

(B) He will cover a certain topic a bit later.

(C) Other students need to speak as well.

(D) The girl made an incorrect statement.

10 **What is the purpose of the talk?**

(A) To compare predators and prey
(B) To describe some animal defenses
(C) To show how predators hunt
(D) To name some common prey animals

11 **What does the teacher mean when he says: "But that's not actually the case"?**

(A) There are more predators than prey.
(B) Sharp teeth and claws are effective.
(C) Prey animals can protect themselves.
(D) Deer can run faster than predators.

12 **What does the teacher imply about sharp teeth and claws?**

(A) Many animals have them.
(B) They can kill prey animals.
(C) They are better than great speed.
(D) Skunks make use of them.

13 **According to the teacher, what is a defense mechanism of the armadillo?**

(A) Sharp claws
(B) Great speed
(C) Sharp quills
(D) Very hard skin

DICTATION 2 Lecture/Discussion

52. MP3

1-5

W _______________ _______________ the Roman Empire was so successful was its _______________. There were more than 120,000 kilometers of roads _______________ the empire. These included the Appian Way, or the Via Appia in Latin. It's _______________ the most famous Roman road. Roman roads were _______________ straight _______________ _______________. Their roads were constructed to let soldiers, travelers, and merchants _______________ from one point to another as _______________ as possible.

Some Roman roads still _______________ today. It seems impossible, doesn't it? But that's a _______________ to their building ability. You're probably _______________ _______________ they managed to construct roads which have _______________ around 2,000 years. Well, let me tell you. Major Roman roads were a _______________ 4.2 meters _______________. This was, in Roman times, wide enough for two _______________ _______________ to pass each other in opposite directions. To make them, first, the Romans _______________ a trench and then put sand or compacted dry soil above it. The next _______________ was large stones or pieces of _______________ around twenty centimeters thick. _______________ that layer was the *rudus*. It contained gravel and mortar to _______________ the stones _______________. The following layer was the *nucleus*. It had _______________ gravel and crushed stones. Last was the *pavimentum*. It contained a layer of stone _______________ closely fitted together. These stones were _______________ slightly from the center, which _______________ rainwater to run off the sides. _______________, wasn't it?

voca

1-5
Roman Empire 로마 제국
successful 성공적인
throughout ~ 전체에
arguably 아마도
construct 건설하다
merchant 상인

exist 존재하다
testament 증거
ability 능력
last 지속하다
standard 표준의
wheeled 바퀴 달린
vehicle 차량
in opposite directions 반대 방향으로
trench 도랑
compact 다지다
soil 흙
layer 층
contain 포함하다
gravel 자갈
mortar 모르타르
bind 결합하다
following 그 다음의
fine (알갱이가) 고운
crush 부수다
slab 판석
closely 촘촘하게
incline 기울이다
allow A to V A가 ~하게 해 주다
rainwater 빗물
run off 흐르다
ingenious 기발한

6-9

M The Great Depression started in the United States in 1929. It ________ ________ ________ ________ World War II began in 1941. This was ________ ________ an economic depression in the U.S. though. It ________ countries around the world. Can anyone tell me ________ ________ ________?

G In October 1929, the stock market ________. This is when people traditionally say that it began. ________, uh, before that time, there were obvious bad financial conditions which ________ ________ the Great Depression happening.

M You're right about that. In the 1920s, people in the United States ________ ________ in the stock market. However, the economic situation then wasn't ________. Unemployment was ________, and people really couldn't ________ ________ be investing in stocks.

G Right. So when the ________ crashed, plenty of people ________ their life savings. Companies went ________, so people also lost their ________. Then, the federal government began ________, particularly by introducing the programs in the New Deal. The New Deal itself ________ the depression ________ last much longer than it should have.

M That's a ________ ________. However, you're getting a bit ________ ________ the discussion. Let's ________ ________ the reasons that the Great Depression started. We can ________ how government interference caused ________ ________ during the depression a bit later.

voca

6-9

Great Depression 대공황
economic 경제의
depression 불황
affect ~에 영향을 주다

stock market 주식 시장
crash 폭락하다
traditionally 전통적으로
obvious 확실한
financial 재정의, 금융의
condition 상태
result in ~을 가져오다

invest 투자하다
unemployment 실업
afford to V ~할 여유가 있다
stock 주식

plenty of 많은
life savings 평생 모은 돈
go bankrupt 파산하다
federal government 연방 정부
interfere 개입하다
particularly 특히
introduce 도입하다
cause A to V A가 ~하게 만들다

ahead of ~보다 앞선
discussion 토론, 논의
focus on ~에 초점을 맞추다
cover 다루다
interference 개입
cause 초래하다, 야기하다

10-13

M Nature is ________. There are predators and ________, and predators are always on the ________ ________ their next meal. We often ________ ________ prey animals ________ ________ being helpless. But that's not actually the case. There are numerous ________ that animals have. Some are pretty standard, ________ ________ sharp teeth and claws. Even ________ ________ such as squirrels, rabbits, and mice have those. They can bite and scratch attackers ________ ________ ________. Other animals, including deer, zebras, and gazelles, have great ________. They can use it to ________ ________ attacking wolves, lions, and other animals. And some animals use ________. They can hide from predators to ________ ________ ________. Rabbits, chameleons, and turtles use this defense mechanism.

There are, however, ________ ________ of defenses which are not standard. These may be ________ ________ a single animal or to a small group of animals. The skunk, ________ ________, can spray liquid that has a ________ ________ at animals. This effectively ________ most predators ________ from it. The porcupine has extremely ________ quills. These can detach and ________ ________ in the bodies of animals attacking it. They're quite ________ and often convince predators to ________ it ________. The armadillo has a very tough ________ that's almost like armor. It can roll itself into a ball when attacked. This ________ it ________ most predators.

voca

10-13

violent 난폭한, 격렬한
predator 포식자
prey 먹이
on the hunt for ~을 찾는, 사냥하는
think of A as B A를 B라고 생각하다
helpless 무력한
numerous 많은
defense 방어
standard 표준적인
scratch 할퀴다
attacker 공격자
gazelle 영양
flee from ~으로부터 도망가다
camouflage 위장
avoid V-ing ~하는 것을 피하다, 모면하다
mechanism 기제

unique to ~에게 독특한
spray 뿌리다
liquid 액체
terrible 끔찍한
effectively 효과적으로
keep away ~이 다가오지 못하게 하다
porcupine 호지
extremely 엄청나게
quill 가시
detach 분리되다
get stuck 박히다
painful 고통스러운
convince A to V A가 ~하도록 만들다
armadillo 아르마딜로
exterior 외피
armor 갑옷
protect A from B A를 B로부터 보호하다

PRACTICE **TEST**

Now you will hear two conversations. Each conversation is followed by three or more questions. Choose the best answer to each question.

1 **What is the boy's problem?**

(A) He cannot do his homework.
(B) He got a low grade on a test.
(C) He is often late for school.
(D) He has too many assignments.

2 **What is probably true about the girl?**

(A) She is the student body president.
(B) She always does her homework.
(C) She is displeased with her math score.
(D) She works with a private tutor.

3 **What kinds of questions are hard for the boy?**

(A) Short answer questions
(B) True-false questions
(C) Word problems
(D) Multiplication problems

4 **What does the girl imply when she says: "I'll do my best"?**

(A) She will do better on the next test.
(B) She will study harder in class.
(C) She will help the boy study math.
(D) She will turn in her homework on time.

5 **What is the subject of the conversation?**

(A) The student magazine
(B) A poem the girl wrote
(C) The girl's extracurricular activities
(D) A recent homework assignment

6 **What does the teacher want to do?**

(A) Get the girl to write an essay
(B) Give the girl an extra assignment
(C) Help improve the girl's writing skills
(D) Have the girl's work published

7 **What does the teacher imply when he says: "It's not a major commitment"?**

(A) The girl will have time to do the work.
(B) He does not mind helping the girl.
(C) The girl must turn in the paper tomorrow.
(D) He would be glad to tutor the girl.

8 **What is the girl going to do tomorrow?**

(A) Revise her essay for the teacher
(B) Come to school earlier than usual
(C) Give the teacher a response
(D) Take a writing test for the teacher

53. MP3

Now you will hear a talk or discussion about an academic topic. The talk or discussion is followed by four or more questions. Choose the best answer to each question.

9 What is the main topic of the talk?

(A) Famous Renaissance artists
(B) The artistic style of Raphael
(C) Raphael's life and works
(D) *The School of Athens*

10 What does the teacher mean when she says: "I, however, am partial to Raphael"?

(A) She likes Raphael more than other artists.
(B) She has seen most of Raphael's works.
(C) Raphael painted during the Renaissance.
(D) Raphael was the greatest artist in history.

11 What does the teacher say about *The School of Athens*?

(A) It is a portrait of Aristotle.
(B) It was created in Urbino.
(C) It was painted on a wall.
(D) It is in a museum in Greece.

12 What will the teacher probably do next?

(A) Ask a student a question
(B) Talk about another artist
(C) Look in depth at a painting
(D) Discuss the Renaissance more

MEMO

MEMO

MEMO

The Best TOEFL Junior®

ANSWERS, SCRIPTS, & TRANSLATIONS

LC

Intermediate

DARAKWON

The Best TOEFL Junior®

ANSWERS, SCRIPTS, & TRANSLATIONS

LC

Intermediate

DARAKWON

DIAGNOSTIC TEST

DIAGNOSTIC TEST			p. 013
1 (D)	2 (C)	3 (B)	4 (B)
5 (D)	6 (B)	7 (D)	8 (B)
9 (B)	10 (C)	11 (D)	12 (C)
13 (A)	14 (A)	15 (D)	16 (C)
17 (A)	18 (B)	19 (C)	20 (A)
21 (B)	22 (A)	23 (D)	24 (B)
25 (C)	26 (B)	27 (B)	28 (C)
29 (D)	30 (A)	31 (A)	32 (B)
33 (B)			

1 Listen to a librarian speaking to a group of students.

W We just subscribed to several newspapers to help students keep up to date on news. We get our local paper now plus four others from around the state. They are online subscriptions, so you can only read them on computer terminals in the library. Let me show you how you can do that.

사서 선생님이 학생들에게 말하는 내용을 들어 보세요.

W 학생들이 최신 뉴스를 접할 수 있도록 여러 신문을 새로 구독했습니다. 이제 우리는 지역 신문 한 부와 주 내의 다른 네 개의 신문을 구독하고 있습니다. 이 신문들은 온라인 구독이기 때문에, 도서관의 컴퓨터 단말기에서만 읽을 수 있습니다. 어떻게 이용할 수 있는지 보여 드릴게요.

2 Listen to a teacher talking to a group of students.

W We're going to have a dress rehearsal for the play tomorrow after school. We're going to practice the entire performance. You need to be in full costume tomorrow. So please bring your outfits from home. We've only got one week before we perform for real, so let's make it a good practice.

선생님이 학생들에게 말하는 내용을 들어 보세요.

W 내일 방과 후에 연극을 위한 총연습을 할 것입니다. 전체 공연을 연습할 예정입니다. 내일은 완전한 의상을 착용해야 합니다. 그러니 집에서 의상을 꼭 가져오세요. 실제로 공연하기까지 일주일밖에 남지 않았으니, 좋은 연습이 되도록 합시다.

3 Listen to a science teacher speaking to her class.

W Tomorrow, we're going to conduct an experiment. I need you to bring a few items from home. Let me write down what you need on the whiteboard. You must bring everything, or you won't be able to do the experiment. All of the items on this list should already be at your home, so you won't have to buy anything.

과학 선생님이 반 학생들에게 말하는 내용을 들어 보세요.

W 내일 우리는 실험을 할 거예요. 여러분이 집에서 몇 가지 물건을 가져와야 해요. 필요한 것을 화이트보드에 적어 줄게요. 모든 것을 가져와야 합니다. 그렇지 않으면 실험을 할 수 없을 거예요. 이 목록에 있는 모든 물건은 이미 여러분 집에 있을 테니, 아무것도 살 필요는 없을 거예요.

4 Listen to a teacher making an announcement.

M Yesterday, I mentioned that your midterm exam will be this Friday, the tenth. This morning, Principal McKinney informed me that the midterm exams will take place next week. So please be advised that our test is not this week. Instead, it's going to take place next Tuesday, the fourteenth. Do you have any questions?

선생님이 공지하는 내용을 들어 보세요.

M 어제, 중간고사가 이번 주 금요일, 10일에 있을 거라고 말했습니다. 오늘 아침에 McKinney 교장 선생님께서 중간고사가 다음 주에 치러질 거라고 알려 주셨습니다. 그러니 우리 시험은 이번 주가 아니라는 것을 알아 두세요. 대신 다음 주 화요일, 14일에 있을 것입니다. 질문 있나요?

5 Listen to a teacher making an announcement.

W Tomorrow, we're going to have a quiz at the beginning of class. You will be tested on the material that we learned today. That means you need to know the names of all fifty states as well as their capitals. The quiz will be worth twenty points and will take about ten minutes.

선생님이 공지하는 내용을 들어 보세요.

W 내일 수업이 시작되면 쪽지 시험을 볼 예정입니다. 오늘 배운 내용에 대해 시험을 볼 것입니다. 즉, 여러분은 모든 50개 주의 이름과 주도를 알아야 한다는 뜻입니다. 퀴즈는 20점의 가치가 있으며 10분 정도 걸릴 것입니다.

6 Listen to a school principal making an announcement.

M The groundskeepers just informed me that they planted new grass on the football field. Nobody is permitted on the field for the next two weeks. We want to make sure that the grass grows well during that time. If anyone goes on the field, that student will receive detention. Thank you for your cooperation.

교장 선생님이 공지하는 내용을 들어 보세요.

M 관리 직원들이 방금 저에게 축구장에 새 잔디를 심었다고 알려 주셨습니다. 앞으로 2주 동안은 아무도 축구장에 들어가면 안 됩니다.

그 기간 동안 잔디가 잘 자라도록 하기를 원합니다. 만약 누가 축구장에 들어가면, 그 학생은 방과 후에 남는 벌을 받게 될 것입니다. 협조해 주셔서 감사합니다.

7 Listen to an art teacher speaking to a group of students.

M I would like to have class outside today. I want all of you to take your sketchpads and some colored pencils when we leave the classroom. We're heading behind this building so that we can see the forest. I want you to make a landscape drawing of the forest. Do you have any questions?

미술 선생님이 학생들에게 말하는 내용을 들어 보세요.

M 오늘은 수업을 교실 밖에서 진행하고자 합니다. 교실을 나갈 때 여러분 모두 스케치북과 색연필 몇 개를 가져갔으면 해요. 우리는 숲을 볼 수 있도록 이 건물 뒤로 갈 예정입니다. 숲의 풍경을 그림으로 그리길 바랍니다. 질문 있나요?

8 Listen to a science teacher speaking to her students.

W Yesterday, a couple of students conducted a science experiment in the lab without any supervision. You simply cannot do that. The chemicals in the lab are dangerous. Some can explode, and others can burn you if they are mixed improperly. Please do not do anything in the lab unless another teacher or I am there.

과학 선생님이 학생들에게 말하는 내용을 들어 보세요.

W 어제 두어 명의 학생이 감독 없이 실험실에서 과학 실험을 진행했습니다. 여러분은 그런 행동을 절대 해서는 안 됩니다. 실험실의 화학 물질은 위험합니다. 일부는 폭발할 수 있고, 다른 것들은 잘못 섞이면 여러분에게 화상을 입힐 수도 있습니다. 다른 선생님이나 제가 있지 않다면 실험실에서 아무것도 하지 마세요.

9-12 Listen to a conversation between two friends.

G Peter, Chris told me that you collect coins. Is that true?

B Yes, it is. I collect old American coins and coins from foreign countries. I also have some coins from ancient Rome and Greece.

G That's fascinating. How did you get interested in collecting them?

B My dad used to travel abroad frequently for business. Whenever he returned, he would give me the coins he had. I thought they were pretty cool, so I began learning about coin collecting.

G But aren't coins from ancient times really expensive?

B They can be. But you can also get old Roman and Greek coins for fairly inexpensive prices. It's just, uh, the quality isn't that good.

G I see. I'd like to see some of your old coins if you don't mind.

B I definitely don't mind. I can bring them to school later in the week.

G Thanks. I appreciate that.

B Do you have a hobby?

G Yes, I do. I paint a lot. I took a class last summer and discovered I've got a bit of talent at it.

B Cool. What kinds of paintings do you make?

G I prefer to do still lifes. I enjoy arranging flowers in a vase and then painting what I see. It's not easy, but I find it fun.

두 친구가 나누는 대화를 들어 보세요.

G Peter, 네가 동전 수집한다고 Chris가 그러던데. 진짜야?

B 응, 맞아. 나는 오래된 미국 동전이랑 외국 동전을 모아. 고대 로마랑 그리스 동전도 몇 개 있어.

G 멋지다. 동전 수집에 어떻게 관심 가지게 된 거야?

B 아빠가 예전엔 해외로 출장 자주 갔거든. 돌아올 때마다 가진 동전들을 주셨어. 난 그게 멋지다고 생각해서 동전 수집을 배우기 시작했어.

G 근데 고대 동전들은 진짜 비싸지 않아?

B 비쌀 수도 있지. 근데 옛날 로마나 그리스 동전은 꽤 저렴하게도 살 수 있어. 다만, 음, 상태가 그렇게 좋진 않아.

G 알겠다. 괜찮으면 네 오래된 동전들 좀 보고 싶어.

B 물론이지. 이번 주 나중에 학교에 가져올 수 있어.

G 고마워, 정말 고마워.

B 너는 취미 있어?

G 응, 있어. 나는 그림을 많이 그려. 지난 여름에 수업 들었는데, 조금 재능 있는 걸 발견했어.

B 멋지다. 무슨 그림을 그려?

G 나는 정물화 그리는 걸 좋아해. 꽃을 꽃병에 꽂고 그걸 그림으로 옮기는 걸 즐겨. 쉽진 않지만 재미있어.

13-16 Listen to a conversation between a student and a teacher.

B Ms. Hanlon, I have decided on my presentation topic.

W That's good to hear, Tom. What are you going to speak about?

B I'm going to focus on the westward push by settlers across the Mississippi River in the 1800s. Is that an acceptable topic?

W It's a good start, but I'd like for you to look at just one particular aspect of it.

B Such as?

W Well, you could talk about the settling of an individual territory before it became a state. Or you could discuss the history of the Oregon Trail. Something like that.

B Ah, I get it. I'll do some more thinking and then give you a specific topic tomorrow morning. Is that okay?

W Sure. That's fine.

B Thank you. Oh, uh . . . There's one more thing. I, um

. . . I get really nervous when I have to speak in front of the class. What happens if I get so nervous that I can't talk? I'm very worried about that.

W Well, let's hope that doesn't happen. Just relax and don't think about the students watching you. Try to focus on your presentation and what you're going to say, and you'll forget about everyone. I'm sure you'll do a fantastic job.

B I sure hope so.

학생과 선생님이 나누는 대화를 들어 보세요.

B Hanlon 선생님, 발표 주제를 결정했어요.

W 잘됐네, Tom. 무엇에 대해 발표할 거야?

B 1800년대 미시시피 강을 넘어 서쪽으로 이동한 개척자들에 대해 집중할 거예요. 그게 적절한 주제일까요?

W 시작으로는 괜찮지만, 네가 특정한 한 측면만 살펴보면 좋겠어.

B 예를 들면 어떤 걸까요?

W 음, 개척 영토가 주가 되기 전 정착 과정에 대해 이야기할 수도 있고, 오리건 산길의 역사에 대해 다룰 수도 있어. 그런 식으로.

B 아, 알겠어요. 더 생각해 보고 내일 아침에 구체적인 주제를 알려 드릴게요. 괜찮을까요?

W 물론, 좋아.

B 감사합니다. 아… 그리고 하나 더 있어요. 저는, 음… 반 학생들 앞에서 말할 때 정말 긴장돼요. 너무 긴장해서 말을 못 하면 어떻게 하죠? 그게 많이 걱정돼요.

W 글쎄, 그런 일이 없길 바라자. 그냥 긴장 풀고 학생들이 보고 있는 것에 대해 생각하지 마. 발표와 말할 내용에 집중해. 그러면 다른 사람에 대해서는 다 잊게 될 거야. 잘할 거라고 확신해.

B 그러길 바라요.

17-20 Listen to a conversation between a student and a teacher.

M Amanda, I'd like a word with you, please.

G Of course, Mr. Carmichael. I have a few minutes before my next class.

M That's good to hear. So, uh, I've been very impressed with the work you've done in my math class this year. You've shown great improvement and an ability to understand the fundamentals of geometry.

G Thank you for saying that.

M So I've decided I'd like you to be on the school's math team.

G I didn't think the school had a math team.

M It's a brand-new team I'm starting this semester. That's why you've never heard of it. There are going to be eight students on the team. Our first competition is two weeks from today. Can you do it?

G Sure. I suppose so. What do I need to do?

M Well, the contests involve students trying to solve math problems as quickly as possible. I've noticed you have a talent for doing that, so I think you'll do well.

G Do we have practice?

M Yes, we do. We're going to meet after school tomorrow and once again next week. I'll show you some typical problems asked on the test. I'll also explain what to do at the competition.

G Okay. Just let me know where to go.

학생과 선생님이 나누는 대화를 들어 보세요.

M Amanda, 잠깐 이야기 좀 했으면 해.

G 물론이에요, Carmichael 선생님. 다음 수업 전까지 시간 있어요.

M 잘됐네. 음, 올해 내 수학 수업에서 네가 한 것을 보면서 정말 감명 받았어. 향상된 실력과 기하학의 기본 원리를 이해하는 능력을 보여 줬거든.

G 그렇게 말씀해 주셔서 감사합니다.

M 그래서 네가 학교 수학 팀에 들어왔으면 좋겠다고 생각했어.

G 학교에 수학 팀이 있는 줄 몰랐어요.

M 내가 새로 이번 학기에 시작하는 팀이야. 그래서 들어 본 적이 없지. 팀에는 여덟 명의 학생이 들어갈 거야. 첫 대회는 오늘로부터 2주 뒤야. 할 수 있겠어?

G 네, 할 수 있을 것 같아요. 뭘 하면 되나요?

M 대회는 학생들이 수학 문제를 가능한 한 빨리 푸는 것을 포함해. 네가 그것에 재능이 있는 것 같아서 잘할 거라고 생각해.

G 연습도 있나요?

M 응, 내일 방과 후랑 다음 주에 한 번 더 만날 거야. 시험에서 나오는 전형적인 문제들을 보여 줄 거고, 대회에서 무엇을 해야 하는지도 설명할 거야.

G 알겠습니다. 어디로 가야 하는지만 알려 주세요.

21-25 Listen to a part of a radio program about science.

M The largest commercial airliner weighs nearly 570,000 kilograms on takeoff. Compare that with the *Wright Flyer*, the first plane ever to take off and land. It had a maximum weight of 338 kilograms. Despite the huge difference in weight, both planes—and every other one, too—rely upon the same principles in order to achieve flight and to stay in the air.

The four forces required for flight are lift, weight, thrust, and drag. All four of these forces interact with one another to enable a plane to fly. Lift refers to the upward force created by air moving both above and below a plane's wings. Air moves faster above the wings and slower below them. This, in turn, makes a difference in air pressure that helps keep a plane in the air. Weight refers to the force of gravity, which pulls the plane down toward the ground. The amount of lift must exceed the pull of gravity in order for a plane to become airborne and to stay aloft. Thrust is the force that a plane's engines or propellers creates. Thrust allows a plane to move forward through the air. Finally, drag is basically air resistance. It works in opposition to thrust by slowing down the plane as it attempts to move forward.

과학에 대한 라디오 프로그램의 일부를 들어 보세요.

M 가장 큰 상업용 여객기는 이륙할 때 무게가 거의 570,000킬로그램에 달합니다. 처음으로 이착륙한 비행기인 Wright Flyer와 비교해 보세요. 그 비행기는 최대 무게가 338킬로그램에 불과했습니다. 무게 차이가 매우 크지만, 두 비행기와 다른 모든 비행기는 날기 위해, 그리고 공중에 머물기 위해 동일한 원리에 의존합니다.

비행에 필요한 네 가지 힘은 양력, 무게, 추진력, 항력입니다. 이 네 가지 힘은 서로 상호작용하여 비행기가 날 수 있도록 합니다. 양력은 비행기의 날개 위아래를 움직이는 공기에 의해 발생하는 위쪽으로 향하는 힘을 말합니다. 공기는 날개 위에서는 빠르게, 아래에서는 느리게 움직입니다. 이로 인해 공기 압력의 차이가 생기며, 이는 비행기를 공중에 떠 있게 하는 데 도움을 줍니다. 무게는 비행기를 지면으로 끌어당기는 중력의 힘을 말합니다. 비행기가 이륙하고 공중에 머물기 위해서는 양력이 중력의 끌어당김보다 커야 합니다. 추진력은 비행기의 엔진이나 프로펠러가 만들어 내는 힘입니다. 추진력은 비행기가 공기를 뚫고 앞으로 나아가게 합니다. 마지막으로 항력은 기본적으로 공기 저항입니다. 항력은 비행기가 앞으로 나아가려 할 때 속도를 늦추며 추진력과 반대로 작용합니다.

28-29 Listen to part of a discussion in an English class.

W Let's talk about *The Call of the Wild* by Jack London. The main character of this novel is not a human but the dog Buck. The story mostly takes place in the Yukon during the gold rush that happened there in the 1890s. Kevin, your hand is up.

B This was easily the best book we've read this semester. I've never been to the Yukon, but London's descriptions of it were so realistic. I wonder how he managed to accomplish that.

W He actually went there. London lived in an age when writers didn't just sit at their desks and write. They went on adventures. For instance, Herman Melville, the author of *Moby-Dick*, spent time on whaling ships. And Stephen Crane was a war correspondent. London himself therefore had firsthand knowledge of the Yukon and what it was like. He knew about the difficulties of searching for gold and how harsh the environment there was. Now, what would you say the theme of the book is?

B It's about Buck's transformation from being civilized to being wild. His life was easy at the beginning. But in the Yukon, life became about survival of the fittest. Buck learns to use his strength not only to survive but also to thrive in the wilderness.

W Well stated, Kevin. There's another theme. Let me give you a hint, and then you can try to figure it out.

영어 수업 중 토론 내용의 일부를 들어 보세요.

W 잭 런던의 『야생의 부름』에 대해 이야기해 보죠. 이 소설의 주인공은 인간이 아니라 개인 벅입니다. 이야기는 주로 1890년대 골드러시가 일어난 유콘에서 전개됩니다. Kevin, 손 들었네.

B 이번 학기에 읽은 책 중에서 단연 최고였어요. 유콘에 가 본 적은 없지만, 런던의 묘사가 너무 사실적이었어요. 어떻게 그렇게 할 수 있었는지 궁금해요.

W 사실 그는 직접 거기에 갔어. 런던은 작가들이 단순히 책상에 앉아 글만 쓰지 않았던 시대에 살았어. 그들은 모험을 떠났지. 예를 들어, 『모비 딕』의 저자 허먼 멜빌은 포경선에서 시간을 보냈고, 스티븐 크레인은 전쟁 특파원이었어. 런던 자신도 유콘과 그곳의 환경을 직접 경험해서 알고 있었어. 그는 금을 찾는 어려움과 그곳의 혹독한 환경에 대해 잘 알고 있었지. 이제, 이 책의 주제가 무엇이라고 생각하니?

B 벅이 문명화된 상태에서 야생으로 변해가는 과정을 다루고 있어요. 처음에는 그의 삶이 편했지만, 유콘에서는 적자생존의 삶이 되었죠. 벅은 생존할 뿐만 아니라 황야에서 번성하기 위해 자신의 힘을 사용하는 법을 배우게 돼요.

W 잘 말했어, Kevin. 또 다른 주제도 있어. 힌트를 줄 테니, 한번 생각해 보렴.

30-33 Listen to part of a talk in a history class.

M Let's move on to another great British explorer, James Cook. He's more commonly known as Captain Cook. He was born in 1728 and died in 1779, so he lived after the Age of Exploration ended. That, by the way, happened in 1620. Still, Captain Cook was a great explorer remembered for his voyages in the Pacific Ocean.

Before I tell you about his three main expeditions, I want to mention something of great importance that Captain Cook was responsible for. One problem that sailors suffered from on long expeditions was scurvy. It was a horrible disease which caused men to lose teeth, to suffer gum problems, and eventually to die. It was caused by a lack of vitamins, particularly vitamin C. Cook provided lots of fresh fruit, particularly citrus fruit, for his sailors. As a result, none of them suffered from scurvy. His actions were later imitated by others, saving countless lives over time.

Now, how about Captain Cook's first expedition . . . ? The first place he visited was Tahiti, an island in the South Pacific Ocean. He was sent there to make astronomical observations of Venus. He also visited both of the main islands of New Zealand, which he mapped in great detail. Last, he sailed around the east coast of Australia. He and his crew finally returned home after three years at sea.

역사 수업 내용의 일부를 들어 보세요.

M 이제 또 다른 위대한 영국 탐험가, 제임스 쿡에 대해 이야기해 보죠. 그는 보통 쿡 선장으로 더 잘 알려져 있습니다. 그는 1728년에 태어나 1779년에 사망했으니, 대항해시대가 끝난 후에 살았습니다. 참고로 대항해시대는 1620년에 일어났습니다. 그럼에도 불구하고 쿡

선장은 태평양에서의 항해로 기억되는 위대한 탐험가입니다.

그의 세 가지 주요 원정에 대해 이야기하기 전에, 쿡 선장이 원인을 제공했던 아주 중요한 일을 하나 언급하고 싶습니다. 긴 항해 동안 선원들이 겪었던 문제 중 하나가 괴혈병이었습니다. 그것은 선원들이 이를 잃고 잇몸 문제가 생기며, 결국 사망하게 되는 무서운 병이었습니다. 비타민, 특히 비타민 C가 부족해서 생겼습니다. 쿡 선장은 선원들에게 많은 신선한 과일, 특히 감귤류 과일을 제공했습니다. 그 결과, 누구도 괴혈병으로 고생하지 않았습니다. 그의 이런 행동은 나중에 다른 사람들에게 모방되어, 시간이 흐르면서 수많은 생명을 구했습니다.

자, 그럼 쿡 선장의 첫 번째 원정은 어땠는지 살펴볼까요…? 그가 처음 방문한 곳은 남태평양의 섬, 타히티였습니다. 그는 거기에 금성의 천문 관측을 하기 위해 보내졌습니다. 또한 그는 뉴질랜드의 주요 두 섬을 모두 방문했는데, 그곳들을 아주 자세하게 지도화했습니다. 마지막으로 그는 호주 동해안을 항해했습니다. 그는 선원들과 함께 3년간의 항해 끝에 마침내 집으로 돌아왔습니다.

CHAPTER 01 MAIN IDEA

PRACTICE 1 Short Talk			p. 025
1 (C)	2 (A)	3 (C)	4 (D)
5 (A)	6 (C)	7 (D)	8 (C)

1 Listen to a history teacher speaking to his students.

M It's time to take your midterm exams. Please close your books and put them under your desk. You need to write the answers with a pencil or a pen. Do not speak to anyone else. Do not look at your phone or book or at another student's test paper. When you finish, you may hand in your exam.

역사 선생님이 학생들에게 말하는 내용을 들어 보세요.

M 중간고사를 볼 시간입니다. 책을 덮고 책상 밑에 넣으세요. 답은 연필이나 펜으로 작성해야 합니다. 다른 사람과 이야기하지 마세요. 휴대폰이나 책이나 다른 학생의 시험지를 보지 마세요. 시험을 끝내면 시험지를 제출할 수 있습니다.

2 Listen to a teacher making an announcement at the end of the day.

W Our school is starting a new program. I hope some of you decide to participate in it. We want students to work as tutors for young children. Volunteer tutors will visit the nearby elementary school twice a week. They will provide tutoring in math, science, and English. Tutors will work one on one with students. Is anyone interested?

종례 때 선생님이 공지하는 내용을 들어 보세요.

W 우리 학교에서 새로운 프로그램을 시작합니다. 몇몇 학생들이 참여하기로 결정하길 바랍니다. 우리는 학생들이 어린 아이들을 가르치는 개인 지도 교사로 활동하길 원합니다. 지원봉사 개인 지도 교사는 인근 초등학교를 주 2회 방문합니다. 수학, 과학, 영어를 가르치게 됩니다. 개인 지도 교사는 학생과 일대일로 수업을 진행합니다. 관심 있는 사람 있나요?

3 Listen to a principal making an announcement.

M Students need to stop running in the halls at once. There have been several near collisions because of students running. This is dangerous and needs to stop immediately. Running students may also slip and get hurt. That is especially true on rainy days like today. The floors are wet, so please be careful and behave better.

교장 선생님이 공지하는 내용을 들어 보세요.

M 학생들은 복도에서 뛰는 것을 당장 그만둬야 합니다. 학생들이 뛰어서 몇 차례 충돌할 뻔한 상황이 발생했습니다. 이것은 위험하므로 즉시 멈춰야 합니다. 뛰는 학생은 또한 미끄러져 다칠 수 있습니다. 오늘처럼 비 오는 날에는 특히 그렇습니다. 바닥이 젖어 있으니 조심하고 더 잘 행동하세요.

4 Listen to a science teacher talking to her students.

W Everyone, please listen up. I need to leave the classroom for a few minutes to speak with the principal. While I'm gone, do not use any of the lab equipment. Some of this equipment is very expensive. It's also fragile and can break easily. Please wait until I return to start your experiments.

과학 선생님이 학생들에게 말하는 내용을 들어 보세요.

W 여러분, 잘 들으세요. 제가 교장 선생님과 잠깐 이야기하러 몇 분 동안 교실에서 나가야 해요. 제가 없는 동안에는 실험 기구를 사용하지 마세요. 일부 기구는 매우 비싸고, 또한 약해서 깨지기 쉽습니다. 제가 돌아올 때까지 실험을 시작하지 말고 기다리세요.

5 Listen to a librarian talking to a group of students.

M In order to find a book here, use the online catalogue. Searching for a book is very simple. If you know the title, type it in. If you know the author, you can type the author's name. If you aren't looking for a specific book, type the subject you want. Then, you'll get a list of possible books.

사서 선생님이 학생들에게 말하는 내용을 들어 보세요.

M 여기서 책을 찾으려면 온라인 도서 목록을 사용하세요. 책을 찾는 것은 매우 간단합니다. 제목을 알고 있다면 입력하세요. 저자를 알고 있다면 저자 이름을 입력할 수 있습니다. 특정한 책을 찾고 있는 것이 아니라면 원하는 주제를 입력하세요. 그러면 가능한 책들의 목록이 나올 것입니다.

6 Listen to a teacher making an announcement.

W For your final project, you are all going to give class presentations. You'll work with a partner on this assignment. You must first choose a topic. It should be from something we studied this year. Then, prepare a presentation about that topic. Your presentation should be ten minutes long. If you need any assistance, please ask me.

선생님이 공지하는 내용을 들어 보세요.

W 기말 프로젝트로, 여러분은 모두 학급 발표를 하게 될 것입니다. 이 과제는 짝과 함께 하게 됩니다. 먼저 주제를 선택해야 합니다. 주제는 올해 공부한 내용 중에서 선택해야 합니다. 그 다음, 그 주제에 대해 발표를 준비하세요. 발표 시간은 10분이어야 합니다. 도움이 필요하면 저에게 물어보세요.

7 Listen to a school nurse making an announcement.

M This has been a long semester, so everyone is tired. Please make sure to get enough rest. That will help you avoid coming down with a cold or the flu. Your body needs rest in order to remain healthy. Don't stay up late. Instead, go to bed early and try to get eight hours of sleep a night.

학교 보건 선생님이 공지하는 내용을 들어 보세요.

M 이번 학기는 길었기 때문에, 모두가 피곤한 상태입니다. 충분한 휴식을 취하도록 하세요. 그래야 감기나 독감에 걸리는 것을 피할 수 있습니다. 건강을 유지하려면 몸이 휴식을 필요로 합니다. 늦게까지 깨어 있지 말고, 대신 일찍 잠자리에 들고 밤에 8시간 정도 자도록 하세요.

8 Listen to a teacher talking in an English class.

W I have some wonderful news, everyone. Tomorrow, we're going to have a guest speaker. Her name is Elizabeth Wilson, and she's a professor of English at the local university. She's also a famous novelist. Some of you might have read her books. She's going to speak about writing to us tomorrow. I hope you all listen carefully.

영어 시간에 선생님이 말하는 내용을 들어 보세요..

W 여러분, 멋진 소식이 있어요. 내일 초청 강연자가 오실 거예요. 그분의 이름은 Elizabeth Wilson이고, 지역 대학에서 영어를 가르치는 교수님이세요. 또한 유명한 소설가이기도 합니다. 여러분 중 몇 명은 그분의 책을 읽어 본 적이 있을지도 모르겠네요. 그분은 내일 우리에게 글쓰기와 관련해 이야기해 주실 거예요. 모두 잘 들어 주시길 바랍니다.

PRACTICE 2 Conversation			p. 029
1 (C)	2 (B)	3 (D)	4 (A)
5 (C)	6 (B)	7 (A)	8 (A)

1-4 Listen to a conversation between two students at school.

B Abigail, did you understand the homework that we had to do for science class? I couldn't figure it out.

G Yes, it wasn't really too hard. You just needed to do the lab experiment to understand it.

B Lab experiment? What are you talking about?

G What do you mean? We did a lab experiment in class two days ago. Weren't you there?

B Oh. Actually, I came to school late on Monday, so I arrived in science class about five minutes before it ended. I guess I must have missed the lab.

G Well, you'd better talk to Mr. Rhodes about it immediately. He said that it's an important lab.

B Okay. I'll do that. But I still need some help with the homework. I don't want to get a poor grade on it. Do you think you can help me?

G I guess I can tell you about the lab. I don't think that would be a problem.

B Thanks so much. I really appreciate it.

G Should we go to the library now? That would be the best place to talk about it.

B Good thinking.

학교에서 두 학생이 나누는 대화를 들어 보세요.

B Abigail, 과학 수업에서 해야 했던 숙제 이해했어? 나는 잘 모르겠더라고.

G 응, 별로 어렵지 않았어. 실험을 해 보면 이해할 수 있어.

B 실험? 무슨 말이야?

G 무슨 뜻이야? 우리 이틀 전에 수업에서 실험했잖아. 너 안 왔어?

B 아. 실은, 월요일에 학교에 늦게 왔거든. 그래서 과학 수업 끝나기 5분쯤 전에 도착했어. 실험을 놓친 것 같네.

G 그럼 바로 Rhodes 선생님께 말씀드리는 게 좋겠어. 중요한 실험이라고 하셨거든.

B 알겠어. 그럴게. 근데 숙제에 아직 좀 도움이 필요해. 나쁜 점수를 받고 싶지 않거든. 도와줄 수 있을 것 같아?

G 실험 내용은 말해 줄 수 있겠지. 문제 없을 것 같아.

B 고마워. 진짜 고마워.

G 지금 도서관 갈까? 거기가 이야기하기 제일 좋은 장소일 거야.

B 좋은 생각이야.

5-8 Listen to a conversation between a student and a teacher.

G Mr. Gardner, I'm so glad I just ran into you. I have some great news.

M You do? What is it, Tiffany?

G Do you remember that online speech contest I entered two months ago? You helped me with it.

M Sure. Did you get the results?

G Yes, sir. And, well . . . I came in first place in the entire city. I can't believe it.

M Congratulations, Tiffany. You worked really hard on your speech and the presentation, so you deserve it.

G Thanks so much. There's an awards ceremony I have to attend at city hall next week. I'll receive a trophy and a certificate there. Oh, there's something else.

M Yeah? What is it?

G Because I won the city contest, I now qualify to participate in the state speech contest. That's going to take place in the state capital one month from now. It won't be an online event this time. So I was wondering . . . Can you help me with my speech?

M Of course. It would be my pleasure. What are you supposed to talk about?

G I'll find out the topic tomorrow. I'm supposed to get an email from the event organizers then. I'll let you know as soon as I can.

학생과 선생님이 나누는 대화를 들어 보세요.

G Gardner 선생님, 마주치게 되어서 너무 반가워요. 좋은 소식이 있어요.

M 정말? 무슨 소식인데, Tiffany?

G 제가 두 달 전에 참가했던 온라인 스피치 대회 기억나세요? 선생님이 도와주셨잖아요.

M 물론이지. 결과 나왔어?

G 네, 선생님. 그리고, 음… 시 전체에서 1등 했어요. 믿기지가 않아요.

M 축하해, Tiffany. 연설과 발표 준비를 정말 열심히 했으니까 당연한 결과야.

G 정말 감사합니다. 다음 주 시청에서 제가 참석해야 하는 시상식이 있어요. 거기서 트로피와 상장을 받을 거예요. 아, 그리고 또 하나 있어요.

M 그래? 뭔데?

G 시 대회에서 우승했으니 이제 주 스피치 대회에 참가할 자격이 생겼어요. 한 달 뒤 주도에서 열릴 예정이에요. 이번에는 온라인 행사가 아니에요. 그래서 생각해 봤는데…. 선생님께서 제 연설 준비 도와주실 수 있나요?

M 물론이지. 기쁘게 도와줄게. 뭐에 대해 발표해야 해?

G 내일 주제를 알게 돼요. 그때 행사 주최 측에서 이메일을 받을 예정이에요. 최대한 빨리 알려 드릴게요.

PRACTICE 3 Lecture/Discussion			p. 032
1 (B)	2 (A)	3 (B)	4 (D)
5 (C)	6 (B)	7 (A)	8 (D)

1-4 Listen to a teacher talking in a science class.

M So those are nonrenewable resources. There are also renewable resources. As the name suggests, these are resources which can be used again and again. Basically, we won't ever run out of them. Water, air, and soil are three examples of renewable resources. The sun's light and heat are, too, and so is the wind. Plants such as trees as well as crops grown on farms are renewable resources because they can be grown again. Animals are another renewable resource since they can reproduce. Those are just a few examples of renewable resources.

Now, uh, why are renewable resources important? Well, first of all, they sustain human life. We all have to eat daily, so we need renewable resources such as crops and animals. The sun provides the light and heat we need to see and to keep warm. Renewable resources are also vital to our energy needs. Flowing water in rivers can create hydroelectric power. So long as the river continues flowing, electricity can be created from it. The same is true, of course, of solar power. When the sun is shining, electricity can be created from it. I wonder if anyone can give me another example. Who would like to try?

과학 시간에 선생님이 설명하는 내용을 들어 보세요.

M 자, 이것들이 비재생 자원이에요. 재생 가능한 자원도 있어요. 이름에서 짐작할 수 있듯이, 이것들은 반복해서 사용할 수 있는 자원이에요. 기본적으로 우리는 결코 그것들을 다 쓰지 않아요. 물, 공기, 흙이 재생 가능한 자원의 세 가지 예예요. 태양의 빛과 열도 재생 가능한 자원이죠, 바람도 마찬가지예요. 나무와 같은 식물이나 농장에서 재배되는 작물도 다시 재배할 수 있으므로 재생 가능한 자원이랍니다. 동물도 또 다른 재생 가능한 자원이에요. 번식할 수 있으니까요. 이런 것들이 재생 가능한 자원의 몇 가지 예예요.

자, 재생 가능한 자원이 왜 중요할까요? 우선, 인간의 생명을 유지해 주거든요. 우리 모두 매일 먹어야 하니까, 작물과 동물 같은 재생 가능한 자원이 필요해요. 태양은 우리가 보고 따뜻하게 지내기 위해 필요한 빛과 열을 제공해요. 재생 가능한 자원은 에너지 필요에도 중요해요. 강물의 흐름으로 수력 발전을 만들 수 있죠. 강물이 계속 흐르는 한, 거기서 전기를 만들어낼 수 있어요. 물론 태양열 발전도 마찬가지예요. 해가 비치면 전기를 만들 수 있죠. 다른 예를 들어 줄 사람 있을까요. 누가 해 보고 싶나요?

5-8 Listen to part of a discussion in a social studies class.

W We live in a constitutional republic, so adults eighteen years of age or older can vote. There are any number of elections we can vote in. There are national, state, and local elections. I know you're all too young to vote yet. But can you tell me why we vote?

B Voting lets us take part in the political process. When we vote, we get to have a say in who our leaders are. Our leaders make important decisions, and these decisions affect our lives. For instance, they determine laws, taxes, and foreign policy. If the people we vote for win, then we should see results that we prefer.

W I see you have done the reading, Allen. Good job. I know some of you think voting is useless. But do you remember the election for mayor of this city last month? What happened?

B It was a really close election. The winner of the election only had five more votes than his opponent. So people's votes really were important in that case.

W That's right. So, uh, basically, if only six more supporters of his opponent had voted, we would have a different mayor. Six people isn't very many if you think about it.

사회 수업 중 토론 내용의 일부를 들어 보세요.

W 우리는 입헌 공화국에 살고 있기 때문에, 18세 이상의 성인은 투표할 수 있어요. 우리가 참여할 수 있는 선거는 아주 많아요. 전국, 주, 지방 선거가 있죠. 여러분은 아직 투표하기에는 너무 어리다는 것을 알고 있어요. 하지만 우리가 왜 투표하는지 말해 줄 수 있나요?

B 투표는 우리가 정치 과정에 참여할 수 있게 해 줘요. 투표할 때 우리는 누가 우리 지도자가 될지 의견을 낼 수 있어요. 지도자들은 중요

한 결정을 내리고, 이 결정들은 우리의 삶에 영향을 미치죠. 예를 들어, 법률, 세금, 외교 정책 등을 결정해요. 우리가 투표한 사람이 당선되면, 우리가 원하는 결과를 보게 되겠죠.

W Allen, 책을 잘 읽어 왔네. 잘했어. 여러분 중 어떤 사람들은 투표가 쓸모없다고 생각할 수도 있다는 걸 알아요. 하지만 지난달 이 도시 시장 선거를 기억하나요? 무슨 일이 있었죠?

B 정말 접전이었어요. 선거에서 이긴 사람은 상대 후보보다 단 5표 더 득표했어요. 그래서 그 경우에는 사람들의 투표가 정말 중요했어요.

W 맞아요. 그러니까, 기본적으로 상대 후보 지지자 여섯 명만 더 투표했어도, 우리는 다른 시장을 갖게 되었을 거예요. 여섯 명은 생각보다 많지 않아요.

PRACTICE TEST p. 036

1 (C)	2 (D)	3 (B)	4 (A)
5 (C)	6 (D)	7 (B)	8 (D)
9 (D)	10 (A)	11 (B)	12 (D)

1 Listen to a social studies teacher talking to a class.

W I'm going to end my lecture for the day. Now, I would like to have a class discussion. We're going to talk about the subject of today's lecture. Everyone, please listen carefully. If you have something to say, just raise your hand and say it. I want everybody to talk out loud as much as possible. Shall we begin?

사회 선생님이 반 학생들에게 말하는 내용을 들어 보세요.

W 오늘 강의를 여기서 마치겠습니다. 이제 반 전체 토론을 진행하고자 합니다. 오늘 강의 주제에 대해 이야기할 거예요. 모두 잘 들으세요. 할 말이 있으면 손을 들고 말하세요. 모두 최대한 큰 소리로 이야기해 주었으면 해요. 시작할까요?

2 Listen to a principal speaking to the students over the intercom.

M [*intercom sound*] Good morning, everybody. I have an important announcement to make. Please do not use the boys' or girls' locker rooms in the gym this week. They are being renovated. When the repairs are complete, they will look much better than before. You'll be able to access them next Monday. We're sorry about the inconvenience, but it's only temporary.

방송을 통해 교장 선생님이 말하는 내용을 들어 보세요.

M [교내 방송 소리] 안녕하세요, 여러분. 중요한 공지가 있습니다. 이번 주에는 체육관의 남녀 탈의실을 사용하지 마세요. 현재 공사 중입니다. 수리가 끝나면 이전보다 훨씬 좋아질 것입니다. 다음 주 월요일에 이용하실 수 있습니다. 불편을 드려 죄송하지만, 이는 일시적인 조치입니다.

3 Listen to a teacher making an announcement.

W I'm pleased to inform you that the school will be having a talent show. It's going to take place on Friday, March 26. Everyone is welcome to compete in it. It doesn't matter what your talent is. It can be singing, dancing, acting, or doing a martial art. Just sign up this week, and you can take part.

선생님이 공지하는 내용을 들어 보세요.

W 학교에서 장기자랑 행사를 개최하게 되었음을 알려드리게 되어 기쁩니다. 행사는 3월 26일 금요일에 열립니다. 누구나 참여할 수 있습니다. 어떤 장기이든 상관없습니다. 노래, 춤, 연기, 또는 무술 등 무엇이든 가능합니다. 이번 주에 신청만 하면 참가할 수 있습니다.

4 Listen to an English teacher talking to a class.

M Everybody should have finished reading *Robinson Crusoe* by now. We're going to have a class discussion about it next Friday. For the weekend, I need you to write a three-page book report about the novel. It should describe the plot and highlight the main events in the story. You need to turn it in on Monday.

영어 선생님이 반 학생들에게 말하는 내용을 들어 보세요.

M 여러분은 지금쯤 『로빈슨 크루소』를 모두 읽었을 것입니다. 다음 주 금요일에 이에 대한 토론 수업을 진행할 예정입니다. 주말 동안, 소설에 대한 3페이지 분량의 독서 보고서를 작성해야 합니다. 줄거리를 설명하고 이야기의 주요 사건을 강조해야 합니다. 월요일에 제출해야 합니다.

5-8 Listen to a conversation between two friends.

B You look really tired these days, Brenda. Are you not getting enough sleep?

G Actually, I get plenty of sleep. I am just a bit busy this semester.

B What are you doing?

G Well, I have three club meetings this week. You know, uh, I'm in the science club, the math club, and the French club.

B Don't you play softball, too?

G Yes, that's correct. I'm the captain of the softball team. We have practice for two hours every day after school.

B Wow, you're pretty busy. Oh, wait a minute. You play in the school orchestra, don't you?

G Yeah. I play the flute. We're going to have a concert next week. And, of course, we have midterm exams soon, so I've been studying for them a lot. Unfortunately, my grades are a bit down this semester.

B Um . . . Don't you think you're trying to do too much?

G Do too much what?

B Well, you might consider doing fewer extracurricular

activities. Then, you can improve your grades. I remember you used to get straight A's in the past.

G Hmm . . . Maybe you're right. Thanks for the advice, Jeff. I appreciate you looking out for me.

두 친구가 나누는 대화를 들어 보세요.

B 요즘 정말 피곤해 보이네, Brenda. 잠을 충분히 못 자는 거 아니야?

G 사실, 난 잠은 충분히 자. 이번 학기에 좀 바쁠 뿐이야.

B 뭘 하는데?

G 이번 주에 동아리 모임이 세 번 있어. 난 과학 동아리, 수학 동아리, 그리고 프랑스어 동아리 회원이야.

B 소프트볼도 하지 않아?

G 응, 맞아. 나는 소프트볼 팀 주장이고, 방과 후 매일 두 시간씩 연습해.

B 와, 진짜 바쁘네. 아, 잠깐만. 학교 오케스트라에서 연주도 하고 있지?

G 응, 나는 플루트를 연주해. 다음 주에 공연이 있어. 물론 곧 중간고사도 있어서 공부도 많이 하고 있어. 안타깝게도 이번 학기 성적이 좀 떨어졌어.

B 음… 너무 많이 하려고 하는 거 아니야?

G 뭐를 너무 많이 한다는 거야?

B 음, 과외 활동을 조금 줄이는 걸 고려해 볼 수 있잖아. 그러면 성적을 올릴 수 있을 거야. 예전에는 네가 항상 A를 받았던 걸로 기억해.

G 흠…. 네 말이 맞을지도 모르겠다. 조언 고마워, Jeff. 신경 써 줘서 고마워.

9-12 Listen to a talk in a social studies class.

W There are canals all over the world. A canal is an artificial waterway connecting two bodies of water. These can be oceans, seas, rivers, or lakes. Many canals are for ships to sail on; however, there are also irrigation canals. They provide fresh water for farmers.

Right now, I'm interested in talking about canals which ships use. There are many canals which I'm sure you've heard of. The Panama Canal connects the Atlantic and Pacific oceans. The Suez Canal joins the Mediterranean Sea with the Red Sea. And here in the United States, the Erie Canal connects the Hudson River with Lake Erie. Each is large enough for ships to travel on them.

The primary advantage of canals is that they shorten the time that it takes to go from one waterway to another. Think about the Panama Canal. Located in Panama, it's fifty-one miles long. Before it existed, to get from the eastern U.S. to the western side, ships had to sail down to the southern tip of South America. Then, they had to sail back north. That trip could take weeks or even months and was dangerous, too. Today, most ships require between eight and ten hours to get through the Panama Canal. That's an enormous difference. Now, how about the Suez Canal?

사회 수업 중 강의 내용을 들어 보세요.

W 전 세계에 운하가 있습니다. 운하는 두 개의 수역을 연결하는 인공 수로입니다. 이 수역들은 대양, 바다, 강, 호수 등이 될 수 있습니다. 많은 운하가 선박이 항해할 수 있도록 만들어졌지만, 관개용 운하도 있습니다. 관개용 운하는 농부들에게 담수를 제공합니다.

지금은 선박이 사용하는 운하에 대해 이야기하는 데 관심이 있습니다. 여러분이 들어 본 운하가 많을 것입니다. 파나마 운하는 대서양과 태평양을 연결합니다. 수에즈 운하는 지중해와 홍해를 잇습니다. 그리고 여기 미국에서는 이리 운하가 허드슨 강과 이리호를 연결합니다. 각각의 운하는 선박이 항해할 수 있을 만큼 큽니다.

운하의 주요 장점은 한 수로에서 다른 수로로 이동하는 시간을 단축해 준다는 점입니다. 파나마 운하를 생각해 보세요. 파나마에 위치하며 길이가 51마일입니다. 운하가 생기기 전에는 미국 동부에서 서부로 가려면 선박이 남미 최남단까지 내려가야 했습니다. 그리고 다시 북쪽으로 돌아와야 했습니다. 그 여정은 몇 주 혹은 몇 달이 걸릴 수 있었고, 위험하기도 했습니다. 오늘날 대부분의 선박은 파나마 운하를 통과하는 데 8~10시간이 걸립니다. 엄청난 차이죠. 그렇다면 수에즈 운하는 어떨까요?

CHAPTER 02 DETAIL

PRACTICE 1 Short Talk p. 041

1 (B)	2 (B)	3 (D)	4 (D)
5 (C)	6 (A)	7 (C)	8 (D)

1 Listen to a teacher speaking to a class.

W I know many people are sick nowadays, and that includes students here at school. If you don't feel well, please visit the school nurse. She can give you some medicine and let you lie down until one of your parents comes to pick you up. Don't worry about your schoolwork for now. Just try to get healthy.

선생님이 반 학생들에게 말하는 내용을 들어 보세요.

W 요즘 많은 사람들이 아프다는 것을 알고 있으며, 이곳 학교 학생들도 포함됩니다. 몸이 좋지 않으면 학교 보건실을 방문하세요. 보건교사가 약을 주고, 부모님 중 한 분이 데리러 올 때까지 누워 있게 해 줄 것입니다. 지금은 학교 공부에 대해 걱정하지 마세요. 그저 건강을 회복하는 데 집중하세요.

2 Listen to a school principal making an announcement.

W Your attention, please. Starting on Monday, the lunch menu will undergo some changes. We'll have more nutritious food with a focus on meat, fruits, and vegetables. However, the price of a meal is going to increase by fifty cents. I think you're really going to love the new cafeteria food. Please inform your parents about this change.

교장 선생님이 공지하는 내용을 들어 보세요.

W 모두 주목하세요. 월요일부터 점심 메뉴에 변화가 있을 예정입니다. 고기, 과일, 채소 중심으로 더 영양가 있는 음식이 제공될 거예요. 하지만 식사 가격이 50센트 올라갈 거예요. 여러분이 새로운 급식 메뉴를 정말 좋아할 거라고 생각합니다. 이 변화에 대해 여러분 부모님께 알려 드리세요.

3 Listen to a science teacher speaking to a class.

M I'd like to do some group work now. At the start of class, I gave everybody a handout. It's a picture of the bones in a human hand and arm. Right now, please find a partner. With your partner, you need to label all of the bones by writing their correct names in the blanks. You have ten minutes.

과학 선생님이 반 학생들에게 말하는 내용을 들어 보세요.

M 이제 그룹 활동을 하고자 합니다. 수업 시작할 때, 여러분 모두에게 유인물을 나눠 줬죠. 사람 손과 팔의 뼈 그림입니다. 지금 바로 짝을 찾으세요. 여러분은 짝과 함께, 모든 뼈의 정확한 이름을 빈칸에 적어 표기해야 합니다. 시간은 10분입니다.

4 Listen to a school coach making an announcement.

W I want to commend Stephanie Watson for her performance at the track meet this past weekend. She came in first place in the 100-meter dash, so she is the new state champion. She also came in second in the 200-meter dash and placed third in the long jump. Please be sure to congratulate Stephanie when you see her today.

학교 코치 선생님이 공지하는 내용을 들어 보세요.

W 지난 주말 육상 대회에서 훌륭한 성과를 거둔 Stephanie Watson을 칭찬하고 싶습니다. 그녀는 100미터 달리기에서 1등을 차지하여 새로운 주 챔피언이 되었습니다. 또한 200미터 달리기에서 2등, 멀리뛰기에서 3등을 차지했습니다. 오늘 Stephanie를 만나면 꼭 축하해 주세요.

5 Listen to a math teacher speaking to his students.

M Everyone, please take out your math notebooks and open them to the page with your homework on it. Then, give your notebook to the person sitting beside you. We're going to go over last night's homework now. Each person needs to check another student's homework. Please be sure to mark both correct and incorrect answers.

수학 선생님이 학생들에게 말하는 내용을 들어 보세요.

M 여러분, 수학 공책을 꺼내서 숙제가 있는 페이지를 펴세요. 그런 다음, 공책을 옆에 앉은 친구에게 주세요. 이제 어젯밤 숙제를 같이 확인할 거예요. 각자 다른 학생의 숙제를 확인해야 합니다. 맞은 답과 틀린 답 모두 표시하도록 하세요.

6 Listen to a teacher making an announcement at the end of the day.

M Please don't forget that you have a vocabulary test first thing tomorrow morning. You must be able to spell all twenty of the words that we learned in class on Monday. You should also know which part of speech they are and what their definitions are. The test will be worth fifty points.

종례 때 선생님이 공지하는 내용을 들어 보세요.

M 내일 아침 제일 먼저 단어 시험이 있다는 것을 잊지 마세요. 월요일 수업에서 배운 20개의 단어 전부의 철자를 쓸 수 있어야 합니다. 또한 각 단어의 품사와 정의도 알아야 합니다. 시험은 50점에 해당합니다.

7 Listen to a teacher talking to her class.

W I'd like to inform you of an exciting opportunity happening this summer. The local university is hosting a special summer program for middle school and high school students. Students will live in a dormitory on campus for four weeks and take classes with professors at the school. If you're interested, I can give you an application form.

선생님이 반 학생들에게 말하는 내용을 들어 보세요.

W 이번 여름에 진행되는 흥미로운 기회에 대해 알려 주려고 해요. 지역 대학에서 중학생과 고등학생을 위한 특별 여름 프로그램을 개최해요. 학생들은 4주 동안 캠퍼스 기숙사에서 생활하며 학교 교수님들과 함께 수업을 듣게 됩니다. 관심 있으면 신청서 양식을 줄게요.

8 Listen to a school principal making an announcement.

M Next Saturday, April 14, we are having a special fundraiser in the school auditorium. It will be a silent auction. There are tons of great items which will be available to bid on. You can see each of them on our school webpage. Please inform your parents about this fun event. All money raised will be used to improve the school.

교장 선생님이 공지하는 내용을 들어 보세요.

M 다음 주 토요일, 4월 14일에 학교 강당에서 특별 모금 행사를 진행합니다. 이번 행사는 입찰식 경매가 될 것입니다. 입찰할 수 있는 멋진 물품이 많이 있습니다. 각 물품은 학교 홈페이지에서 확인할 수 있습니다. 이 재미있는 행사에 대해 부모님께 알려 드리세요. 모금된 모든 금액은 학교를 개선하기 위해 사용될 것입니다.

PRACTICE 2 Conversation p. 045

1 (A)	2 (C)	3 (B)	4 (D)
5 (A)	6 (A)	7 (D)	8 (B)

1-4 Listen to a conversation between two friends at school.

B I'm so glad we have final exams next week. I'm really looking forward to winter vacation. My family is planning to go skiing for a few days as soon as the last test finishes.

G That sounds like a wonderful plan. But don't think too much about your skiing trip. After all, our tests are not going to be easy.

B You can say that again. Have you started studying yet? I went over the first couple of chapters in our science book last night.

G You're ahead of me. I was planning to begin reviewing my notes tonight.

B Which test are you the most confident about?

G History for sure. It's my best subject. I seem to have a knack for remembering names, dates, and places.

B Yeah, Mr. Owens loves you, so I'm sure you'll do well in his class.

G How about you?

B My best subject is math, so I don't really need to study hard for it. But I'm having trouble in science this year, so I have to review a lot for that test. I'm just glad science is the first final we have to take.

G Yeah, I'll have to study hard for that test as well to make sure I can get an A on it.

학교에서 두 친구가 나누는 대화를 들어 보세요.

B 다음 주에 기말고사가 있어서 정말 기뻐. 겨울 방학이 너무 기대돼. 마지막 시험이 끝나자마자 우리 가족은 며칠 동안 스키 타러 갈 계획이야.

G 그거 정말 멋진 계획처럼 들리네. 하지만 스키 여행만 너무 생각하지 마. 어쨌든 우리 시험이 쉽지 않을 거야.

B 맞아, 정말 그래. 너 공부 시작했어? 난 어젯밤에 과학책 첫 두 단원을 훑어봤어.

G 너는 나보다 빠르네. 난 오늘 밤에 노트 복습을 시작하려고 했어.

B 너는 어느 시험이 제일 자신 있어?

G 당연히 역사야. 내 제일 잘하는 과목이거든. 이름, 날짜, 장소를 기억하는 데 재주가 있는 것 같아.

B 맞아, Owens 선생님이 너를 좋아하시잖아. 네가 그분 수업 시간에 잘할 게 분명해.

G 너는 어때?

B 내가 제일 잘하는 과목은 수학이야. 그래서 열심히 공부할 필요는 없어. 하지만 올해 과학이 좀 힘들어서 그 시험을 위해 많이 복습해야 해. 과학이 첫 번째 기말 시험이라서 다행이야.

G 그래, 나도 그 시험을 위해 열심히 공부해야겠어. A 받을 수 있도록 말이야.

5-8 Listen to a conversation between two friends.

G Hey, Jimmy. What are you doing for the Thanksgiving holiday?

B My family is flying out to visit my grandparents. We're going to leave on Wednesday morning.

G We have school on that day.

B Yeah, my parents already let the school know what we're doing. We're having a family reunion, so about fifty relatives should be at my grandparents' farm. I haven't seen a few of them in several years.

G It sounds like you're going to have loads of fun.

B I sure hope so. What about you, Tina? Are you doing anything special?

G We're not going anywhere because we have some family members coming to our house. My dad's brother and his family are coming, and so are my mom's brother and his family.

B That's going to be a crowded house.

G Yeah, it will be pretty crowded, but they're only staying for three days. So I think everything will be okay. I'm just worried about all of the cooking we're going to have to do.

B Yeah, I'm not sure how we're going to feed fifty

people. I'm kind of curious how that's going to work out.

G Let me know about it when you get back.

B Sure.

두 친구가 나누는 대화를 들어 보세요.

G 안녕, Jimmy. 추수감사절 연휴에는 뭐 할 거야?

B 우리 가족은 조부모님 댁에 비행기 타고 가기로 했어. 수요일 아침에 출발할 거야.

G 그날 학교 수업 있잖아.

B 응, 부모님이 이미 학교에 우리 계획을 알렸어. 가족 모임을 할 거라서, 조부모님 농장에 친척이 약 50명쯤 모일 거야. 몇몇은 몇 년 동안 못 봤어.

G 엄청 재밌을 것처럼 들린다.

B 그러길 바라. 너는 어때, Tina? 특별한 계획 있어?

G 우리는 아무데도 안 가. 가족 몇 명이 우리 집에 오거든. 아빠 형과 가족, 그리고 엄마 남동생과 가족이 올 거야.

B 집이 꽤 복잡하겠네.

G 맞아, 꽤 붐빌 거야. 하지만 3일만 머물 거야. 그래서 괜찮을 것 같아. 단지 우리가 해야 할 그 모든 요리가 걱정이야.

B 응, 나도 우리가 50명을 어떻게 먹일지 잘 모르겠네. 그게 어떻게 될지 궁금하다.

G 다녀와서 알려 줘.

B 알겠어.

PRACTICE 3 Lecture/Discussion			p. 048
1 (D)	**2** (D)	**3** (B)	**4** (A)
5 (B)	**6** (C)	**7** (A)	**8** (D)

1-4 Listen to a talk in a science class.

M The three main types of clouds are cumulus, stratus, and cirrus. Cumulus clouds are white and look fluffy while stratus clouds resemble flat sheets floating in the air. As for cirrus clouds, they're thin and have a wispy look. Now, uh, you're probably aware that there are more than three names for clouds. Take a look at page 145 in your books, and you'll see names like altocumulus and cirrostratus. You see, the altitude of a cloud is important when determining its name.

There are low-level clouds, middle-level clouds, and high-level clouds. Low-level clouds form at an altitude 6,500 feet above the ground or lower. The word "stratus" is often used for these clouds. Middle-level clouds are between 6,500 and 20,000 feet above the ground and have the word "alto" in their names. Lastly, high-level clouds form above 20,000 feet and may have "cirro" or "cirrus" in their names.

Let's start with low-level clouds first. Stratus clouds are low-level clouds which are flat and usually gray. They also typically cover most of the sky but only drop a small amount of rain. Stratocumulus clouds, on the other hand, are low and puffy gray-colored clouds. They sometimes result in rain but may also transform into clouds that produce thunderstorms. The cloud cover we have outside now is made of stratocumulus clouds by the way.

과학 수업 중 강의 내용을 들어 보세요.

M 구름의 세 가지 주요 종류는 적운, 층운, 권운입니다. 적운은 하얗고 푹신해 보이는 반면, 층운은 공중에 떠 있는 평평한 시트처럼 보입니다. 권운으로 말하자면 얇고 성긴 모양입니다. 음, 여러분도 아시겠지만 구름 이름은 세 가지보다 훨씬 많습니다. 교과서 145쪽을 보세요. 그러면 고적운이나 권층운 같은 이름이 보일 것입니다. 구름 이름을 결정할 때 구름의 고도가 중요합니다.

하층운, 중층운, 상층운이 있습니다. 하층운은 지상 6,500피트 이하에서 생깁니다. 이런 구름에는 '층운'이라는 단어가 자주 사용됩니다. 중층운은 지상 6,500~20,000피트 사이에 생기고 이름에 '고'가 들어갑니다. 마지막으로, 상층운은 20,000피트 이상에서 생기고 이름에 '권'이나 '권운'이 들어갈 수 있습니다.

먼저 하층운부터 시작하죠. 층운은 평평하고 보통 회색인 낮은 고도의 구름입니다. 보통 하늘 대부분을 덮지만 비는 조금만 내립니다. 반면에 층적운은 낮고 푹신한 회색 구름입니다. 때로는 비를 내리기도 하고, 뇌우를 일으키는 구름으로 변하기도 합니다. 참고로 지금 밖에 있는 하늘을 덮고 있는 구름은 층적운입니다.

5-8 Listen to part of a discussion in a history class.

M President Thomas Jefferson purchased the Louisiana Territory from France in 1803. The Louisiana Territory was land west of the Mississippi River and essentially covered the middle section of what is the United States today. The following year, he sent the Lewis and Clark Expedition west. Who can tell me why? Tabitha?

G There were several reasons the expedition was sent out, but three were of great importance. First, this was mostly unexplored land, so one task of the expedition was to map the land for future settlers. Secondly, Lewis and Clark wanted to find a route—uh, preferably by water—all the way to the Pacific Ocean.

M You are correct about both of those. And what about the third important reason?

G Well, there were many native American tribes living on the land. Lewis and Clark were asked to make contact with them and to establish peaceful relations. They brought various gifts for the tribes to show that they wanted peace, not war.

M Right again. Most of the tribes the explorers met on the way were peaceful, and some even helped the expedition during its journey.

역사 수업 중 토론 내용의 일부를 들어 보세요.

M 토머스 제퍼슨 대통령은 1803년에 프랑스로부터 루이지애나 영토를 구입했어요. 루이지애나 영토는 미시시피강 서쪽에 있는 땅으로, 오늘날 미국 중부 지역 대부분을 포함하고 있었습니다. 그 다음 해에, 그는 루이스와 클락 원정대를 서쪽으로 보냈습니다. 왜였는지 아는 사람 있나요, Tabitha?

G 원정대를 보낸 이유는 여러 가지가 있었지만, 세 가지가 특히 중요했어요. 첫째로, 이 지역은 대부분 탐험되지 않은 땅이었기 때문에, 원정대의 임무 중 하나는 미래 정착민들을 위해 지도를 작성하는 것이었죠. 둘째로, 루이스와 클락은 태평양까지 가는 경로를, 가능하면 수로를 찾고자 했어요.

M 둘 다 맞아요. 그렇다면 세 번째 중요한 이유는 무엇일까요?

G 음, 그 땅에는 많은 원주민 부족들이 살고 있었어요. 루이스와 클락은 그들과 접촉하고 평화로운 관계를 맺도록 요청받았어요. 부족들에게 전쟁이 아니라 평화를 원한다는 뜻을 보여 주기 위해 여러 가지 선물을 가져갔죠.

M 이번에도 맞아요. 탐험가들이 도중에 만난 대부분의 부족들은 평화로웠고, 어떤 부족들은 여정 동안 원정대를 도와주기도 했습니다.

PRACTICE TEST p. 052

1 (D)	2 (C)	3 (B)	4 (A)
5 (C)	6 (B)	7 (A)	8 (D)
9 (A)	10 (C)	11 (C)	12 (C)
13 (A)			

1 Listen to a history teacher speaking to his students.

M I really wish that all of you would read the assigned material before we have a discussion. It's obvious that most of you aren't doing that. Only four of you made good contributions to today's discussion. I would like to see everybody talking, but you can't do that unless you read first.

역사 선생님이 학생들에게 말하는 내용을 들어 보세요.

M 여러분 모두가 토론하기 전에 지정된 자료를 읽어 주었으면 정말 좋겠습니다. 대부분의 학생들이 그렇게 하지 않는 것이 분명하네요. 오늘 토론에서 제대로 기여한 사람은 단 네 명뿐이었습니다. 모든 학생이 발언하는 모습을 보고 싶은데, 먼저 읽지 않으면 그럴 수 없습니다.

2 Listen to a high school principal talking to the school's students.

W There will be a volleyball game in the school gymnasium after school today at five o'clock. We're playing Chandler High School. If our team wins this game, they're going to compete in the state championship game this Saturday. Please show some school spirit by attending the game and cheering for our team.

고등학교 교장 선생님이 학생들에게 말하는 내용을 들어 보세요.

W 오늘 방과 후 다섯 시에 학교 체육관에서 배구 경기가 있을 예정입니다. 우리는 Chandler 고등학교와 경기를 합니다. 우리 팀이 이번 경기에 이기면 이번 토요일 주 챔피언십 경기에 출전하게 됩니다. 경기에 참석해 우리 팀을 응원하며 애교심을 보여 주세요.

3 Listen to a science teacher speaking to her students.

W As you know, your midterm exam will take place this coming Friday. Please study everything we have learned up to this point. That includes all five chapters in the book as well as the handouts I gave you. I hope you took notes when we watched those videos because there will be questions about them on the test, too.

과학 선생님이 학생들에게 말하는 내용을 들어 보세요.

W 여러분이 알고 있듯이, 중간고사는 이번 금요일에 치러집니다. 지금까지 배운 모든 내용을 공부하세요. 여기에는 교재의 다섯 개 장 모두와 제가 나눠 준 유인물도 포함됩니다. 우리가 그 동영상을 볼 때 필기했기를 바랍니다. 시험에 그 동영상과 관련된 질문도 나올 예정이거든요.

4 Listen to a school nurse speaking to a group of students.

M This spring has been hotter than usual, and summer is rapidly approaching. You should be sure to drink a lot of fluids every day. That will keep you hydrated and be good for your body. If you feel like fainting when you're out in the sun, get into the shade and sit down. You should feel better soon afterward.

보건 선생님이 학생들에게 말하는 내용을 들어 보세요.

M 올봄은 평소보다 더 더웠고, 여름이 빠르게 다가오고 있습니다. 매일 충분히 수분을 섭취해야 합니다. 그것이 수분을 유지하게 하고 몸에 좋습니다. 햇볕 아래 있다가 기절할 것 같은 느낌이 들면, 그늘로 들어가 앉으세요. 곧 기분이 나아질 것입니다.

5-8 Listen to a conversation between a student and her father.

G Dad, some of my friends are planning to go on a trip this Saturday, and they invited me to go along with them. May I go?

M Where exactly are you going?

G Oh, yeah. Sorry. We're planning to go to Lake Mitchell. Sandy's family owns a house right by the lake, so we'll go there in the morning.

M And what are you planning to do?

G We're mostly going to do some swimming and maybe going out in her family's speedboat. I really want to go waterskiing. So is it all right if I go?

M Hmm . . . Are Sandy's parents going to be present while all of you kids are there? I don't want you going anywhere without adult supervision. And when are you planning to come back?

G I . . . I don't know if her parents will be there or not. She didn't mention that. And I was hoping you could drive me there in the morning and then pick me up a little after dinnertime.

M The times you mentioned are acceptable. But you can't go if no adults are going to be there.

G I'll give her a call right now and find out.

M Great. Let me know what she says.

학생과 아버지가 나누는 대화를 들어 보세요.

G 아빠, 이번 토요일에 친구들 몇 명이 여행을 갈 계획인데, 저도 같이 가자고 초대했어요. 가도 될까요?

M 정확히 어디로 가는데?

G 아, 맞다. 죄송해요. 저희는 미첼 호수에 갈 계획이에요. Sandy네 가족이 호숫가에 집을 가지고 있어서 아침에 거기로 갈 거예요.

M 그리고 뭘 할 계획이야?

G 주로 수영을 하고, 아마 걔네 가족의 모터보트를 탈 것 같아요. 저는 수상 스키를 정말 하고 싶어요. 그럼 가도 괜찮을까요?

M 음…. Sandy 부모님이 너희가 거기 있는 동안 계실 거야? 어른 감독 없이 아무 데도 가지 않길 바라거든. 그리고 언제 돌아올 계획이야?

G 그게… 그 애 부모님이 거기 계실지 아닐지는 모르겠어요. 그 애가 말하지 않았어요. 그리고 저는 아빠가 아침에 거기 데려다주시고 저녁 식사 시간이 좀 지나서 데리러 와 주실 수 있기를 바라고 있어요.

M 네가 말한 시간은 괜찮아. 하지만 어른이 거기 없을 거라면 갈 수 없어.

G 그 애한테 지금 전화해서 확인할게요.

M 좋아. 그 애가 뭐라고 하는지 알려 주렴.

9-13 Listen to a teacher talking in a music class.

W That was some really nice music, wasn't it? It was some music from a work called *Water Music*, which was composed by George Frideric Handel. Handel is a personal favorite of mine. He's also widely considered one of the greatest composers of classical music in history.

Handel lived during the Baroque Period. It lasted from around 1600 to 1750. 1750 was, by the way, the year that Johann Sebastian Bach died. Bach, along with Handel and Antonio Vivaldi, was one of the three leading Baroque composers. So, uh, what was Baroque music? First, as you surely noticed in listening to *Water Music*, Baroque music doesn't let up. There are few pauses in it. It's highly ornamental and features flourishes and trills. It also creates different feelings and emotion in its listeners. Another feature is that Baroque music is polyphonic. This means that the musicians are playing different melodies and structures in the music. However, the different sounds come together to create beautiful music.

Something else you might have noticed is the changes in volume. Baroque music can go from loud to soft and then back to loud again very quickly. Now, let's listen to a work by another Baroque composer. This is music by Henry Purcell. It's from his work *The Faerie Queene*.

음악 시간에 선생님이 설명하는 내용을 들어 보세요.

W 방금 들은 음악 정말 좋았죠? 《수상 음악》이라는 작품의 일부였는데, 게오르크 프리드리히 헨델이 작곡했어요. 헨델은 제가 개인적으로 좋아하는 작곡가예요. 또한 그는 역사상 가장 위대한 클래식 음악 작곡가 중 한 명으로 널리 인정받고 있어요.

헨델은 바로크 시대에 살았어요. 바로크 시대는 대략 1600년부터 1750년까지였어요. 참고로 1750년은 요한 제바스티안 바흐가 사망한 해이기도 해요. 바흐는 헨델, 안토니오 비발디와 함께 세 명의 주요 바로크 작곡가 중 한 명이었어요. 그렇다면 바로크 음악이란 무엇이었을까요? 먼저, 《수상 음악》을 들으면서 분명히 느꼈겠지만, 바로크 음악은 느슨해지지 않아요. 쉬어 가는 구간이 거의 없어요. 매우 장식적이고 장식음과 꾸밈음이 특징이에요. 또한 듣는 사람에게 다양한 감정과 느낌을 전달해요. 또 다른 특징은 바로크 음악이 다성 음악이라는 점이에요. 이는 음악가들이 서로 다른 멜로디와 구조를 연주한다는 뜻이에요. 하지만 서로 다른 소리가 어우러져 아름다운 음악을 만들어 내는 거예요.

또 한 가지 눈치챘을 것은 음량의 변화예요. 바로크 음악은 크다가 작게, 다시 크게, 이렇게 빠르게 변화할 수 있어요. 이제 다른 바로크 작곡가의 작품을 들어 봅시다. 헨리 퍼셀의 《요정 여왕》의 일부예요.

CHAPTER 03 INFERENCE

PRACTICE 1 Short Talk p. 057

1 (C)	2 (D)	3 (A)	4 (B)
5 (A)	6 (D)	7 (D)	8 (A)

1 Listen to a teacher speaking to her students.

W It's time to create a username. All students here need one to log on to and to use school computers until they graduate. First, look at the middle of the screen. Click on "New User" right now. A new screen will appear. Please type your name and student ID number into the correct boxes and then hit the enter button.

선생님이 학생들에게 말하는 내용을 들어 보세요.

W 이제 사용자 이름을 만들어야 할 시간이에요. 이 학교의 모든 학생은 졸업할 때까지 학교 컴퓨터에 로그인하고 사용하기 위해 사용자 이름이 필요해요. 먼저 화면 중앙을 보세요. 지금 바로 '새 사용자'를 클릭하세요. 새 화면이 나타날 거예요. 이름과 학번을 해당 칸에 입력한 다음 엔터 버튼을 누르세요.

2 Listen to a teacher making an announcement at the end of the day.

M Before you leave, I have an announcement to make. If you are absent, it is your responsibility to find out what you missed in class. This includes any homework assignments. You can check the class website, ask a classmate, or even email me. Absence is not an excuse for not doing assignments. Does everyone understand?

종례 때 선생님이 공지하는 내용을 들어 보세요.

M 여러분이 가기 전에 공지할 것이 있어요. 결석한 경우, 수업에서 놓친 내용을 알아내는 것은 여러분의 책임이에요. 여기에는 숙제도 포함됩니다. 수업 웹사이트를 확인하거나, 같은 반 친구에게 물어보거나, 심지어 저에게 이메일을 보내도 돼요. 결석은 과제를 하지 않은 것에 대한 변명이 되지 않아요. 모두 이해했나요?

3 Listen to a social studies teacher speaking to her students.

W We have a long weekend coming up, so I know everyone is happy. However, we will have our midterm exam on Tuesday. Even though Monday is a holiday, I still expect you to be prepared for the test. There's nothing I can do about the test schedule, so please don't ask. Just come here ready for the test, and you'll do well.

사회 선생님이 학생들에게 말하는 내용을 들어 보세요.

W 곧 긴 주말이 다가오니 모두 기분이 좋겠죠. 하지만 화요일에 중간고사가 있어요. 월요일이 휴일임에도 불구하고 여러분이 시험 준비를 해 오기를 기대해요. 시험 일정에 대해서는 제가 어쩔 수 없으니 묻지 마세요. 그냥 시험 볼 준비를 하고 오세요. 그러면 잘할 수 있을 거예요.

4 Listen to a history teacher talking to a class.

M I no longer want you to print your reports and then submit them to me in person. Instead, I would prefer that you email them to me before the due date. It's faster for me to read your reports and to make corrections to them on the computer. Plus, we should do our part to reduce paper usage to help save forests.

역사 선생님이 반 학생들에게 말하는 내용을 들어 보세요.

M 이제 더 이상 보고서를 출력해서 직접 제출하지 않아도 돼요. 대신, 제출 기한 전에 이메일로 보내 주면 좋겠어요. 제가 컴퓨터에서 보고서를 읽고 수정하는 것이 더 빠르거든요. 게다가, 산림 보호를 돕기 위해 종이 사용을 줄이는 일에도 함께 힘써야 합니다.

5 Listen to a school coach talking to a basketball team.

W You're doing wonderfully now. We're ten points up, but we still have an entire half of basketball to play. Just keep passing the ball and taking open shots when you have them. We need to stop number ten on their team. She's scoring a lot, so we're going to double-team her every time she gets the ball.

학교 코치 선생님이 농구 팀원들에게 말하는 내용을 들어 보세요.

W 지금 정말 잘하고 있어. 우리 팀이 10점 앞서고 있지만, 아직 농구 경기의 절반이 남아 있어. 계속 공을 패스하고 기회가 있을 때 열린 슛을 쏴. 상대 팀 10번 선수를 막아야 해. 그 친구가 득점을 많이 하고 있으니, 그 선수가 공을 잡을 때마다 두 명이 동시에 수비할 거야.

6 Listen to a school librarian making an announcement.

M As you all know, the library suffered water damage during the storm this past weekend. A large percentage of our collection has been ruined, so those books are unreadable now. We need more books at once, but we don't have enough money to purchase many. Please consider donating any unwanted books at home to the library.

학교의 사서 선생님이 공지하는 내용을 들어 보세요.

M 여러분도 알다시피, 지난 주말 폭풍으로 도서관이 수해를 입었어요. 소장 도서의 상당 부분이 손상되어 그 책들은 현재 읽을 수 없는 상

태입니다. 지금 당장 더 많은 책이 필요하지만, 많은 책을 구매할 예산이 없어요. 집에 필요 없는 책이 있다면 도서관에 기부하는 것을 고려해 주세요.

7 Listen to a principal speaking to the students over the intercom.

W [*intercom sound*] Your attention, please. Tomorrow, you will not be able to use any of the vending machines to buy drinks and snacks in the cafeteria or anywhere else in the school. All of the machines are being replaced. So one company will remove them in the morning, and a different one will install new machines in the afternoon. Please make alternative arrangements.

방송을 통해 교장 선생님이 학생들에게 말하는 내용을 들어 보세요.

W [교내 방송 소리] 여러분, 집중해 주세요. 내일은 구내식당이나 학교 내 어디에서도 자판기를 이용해 음료나 간식을 구매할 수 없을 것입니다. 모든 자판기가 교체될 예정이에요. 오전에는 한 회사가 기존 자판기를 철거하고, 오후에는 다른 회사가 새 자판기를 설치할 겁니다. 미리 다른 방법을 마련해 주세요.

8 Listen to a teacher making an announcement.

M Let me remind you that the school play is being held tonight at 8:00. I urge everybody to attend to support our student actors. The students have worked hard rehearsing for the past two months. I know they're going to put on a great show. Be sure to wish the performers good luck if you see them today.

선생님이 공지하는 내용을 들어 보세요.

M 여러분, 학교 연극이 오늘 밤 8시에 열린다는 것을 다시 알려 드립니다. 학생 배우들을 응원하기 위해 모두 꼭 참석해 주시기 바랍니다. 학생들은 지난 두 달 동안 열심히 연습했습니다. 훌륭한 공연을 보여줄 거예요. 오늘 배우들을 만나면 꼭 행운을 빌어 주세요.

PRACTICE 2 Conversation p. 061

1 (A)	2 (B)	3 (D)	4 (D)
5 (C)	6 (B)	7 (A)	8 (D)

1-4 Listen to a conversation between a student and a school counselor.

M Hello, Katie. Ms. Kingwood said you've been looking for me all day. What can I do for you?

G Good afternoon, sir. I need to talk about my math class.

M Remind me, please . . . Which math class are you enrolled in, and who's your instructor?

G I'm taking Algebra 1 with Mr. Jefferson. I'm in his class in third period.

M Ah, that's right. So . . . what's wrong with his class? Are you having problems understanding the material?

G On the contrary, the class is too easy. I mean, uh, I haven't missed a single question in the three weeks I've been taking it. I also looked through the book. I already know how to do everything we'll be learning this year.

M I see. So you'd like to take a harder class. Is that correct?

G Yes, sir. I'd love to take Ms. Weston's advanced algebra class. She teaches it during third period, so it fits perfectly with my schedule. But I was told I need to get her permission as well as yours to take the class. And, uh . . . I've never spoken to her before.

M Ah, sure. Why don't we go and have a chat with her now? She's on break, so she should be in her office.

G Thank you, sir.

학생과 학교 상담 선생님이 나누는 대화를 들어 보세요.

M 안녕, Katie. Kingwood 선생님께서 네가 오늘 하루 종일 나를 찾고 있다고 하시던데. 무슨 일이니?

G 안녕하세요, 선생님. 제 수학 수업에 대해 이야기하고 싶어요.

M 다시 한번 알려 줄래…. 어떤 수학 수업을 듣고 있고, 담당 선생님은 누구시지?

G 저는 Jefferson 선생님이 가르치는 대수 1 수업을 듣고 있어요. 3교시에 그분 수업을 들어요.

M 아, 맞아. 그렇다면… 수업에 무슨 문제가 있니? 내용 이해에 어려움이 있나?

G 반대로, 수업이 너무 쉬워요. 그 수업을 들은 지난 3주 동안 한 문제도 틀린 적이 없어요. 교과서도 이미 살펴봤는데, 올해 배우게 될 내용은 모두 어떻게 하는지 알고 있어요.

M 그렇구나. 그러니까 더 어려운 수업을 듣고 싶다는 거지. 맞니?

G 네, 선생님. Weston 선생님의 고급 대수 수업을 듣고 싶어요. 그분이 3교시에 그 수업을 하셔서 제 시간표랑 딱 맞아요. 그런데 그 수업을 듣기 위해서는 그 선생님과 선생님의 허락을 받아야 한다고 들었어요. 그리고, 어… 사실 그분과는 한 번도 이야기해 본 적이 없어요.

M 아, 좋아. 그럼 지금 가서 그분과 이야기해 보면 어떻겠니? 지금 쉬는 시간이라 사무실에 계실 거야.

G 감사합니다, 선생님.

5-8 Listen to a conversation between two friends.

B Wendy, were you at the shopping center on Sunday evening? I thought I saw you there.

G Yeah, I went there with a couple of my friends. Where did you see me?

B You were near the movie theater around, uh, seven.

G David, Cathy, and I were about to go in to watch a movie. We saw that new superhero movie everyone is talking about.

B Cool. How was it?

G Don't waste your time on it.

B Oh . . . That's too bad. I was thinking of seeing it later this week.

G What were you doing at the mall? You should have come over and said hi to us.

B I couldn't. I was with my parents and my grandmother. It was my mother's birthday, so we had dinner at the new Italian restaurant on the third floor. It was amazingly good. You ought to check it out if you can.

G Thanks for the tip. I'll let my parents know what you said. They were discussing going out to eat tonight.

B Sounds good. Anyway, the bell is about to ring. I'd better get to my class. You know how Mr. Sorenson gets when students arrive after the bell.

G You don't have to remind me. See you at lunch.

두 친구가 나누는 대화를 들어 보세요.

B Wendy, 일요일 저녁에 쇼핑 센터에 있었어? 거기서 널 본 것 같아서.

G 응, 친구들 두 명이랑 같이 갔어. 어디서 봤는데?

B 영화관 근처에서, 음, 7시쯤이었어

G David랑 Cathy랑 나랑 영화 보러 들어가려던 참이었어. 다들 얘기하는 새로 나온 슈퍼히어로 영화를 봤어.

B 멋지다. 어땠어?

G 시간 낭비하지 마.

B 아… 아쉽네. 이번 주에 보려고 했거든.

G 쇼핑몰에선 뭐 하고 있었어? 우리한테 와서 인사하지 그랬어.

B 못 했어. 부모님이랑 할머니랑 같이 있었거든. 엄마 생신이라 3층에 새로 생긴 이탈리안 레스토랑에서 저녁 먹었어. 진짜 맛있었어. 가능하면 가 봐.

G 정보 고마워. 부모님께 네가 한 말 말해 드릴게. 오늘 저녁 외식할까 얘기 중이셨거든.

B 좋아. 어쨌든 곧 종 울리겠네. 수업 가야겠어. Sorenson 선생님이 종 울린 후에 학생들이 오면 어떻게 하는지 알잖아.

G 알고말고. 점심때 봐.

PRACTICE 3 Lecture/Discussion p. 064

1 (C)	2 (A)	3 (B)	4 (A)
5 (D)	6 (B)	7 (B)	8 (A)

1-4 Listen to a part of a radio program about animals.

M There are more than eighty species of whales, including blue whales, sperm whales, killer whales, and narwhals. Whales can be found living in all of the world's oceans. Some species are among the largest animals ever to live on the Earth. For instance, the largest blue whale ever recorded was 111 feet long. Some blue whales can weigh up to 200 tons, too.

Whales are divided into two separate types: baleen whales and toothed whales. There are fourteen species of baleen whales, such as blue whales, humpback whales, and fin whales. Baleen whales tend to be larger than toothed whales. Despite their enormous sizes, baleen whales mostly eat krill, a small shrimp-like crustacean. Baleen are plates made of keratin found in the mouths of baleen whales. Basically, when they feed, baleen whales open their mouths and take in large amounts of water. When they expel the water, their baleen filters out krill, zooplankton, and various small fish, which they eat.

Toothed whales are all of the other whales. Among them are sperm whales, killer whales, dolphins, and porpoises. They are social animals and often live in groups called pods. Toothed whales actively hunt fish and marine creatures in the oceans. However, the types of creatures they pursue differ. For instance, sperm whales dive deep to hunt giant squid. What about killer whales?

동물에 대한 라디오 프로그램 내용의 일부를 들어 보세요.

M 고래는 80종이 넘는데, 여기에는 흰긴수염고래, 향유고래, 흰줄박이물돼지, 일각고래가 포함돼요. 고래는 전 세계 모든 바다에서 살고 있습니다. 일부 종은 지구상에서 살아 온 동물 중 가장 큰 것들에 속해요. 예를 들어, 기록된 가장 큰 흰긴수염고래는 길이가 111피트였습니다. 일부 흰긴수염고래는 무게가 200톤에 달하기도 합니다.

고래는 수염고래와 이빨고래 두 가지 유형으로 나뉘어요. 수염고래는 흰긴수염고래, 혹등고래, 긴수염고래 등 14종이 있습니다. 수염고래는 이빨고래보다 몸집이 큰 편이에요. 엄청나게 크지만, 수염고래는 주로 크릴이라는 작은 새우 같은 갑각류를 먹습니다. 수염은 수염고래 입안에 있는 케라틴으로 된 판입니다. 기본적으로 먹이를 먹을 때 수염고래는 입을 크게 벌리고 많은 양의 물을 들이마셔요. 물을 내보낼 때 수염이 크릴, 동물성 플랑크톤, 다양한 작은 물고기를 거르고, 고래는 그것들을 먹습니다.

이빨고래는 나머지 모든 고래를 말합니다. 향유고래, 흰줄박이물돼지, 돌고래, 참돌고래 등이 이에 속합니다. 이빨고래는 사회적 동물로, 종종 '포드'라고 불리는 무리에서 생활해요. 이빨고래는 바다에서 물고기와 해양 생물을 적극적으로 사냥합니다. 다만, 사냥하는 생물의 종류는 달라요. 예를 들어, 향유고래는 대왕오징어를 잡기 위해 깊이 잠수합니다. 그렇다면 흰줄박이물돼지는요?

5-8 Listen to part of a discussion in a social studies class.

W Many people believe Henry Ford invented the assembly line. They are mistaken, but Ford did make great use of it by manufacturing the Model T, a type of car, on it. We're going to talk more about the assembly line later, but I'd like to find out what you know about it. Who can tell me what some of its advantages are? Jeff, your hand is up.

B It makes the production process go much faster

because each worker specializes in just one or two tasks. Before the assembly line, a single person was involved in every step of the manufacturing process. This was a very slow way of making things. But when Ford's workers began specializing in specific tasks, they could produce cars or other objects quickly.

W Correct, Jeff. By 1913, thanks to the assembly line, the Ford Motor Company was able to make a single Model T in around ninety-three minutes. Imagine that. A single car made in an hour and a half. That would have been unthinkable merely ten or twenty years earlier.

B I also want to say that the assembly line helped improve the quality of manufactured goods. Because workers were so specialized at their tasks, they did those tasks well. So parts became standardized.

W A very good point. Who can tell me what some results of this standardization of parts were?

사회 수업 중 토론 내용의 일부를 들어 보세요.

W 많은 사람들이 헨리 포드가 조립 라인을 발명했다고 믿습니다. 이는 잘못된 생각이에요. 그러나 포드는 모델 T라는 자동차를 생산하는 데 조립 라인을 훌륭하게 활용했습니다. 조립 라인에 대해서는 나중에 더 이야기하겠지만, 먼저 여러분이 아는 것을 알아보고 싶습니다. 조립 라인의 장점에는 어떤 것들이 있을까요? Jeff, 손 들었네요.

B 조립 라인은 생산 과정을 훨씬 빠르게 만들어 줘요. 각 작업자가 한두 가지 작업만 전문적으로 수행하기 때문이죠. 조립 라인이 생기기 전에는 한 사람이 제조 과정의 모든 단계를 담당했어요. 이것은 매우 느린 생산 방식이었어요. 하지만 포드의 직원들이 특정 작업에 전문성을 가지기 시작하면서, 자동차나 다른 제품을 빠르게 생산할 수 있게 되었죠.

W 맞아요, Jeff. 1913년에는 조립 라인 덕분에 포드 자동차 회사가 모델 T 한 대를 약 93분 만에 만들 수 있었어요. 상상해 보세요. 한 시간 반 만에 자동차 한 대를 만든다는 것을, 불과 10년이나 20년 전만 해도 상상할 수 없는 일이었을 거예요.

B 또 한 가지 말하고 싶은 것은, 조립 라인이 제조품의 품질 향상에도 도움을 주었다는 점이에요. 작업자들이 각자의 작업에 전문성을 가지니 그 작업을 잘 수행했고, 그래서 부품이 표준화되었죠.

W 아주 좋은 지적이에요. 그렇다면 이 부품 표준화의 결과로 나타난 것에는 어떤 것들이 있었는지 누가 말해 줄 수 있을까요?

PRACTICE TEST

p. 068

1 (D)	2 (A)	3 (A)	4 (C)
5 (B)	6 (D)	7 (A)	8 (A)
9 (C)	10 (B)	11 (D)	12 (C)

1 Listen to a teacher making an announcement.

W This year, the school has agreed to allow students to celebrate their birthday in class. If you want to have a party, we can do that. Just let me know one week in advance. Tell me what you're planning on bringing and what day your birthday is. We'll figure out a good time to have the party.

선생님이 공지하는 내용을 들어 보세요.

W 올해부터 학교에서는 학생들이 수업 시간에 생일을 축하할 수 있도록 허락했습니다. 파티를 하고 싶다면 그렇게 할 수 있어요. 단, 일주일 전에 알려 주세요. 무엇을 가져올 계획인지, 생일이 언제인지 알려 주세요. 파티를 할 적절한 시간을 정하겠습니다.

2 Listen to a school nurse speaking to a class.

M You should be careful about walking in the forest right behind the school. I saw some poison ivy growing there yesterday. If you touch it, you'll break out in a rash. It can be very itchy and painful and take weeks to go away. Trust me. It's unpleasant. You really don't want to have to deal with this problem.

학교 보건 선생님이 반 학생들에게 말하는 내용을 들어 보세요.

M 학교 바로 뒤 숲속을 걸을 때 조심해야 합니다. 어제 거기서 덩굴옻나무가 자라고 있는 걸 봤거든요. 만지면 발진이 생길 거예요. 가려움과 통증이 심할 수 있고, 사라지는 데 몇 주가 걸릴 수도 있습니다. 정말이에요. 불쾌합니다. 이런 문제를 겪고 싶지 않을 거예요.

3 Listen to a teacher speaking to a group of students.

W I asked you all to come here today for a specific reason. I have seen some of you talking to others during class. Others of you often pass notes to your friends in class. I won't tolerate that sort of activity anymore. If I catch you doing it again, you will get detention and have to stay after school.

선생님이 학생들에게 말하는 내용을 들어 보세요.

W 오늘 여러분을 여기 부른 데에는 특별한 이유가 있습니다. 어떤 학생들이 수업 중에 다른 학생과 이야기하는 모습을 봤어요. 또 다른 학생들은 수업 시간에 친구에게 쪽지를 자주 전달하더군요. 이런 행동을 더 이상 용납하지 않겠습니다. 그런 행동을 하는 걸 제가 보게 되면 여러분은 벌을 받아 방과 후에 남아야 할 것입니다.

4 Listen to a school principal speaking to the students over the intercom.

W [*intercom sound*] During summer vacation, many parents expressed an interest in having the school start a marching band. If at least twenty students want to join the band, we can do this. Mr. Wilson has agreed to be the band instructor and will hold practice after school. If you're interested, please speak with him before the week is over.

방송을 통해 교장 선생님이 학생들에게 말하는 내용을 들어 보세요.

W [교내 방송 소리] 여름 방학 동안 많은 학부모님께서 학교에서 마칭 밴드를 시작하게 하는 것에 대한 관심을 표명하셨습니다. 최소

20명의 학생이 밴드에 참여하기를 원하면, 이것을 할 수 있습니다. Wilson 선생님께서 밴드 지도 교사가 되어 주시기로 하셨고, 방과 후 연습을 진행하실 예정입니다. 관심 있는 학생은 이번 주가 끝나기 전에 선생님께 말씀드리세요.

5-8 Listen to a conversation between a student and his mother.

W Brad, did you remember to pick up the groceries from the store?

B Oh, no, Mom. I totally forgot. I'm so sorry. Do you want me to pick them up now?

W Instead, how about cleaning up the living room first? Your father's boss is coming over for dinner, so the house needs to look nice.

B Sure. I can do that.

W Great. Thanks. It should take you ten minutes to tidy up everything. After that, you can go to the grocery store. I wrote down everything I need on a list to make sure you don't forget anything again.

B Thanks. I'll remember to buy everything this time.

W Please be back before five o'clock. Mr. Rogers and your father should be here by six, and I'll need an hour to prepare everything.

B Five o'clock? It's already a quarter past four.

W Is it? In that case, why don't you go to the store now? When you return, you can take care of the living room. Here's the list.

B Thanks . . . Hmm . . . That's a lot of stuff. I don't have enough money for that.

W Here. Take this card and use it at the store. Hurry back.

B Okay, Mom. I'll go as fast as I can.

학생과 어머니가 나누는 대화를 들어 보세요.

W Brad, 가게에서 장 보는 거 기억했니?

B 아, 이런, 엄마. 완전히 잊어버렸어요. 정말 죄송해요. 지금 가서 사 올까요?

W 그 대신 거실 청소부터 하는 게 어때? 아빠 상사분이 저녁 먹으러 오시니까, 집이 깔끔해 보여야 해.

B 알겠어요. 할게요.

W 좋아. 고마워. 모든 걸 정리하는 데 10분 정도 걸릴 거야. 그 다음에 장 보러 가면 돼. 네가 또 뭔가를 잊지 않도록 필요한 걸 내가 목록에 다 적어 놨어.

B 고마워요. 이번에는 잊지 않고 다 살게요.

W 5시 전에 돌아오도록 해. Rogers 씨랑 아빠가 6시까지 오실 거고, 내가 모든 걸 준비하는 데 한 시간이 필요해.

B 5시요? 지금 벌써 4시 15분이에요.

W 그래? 그럼 지금 바로 가게에 가는 게 어때? 돌아와서 거실 정리하면 돼. 여기 목록 있어.

B 고마워요…. 음…. 물건이 많네요. 돈이 충분하지 않아요.

W 여기. 카드 가져가서 가게에서 사용해. 빨리 다녀와.

B 알겠어요, 엄마. 최대한 빨리 다녀올게요.

9-12 Listen to a talk in a history class.

M Imagine building a single wall from one side of the country to the other. It would be an enormous undertaking, wouldn't it? It would probably take years to accomplish. As a matter of fact, this was done in ancient times. In 122 A.D., the Romans constructed a wall across northern England. It started at the North Sea on the eastern side of the country and extended seventy-three miles westward, where it ended at the Irish Sea.

You probably know I'm referring to Hadrian's Wall. It was ordered to be built by the Roman Emperor Hadrian. It required approximately fourteen years to complete, and historians estimate that at least 15,000 Roman soldiers helped construct it. The wall was between ten and twenty feet wide and between ten and twenty feet high. Along the wall were sixteen forts, each of which held around 600 soldiers. There were viewing points along the wall for soldiers to observe approaching enemies, and soldiers could also patrol along the walls. Historians believe up to 10,000 soldiers used to man the wall.

Even today, you can still see parts of Hadrian's Wall. Somewhere around ten percent of it still remains, which shows what amazing builders the Romans were. Here, uh, let me show you a few pictures so you can see how it looked.

역사 수업 중 강의 내용을 들어 보세요.

M 한 나라의 한쪽 끝에서 다른 쪽 끝까지 하나의 벽을 쌓는다고 상상해 보세요. 엄청난 일이 되겠죠? 실제로 완료하는 데 수년이 걸릴 거예요. 사실, 이런 일이 고대에 실제로 있었습니다. 서기 122년에 로마인들이 영국 북부에 성벽을 세웠습니다. 성벽은 영국 동쪽의 북해에서 시작해 서쪽으로 73마일을 이어 아일랜드 해에서 끝났습니다.

여러분은 아마 제가 하드리아누스 방벽에 대해 말하고 있다는 걸 알겠죠. 그것은 로마 황제 하드리아누스의 명령으로 지어졌습니다. 완공하는 데 약 14년이 걸렸고, 역사가들은 최소 15,000명의 로마 병사들이 건설에 참여했다고 추정합니다. 성벽의 너비는 10~20피트, 높이도 10~20피트였습니다. 성벽을 따라 16개의 요새가 있었고, 각 요새에는 약 600명의 병사가 있었습니다. 성벽에는 접근하는 적을 관찰할 수 있는 전망대도 있었고, 병사들은 성벽을 따라 순찰할 수도 있었습니다. 역사가들은 최대 10,000명의 병사가 성벽을 지켰다고 봅니다.

오늘날에도 하드리아누스 방벽의 일부를 여전히 볼 수 있습니다. 약 10% 정도가 남아 있어 로마인들이 얼마나 놀라운 건축가였는지 보여 줍니다. 여기, 성벽이 어떻게 생겼는지 볼 수 있도록 제가 몇 장의 사진을 보여 드릴게요.

CHAPTER 04 **PREDICTION**

PRACTICE 1 Short Talk p. 073

1 (B)	2 (B)	3 (D)	4 (A)
5 (C)	6 (D)	7 (C)	8 (B)

1 Listen to a teacher making an announcement.

W The bell for lunch will ring in a moment. Before we go, I should tell you about the new cash cards at the cafeteria. You can buy them from the machines by the door. Then, pay the cashier by handing her your card. Cash is no longer an acceptable payment method in the cafeteria. Got it?

선생님이 공지하는 내용을 들어 보세요.

W 점심 시간 종이 곧 울릴 거예요. 가기 전에, 새로운 구내식당용 현금 카드에 대해 알려 드릴게요. 출입문 옆에 있는 기계에서 카드를 구입하면 됩니다. 그런 다음, 계산하시는 분께 카드로 결제하세요. 현금은 구내식당에서는 더 이상 사용 가능한 결제 수단이 아닙니다. 알겠죠?

2 Listen to a teacher speaking to his students.

M I want to show you a documentary about coral reefs today. However, first, I need to give you a handout. It has important information about coral reefs, including where they can be found and what kinds of animals live in them. Please be sure not to lose it because you will be tested on this information.

선생님이 학생들에게 말하는 내용을 들어 보세요.

M 오늘 여러분에게 산호초에 관한 다큐멘터리를 보여 주고 싶습니다. 하지만 먼저, 여러분에게 유인물을 나눠 줘야겠네요. 이 유인물에는 산호초에 대한 중요한 정보가 담겨 있으며, 어디에서 볼 수 있는지와 어떤 동물들이 사는지도 포함되어 있습니다. 이 정보에 대해 시험을 볼 테니 잃어버리지 않도록 하세요.

3 Listen to a school principal speaking to the students over the intercom.

M [*intercom sound*] Good morning, everybody. Arbor Day is this Saturday, and we're going to celebrate it the same way as always. That means we'll be planting some trees on the school grounds. If you want to come and help, please sign the list that your teachers will show you right now.

방송을 통해 교장 선생님이 학생들에게 말하는 내용을 들어 보세요.

M [교내 방송 소리] 여러분, 안녕하세요. 식목일은 이번 토요일이며, 늘 하던 것처럼 기념할 예정입니다. 즉, 학교 운동장에 나무를 심을 거예요. 와서 돕고 싶은 사람은 지금 선생님께서 보여 주실 명단에 이름을 적어 주세요.

4 Listen to a teacher speaking to her students.

W Some of you have inquired about our class project, so I'd like to talk about it. First, your class project is due on November 22. That's six weeks from now, so you have plenty of time to work on it. Now, what about the topic? Well, you can choose from a variety of them. Let me give you some examples.

선생님이 학생들에게 말하는 내용을 들어 보세요.

W 여러분 중 몇 명이 학급 프로젝트에 대해 문의했기에, 그 이야기를 하고자 합니다. 먼저, 학급 프로젝트 제출일은 11월 22일입니다. 지금부터 6주 뒤이니, 충분히 준비할 시간이 있습니다. 그럼 주제는 어떻게 할까요? 다양한 주제 중에서 선택할 수 있습니다. 몇 가지 예를 들어 줄게요.

5 Listen to a teacher making an announcement at the end of the day.

W This weekend, our very own school marching band will be participating in the city's Foundation Day parade. The parade starts at City Hall at 9:00 AM. It will last for around ninety minutes. I'm going to be attending the parade to cheer for our students. I hope many of you go there, too.

종례 때 선생님이 공지하는 내용을 들어 보세요.

W 이번 주말에 우리 학교 마칭 밴드가 시 건립 기념일 퍼레이드에 참가합니다. 퍼레이드는 오전 9시에 시청에서 시작하며, 약 90분간 진행됩니다. 저는 학생들을 응원하러 퍼레이드에 참석할 예정입니다. 여러분도 많이 참석하길 바랍니다.

6 Listen to a history teacher speaking to his students.

M Some of you are not taking notes in class. You absolutely must write down the important things I say in your notebooks. In addition, the information I write on the board is crucial to this class, so write it down. All right. Why don't we get started on today's class? We're discussing the American Revolution today.

역사 선생님이 학생들에게 말하는 내용을 들어 보세요.

M 여러분 중 일부는 수업 시간에 필기를 하지 않고 있습니다. 제가 말하는 중요한 내용은 반드시 공책에 적어야 합니다. 또한, 제가 칠판에 쓰는 내용은 이 수업에서 매우 중요하니 적어 두세요. 자, 그럼 오늘 수업을 시작할까요? 오늘은 미국 독립혁명에 대해 다루겠습니다.

7 Listen to a school coach talking to her team.

W Congratulations on winning the game tonight. You played an amazing game and deserved to win. I know you're tired, so we're going to have an easy practice after school tomorrow. We're only going to meet for around thirty minutes. Now, get cleaned up, go home, and get some rest. Great game, everybody.

학교 코치 선생님이 팀원들에게 말하는 내용을 들어 보세요.

W 오늘 저녁 경기에서 승리한 것을 축하해요. 여러분은 정말 멋진 경기를 펼쳤고 승리할 만했어요. 피곤할 테니 내일 방과 후 연습은 가볍게 하겠습니다. 약 30분 정도만 모일 예정입니다. 이제 정리하고 집에 가서 쉬세요. 훌륭한 경기였어요, 여러분.

8 Listen to a science teacher making an announcement.

M Some of the younger students at our school are having trouble learning science. They need tutoring, so I wonder if any of you are interested in helping. If you have an A or a B in this class, you're qualified to tutor younger kids. I'd like you to stay after class and talk to me if you'd like to help.

과학 선생님이 공지하는 내용을 들어 보세요.

M 우리 학교의 일부 저학년 학생들이 과학 공부에 어려움을 겪고 있습니다. 그들은 개인 지도가 필요합니다. 그래서 여러분 중에 혹시 도와주고 싶은 학생이 있을까 해요. 이 수업에서 A나 B를 받은 학생은 저학년 학생들을 가르칠 자격이 있습니다. 도와주고 싶다면 수업 후에 저와 이야기하러 남아 주길 바랍니다.

PRACTICE 2 Conversation p. 077

1 (D)	2 (A)	3 (D)	4 (B)
5 (D)	6 (B)	7 (B)	8 (C)

1-4 Listen to a conversation between two friends at school.

G My parents keep telling me I should play a sport at school this spring.

B So do mine, but I don't enjoy team sports. Plus, I can't play golf or tennis.

G I feel the same way as you. I guess that means I have to try out for the track and field team.

B I didn't even know that our school had one.

G Yeah, we do, but there aren't many students on the team. Basically, any student who tries out for the team will make it.

B That's not bad. What are you thinking of doing?

G I'm not a good sprinter, and I really can't stand long-distance running. I think I should try to do either the 400-meter run or the 800-meter run.

B Those sound okay. I don't know what I would do though. I can't run fast at all.

G But you're pretty strong. You could throw the discus or the shot put. Those require strength, and you don't have to do any running.

B What a great idea. Why don't we try to find Coach Wilson right now?

G Okay. Let's do it. We still have about fifteen minutes before lunch is over.

학교에서 두 친구가 나누는 대화를 들어 보세요.

G 부모님이 이번 봄에 학교에서 운동을 하라고 나한테 계속 말씀하셔.

B 우리 부모님도 그러시는데, 나는 단체 운동을 별로 안 좋아해. 게다가 골프나 테니스도 못 해.

G 나도 너랑 같은 생각이야. 그럼 육상부에 들어가 봐야 할 것 같아.

B 우리 학교에 그런 팀이 있는지도 몰랐는데.

G 응, 있긴 한데 팀원이 많지 않아. 기본적으로, 선발 테스트를 보는 학생은 누구나 팀에 들어갈 수 있어.

B 나쁘지 않네. 넌 어떤 걸 해 볼 생각이야?

G 나는 뛰어난 단거리 주자도 아니고, 장거리 달리기는 정말 못 참겠어. 400m나 800m 달리기를 해 봐야 할 것 같아.

B 괜찮게 들리네. 하지만 난 뭘 해야 할지 모르겠어. 나는 전혀 빨리 달릴 수가 없어.

G 근데 너 힘이 꽤 세잖아. 원반 던지기나 포환 던지기를 할 수 있을 거야. 힘이 필요하고 달릴 필요는 없어.

B 좋은 생각이네. 우리 지금 바로 Wilson 코치 선생님을 찾아보면 어때?

G 좋아, 그러자. 점심 시간 끝나기까지 아직 15분 정도 남았어.

5-8 Listen to a conversation between a student and a teacher.

W Ken, would you stay here for a moment, please? I'd like to have a word with you.

B Sure thing, Ms. Hampton.

W Have a seat here, Ken . . . I want to talk to you about your performance this semester.

B It hasn't been very good, has it?

W No, it hasn't. And I'm curious about why. After all, you got an A in my history class both semesters last year. You also spoke in class regularly and showed a real affinity for history. I haven't seen any of that this year.

B I'm sorry, Ms. Hampton. I just . . . I just haven't been feeling well these days. So, uh, I haven't really studied as much as I should.

W Well, that explains your poor performance on the test. But what about your lack of interest during class? What's going on?

B Well . . . I'm kind of having some problems at home. I don't want to talk about them if you don't mind though. But things are not very good.

W I'm so sorry to hear that. You know, we have a counselor at this school. You can talk to him if you have problems.

B Yeah . . . That sounds all right.

W Let's go then. Mr. Jackson's office is two doors down from mine.

학생과 선생님이 나누는 대화를 들어 보세요.

W Ken, 잠깐 여기 있어 줄래? 할 말이 있어.

B 알겠어요, Hampton 선생님.

W 여기 앉으렴, Ken…. 이번 학기 너의 성적에 대해 이야기하고 싶어.

B 별로 좋지 않았죠, 그렇죠?

W 응, 그렇지. 왜 그런지 궁금하네. 어쨌거나 작년 두 학기 모두 내 역사 수업에서 A를 받았잖아. 게다가 수업 시간에 자주 말하고 역사에 많은 관심을 보였지. 그런데 올해는 그런 모습이 전혀 보이지 않아.

B 죄송해요, Hampton 선생님. 제가… 요즘 몸 상태가 좋지 않았어요. 그래서 공부를 해야 하는 만큼 하지 못했어요.

W 그럼 시험 성적이 안 좋았던 이유는 이해가 되네. 그런데 수업 시간에 관심이 없는 건 왜 그렇지? 무슨 일이 있어?

B 음…. 집에서 좀 문제가 있어요. 괜찮으시다면 말씀드리고 싶지 않아요. 근데 상황이 별로 좋지 않아요.

W 그 말을 들으니 안타깝다. 우리 학교에 상담 선생님이 있어. 문제가 있으면 그분과 이야기할 수 있어.

B 네…. 괜찮을 것 같아요.

W 그럼 가자. Jackson 선생님 사무실은 내 사무실에서 두 방 더 가면 있어.

PRACTICE 3 Lecture/Discussion p. 080

1 (D)	2 (B)	3 (C)	4 (B)
5 (D)	6 (D)	7 (B)	8 (B)
9 (B)			

1-4 Listen to a talk in a history class.

W The Iron Age started between 1200 and 600 B.C. That's a very broad period of time. The reason is that like the Bronze Age, which came before it, the Iron Age didn't start at the same time everywhere. It took time for the knowledge of how to work with iron to spread. The first places the Iron Age began were in the Mediterranean region and the Middle East. Later, it spread to other places in Europe, Asia, and northern Africa.

What's interesting is that iron isn't as strong or durable as bronze. Bronze, by the way, is an alloy made of copper and tin. So if bronze is superior to iron, why is the Iron Age considered a more advanced time than the Bronze Age . . . ? The answer is that during the Iron Age, people learned to make steel by adding carbon to iron. This allowed people to develop tools superior to those made of bronze, especially weapons, which were strong and long lasting.

You should also know that when the Bronze Age ended and the Iron Age began, many civilizations collapsed. The Mycenaean civilization in Greece was one. The Hittite Empire in the modern-day country of Turkey was another. The city of Troy, famous in stories about the Trojan War, was destroyed as well. Let's look at the reasons why they collapsed now.

역사 수업 중 강의 내용을 들어 보세요.

W 철기 시대는 기원전 1200년에서 600년 사이에 시작되었습니다. 꽤 넓은 기간이에요. 그 이유는, 그 이전에 있던 청동기 시대처럼, 철기 시대도 모든 지역에서 동시에 시작된 것이 아니기 때문이에요. 철을 다루는 법에 대한 지식이 퍼지는 데 시간이 걸렸죠. 철기 시대가 처음 시작된 곳은 지중해 지역과 중동이었고, 이후 유럽, 아시아, 북아프리카로 퍼졌습니다.

재미있는 점은, 철이 청동만큼 강하거나 내구성이 뛰어나지 않다는 거예요. 참고로 청동은 구리와 주석을 섞어 만든 합금입니다. 그러면 청동보다 철이 더 뛰어나지 않은데 왜 철기 시대가 청동기 시대보다 더 발전된 시기로 여겨질까요…? 그 이유는 철기 시대에 사람들이 철에 탄소를 첨가해 강철을 만드는 법을 터득하게 되었기 때문입니다. 이를 통해 청동으로 만든 도구보다 우수한 도구, 특히 강하고 오래가는 무기를 만들 수 있게 되었어요.

또한 알아 두어야 할 점은, 청동기 시대가 끝나고 철기 시대가 시작될 때 많은 문명이 붕괴되었다는 것입니다. 그리스의 미케네 문명이 그랬고, 현재의 튀르키예에 있던 히타이트 제국도 그랬습니다. 트로이 전쟁 이야기로 유명한 도시 트로이도 파괴되었죠. 이제 이들이 왜 붕괴했는지 살펴봅시다.

5-9 Listen to part of a discussion in a science class.

M Since the 1920s, American schoolchildren have been regularly dissecting animals in their science classes. Up to twelve million animals are believed to be dissected each year. Can anyone tell me why we cut up animals in science class?

G It's a kind of hands-on learning that is ideal for biology. Instead of just looking at pictures and diagrams, students can see the insides of various animals for themselves. This kind of activity can interest students who don't particularly enjoy lectures and learning from books. It can also inspire students to decide to pursue careers in biology or zoology.

M Correct, Stephanie. Now, uh, these days, there are computer programs which act as alternatives to animal dissection. These were created because some people complained about animal dissection being inhumane.

G I kind of understand that argument, but what about veterinarians? They have to be able to look at the insides of animals if they want to operate on them or just understand how animals' bodies work. And, uh, it's not like we're dissecting dogs or other similar animals. Last year, we dissected frogs, grasshoppers, and earthworms. Those aren't animals that anyone cares about.

M That's the argument in favor of dissection. Does anyone want to provide a counterpoint to her argument?

과학 수업 중 토론 내용의 일부를 들어 보세요.

M 1920년대 이후로, 미국의 학교 학생들은 과학 수업 시간에 정기적으로 동물 해부를 해 왔습니다. 매년 최대 1,200만 마리의 동물이 해부되는 것으로 추정됩니다. 과학 시간에 동물을 해부하는 이유를 누가 말해 줄 수 있나요?

G 생물학을 위한 이상적인 실습 학습의 한 종류이기 때문이에요. 그림이나 도표만 보는 대신, 학생들이 직접 다양한 동물의 내부를 볼 수 있죠. 이런 활동은 강의나 책으로 배우는 것을 별로 즐기지 않는 학생들의 흥미를 끌 수 있고, 학생들이 생물학이나 동물학 분야로 진로를 결정하는 데에도 영감을 줄 수 있어요.

M 맞아요, Stephanie. 요즘에는 동물 해부를 대체할 수 있는 컴퓨터 프로그램이 있습니다. 일부 사람들이 동물 해부가 비인도적이라고 불평했기 때문에 이런 프로그램이 만들어졌죠.

G 그 주장은 이해가 가지만, 수의사는 어떡하죠? 수의사가 동물을 수술하거나 동물의 몸이 어떻게 작동하는지 이해하려면 동물의 내부를 볼 수 있어야 해요. 그리고 우리가 개나 비슷한 동물을 해부하는 것도 아니잖아요. 작년에는 개구리, 메뚜기, 지렁이를 해부했어요. 아무도 신경 쓰지 않는 동물들이잖아요.

M 그게 해부를 찬성하는 논거입니다. 혹시 그 주장에 반대되는 의견을 말하고 싶은 사람 있나요?

PRACTICE TEST p. 084

1 (D)	2 (A)	3 (D)	4 (C)
5 (A)	6 (C)	7 (D)	8 (C)
9 (B)	10 (A)	11 (C)	12 (B)

1 Listen to a teacher talking to a class.

W I'm very sorry, but I've got a terrible headache. I need to step out of the room to see the school nurse for some aspirin. Please turn to page 108 in your books. I want you to read the story on pages 108 and 109 while I'm gone. I'll be back in five minutes. And please be quiet. Okay?

선생님이 반 학생들에게 말하는 내용을 들어 보세요.

W 미안하지만, 머리가 너무 아파요. 보건 선생님께 가서 아스피린을 받으러 잠시 교실을 나가 있어야겠어요. 책 108쪽을 펴세요. 내가 없는 동안 108쪽과 109쪽에 있는 이야기를 읽으세요. 5분 안에 다녀올게요. 소용히 해 수세요. 알겠죠?

2 Listen to a teacher making an announcement.

M The school gave every teacher a survey for the students to fill out. Please take one of these sheets and then answer the questions. Make sure you respond honestly because we will make changes based on your answers. Don't write your name on the paper. This survey is completely anonymous.

선생님이 공지하는 내용을 들어 보세요.

M 학교에서 학생들이 작성할 설문지를 모든 선생님께 나눠 주었습니다. 이 종이 중 하나를 가져가서 질문에 답해 주세요. 여러분의 답변을 바탕으로 변경 사항을 만들 예정이니 솔직히 답하도록 하세요. 이름은 적지 마세요. 이 설문지는 완전히 익명입니다.

3 Listen to a principal talking to a group of students.

W Welcome to our school's second annual singing contest. We've got fifteen students who are competing in today's event. I personally am really looking forward to listening to our school's singers. I hope you're ready because I sure am. Let's get this contest started with our first contestant.

교장 선생님이 학생들에게 말하는 내용을 들어 보세요.

W 우리 학교 제2회 연례 노래 경연대회에 오신 것을 환영합니다. 오늘 경연에는 15명의 학생이 참가합니다. 저는 개인적으로 우리 학교 학생들의 노래를 듣는 것을 정말 기대하고 있습니다. 저는 준비됐으니 여러분도 준비되셨기를 바라요. 그럼, 첫 번째 참가자와 함께 경연을 시작하겠습니다.

4 Listen to a science teacher speaking to her students.

W Many of you mentioned that I've been using some difficult terms every class. So I made this handout. It contains a list of hard words as well as their definitions. Now, when I say something that you don't understand, you can consult the handout. Let's go over the terms now to make sure everything is clear.

과학 선생님이 학생들에게 말하는 내용을 들어 보세요.

W 여러분 중 많은 학생이 제가 수업 시간마다 어려운 용어를 사용한다고 말했어요. 그래서 제가 이 유인물을 준비했어요. 여기에는 어려운 단어와 그 뜻이 나와 있습니다. 이제 제가 이해가 안 되는 말을 할 때는 유인물을 참고하면 됩니다. 자, 모든 것이 명확하도록 하기 위해 용어들을 함께 살펴보죠.

5-8 Listen to a conversation between a student and a school secretary.

G Mr. Mandell, may I have a word with you, please?

M Sure. What can I do for you?

G I lost something, and my teacher told me that I should speak with you about it.

M That's right. When anyone finds something at school, it gets put in the lost and found box here in the office. What did you lose?

G A ring.

M Can you describe it, please?

G Oh, yeah. Sorry. Um, it's a gold ring that has a red stone in it. I believe it's a ruby. It also has four small diamonds around the ruby. It was my grandmother's ring. I can't believe I lost it. It happened sometime around lunch.

M Well, today's your lucky day because I believe I have it here. Let me see . . . Is this it?

G Oh, my gosh. Yes, that's it. Thank you so, so, so much.

M Don't thank me. Ian Kennedy turned it in a few minutes ago. He told me that he found it in the hallway.

G Oh, I know him. He's in room 108 now. I'll drop by there before my next class. Thanks again.

학생과 교무 직원이 나누는 대화를 들어 보세요.

G Mandell 선생님, 잠깐 말씀 나눌 수 있을까요?

M 그래, 무슨 일이야?

G 제가 뭔가를 잃어버렸는데, 저희 선생님께서 선생님과 이야기하라고 하셨어요.

M 맞아. 학교에서 누군가 물건을 찾으면 여기 사무실에 있는 분실물 보관함에 들어가. 뭘 잃어버렸는데?

G 반지요.

M 자세히 말해 줄래?

G 아, 네. 죄송해요. 음, 금반지인데 빨간 보석이 있어요. 아마 루비인 것 같아요. 루비 주변에는 작은 다이아몬드 네 개가 있어요. 할머니 반지였는데, 잃어버리다니 믿기지 않아요. 점심 때쯤 그런 것 같아요.

M 오늘 운이 좋네. 여기 있는 것 같으니까. 어디 보자…. 이거 맞아?

G 세상에. 네, 맞아요. 정말 정말 감사합니다.

M 나한테 감사할 필요 없어. Ian Kennedy가 몇 분 전에 가져다줬거든. 복도에서 발견했대.

G 아, 그 친구 알아요. 지금 108호에 있어요. 다음 수업 전에 들러야겠네요. 다시 한번 감사드려요.

9-12 Listen to a talk in an English class.

M Thousands of years ago, humans didn't understand the natural world. They didn't know why the sun rose and set. They didn't know why earthquakes happened. And they had no idea why eclipses took place. So they created stories explaining what was going on. For instance, the Greeks said that Helios, the sun god, drove a fiery chariot across the sky every day. That explained why the sun appeared during the day and disappeared at night.

Stories like that are called myths. A myth is a story—or a group of stories—that features gods, heroes, supernatural creatures, and figures from the past. Myths were created to explain natural phenomena, the creation of the world, human behavior, and cultural beliefs. Throughout history, every society has developed its own myths.

In modern times, most people consider myths stories with no truth to them. But that's not necessarily true. Now, uh, myths aren't entirely true, but there is truth behind many of them. And many myths have survived into modern times. Take the story of Atlantis as an example. Plato wrote about the mythical island that sank into the ocean more than 2,300 years ago, but people still search for it today.

With that in mind, open your books to page 242. Read the myth on that page. While you're doing that, think about what I said about myths and truth.

영어 수업 중 강의 내용을 들어 보세요.

M 수천 년 전, 사람들은 자연 세계를 잘 이해하지 못했습니다. 왜 해가 뜨고 지는지, 왜 지진이 일어나는지 몰랐죠. 왜 일식과 월식이 일어나는지 전혀 몰랐습니다. 그래서 사람들은 현상을 설명하기 위해 이야기를 만들어 냈습니다. 예를 들어, 그리스인들은 태양신 헬리오스가 매일 불타는 전차를 몰고 하늘을 가로지른다고 했습니다. 이것이 낮에 해가 보이고 밤에는 사라지는 이유를 설명해 주었습니다.

이런 이야기를 신화라고 합니다. 신화는 신, 영웅, 초자연적 존재, 과거의 인물이 등장하는 이야기 혹은 이야기 모음입니다. 신화는 자연 현상, 세상의 창조, 인간의 행동, 문화적 믿음을 설명하기 위해 만들어졌습니다. 역사를 통틀어, 모든 사회는 자신만의 신화를 발전시켜 왔습니다.

현대에 들어와서는 대부분의 사람들은 신화를 사실무근의 이야기로 생각합니다. 하지만 반드시 그렇지만은 않습니다. 신화가 완전히 사실은 아니지만, 많은 신화의 이면에는 사실이 담겨 있습니다. 그리고 많은 신화가 현대까지 전해져 오고 있습니다. 예를 들어, 아틀란티스 이야기를 보겠습니다. 플라톤이 2,300년보다 더 전에 바다에 잠긴 신화 속 섬에 대해 썼지만, 사람들은 오늘날에도 그 섬을 찾고 있습니다.

이것을 염두에 두고 교과서 242페이지를 펴세요. 그 페이지에 있는 신화를 읽으세요. 그러는 동안 신화와 진실에 대해 제가 말한 내용을 생각해 보기 바랍니다.

CHAPTER 05 SPEAKER'S PURPOSE

PRACTICE 1 Short Talk			p. 089
1 (D)	2 (B)	3 (A)	4 (D)
5 (B)	6 (A)	7 (B)	8 (A)

1 Listen to a teacher making an announcement.

M Yesterday, after everyone left the classroom, I found a textbook on the floor. Unfortunately, the book didn't have a name written in it. So I don't know who it belongs to. Did any of you lose your science book yesterday? If you did, I've got it right here.

선생님이 공지하는 내용을 들어 보세요.

M 어제 모두가 교실을 떠난 후, 교실 바닥에서 교과서를 하나 발견했어요. 안타깝게도 책 안에 이름이 적혀 있지 않아서 누구의 것인지 모르겠네요. 어제 과학책을 잃어버린 학생 있나요? 만약 있다면, 여기 내가 가지고 있어요.

2 Listen to a teacher making an announcement at the end of the day.

W This is a reminder about the open house we're having tomorrow night. Your parents are invited to attend. It begins at seven and should last until eight thirty. Your parents can meet me and your other teachers. They can ask questions and learn what you do here. It's a very educational event, so I hope they come.

종례 때 선생님이 공지하는 내용을 들어 보세요.

W 내일 저녁에 있을 학부모 초청 행사에 대한 안내예요. 학부모님들께서 참석하실 수 있습니다. 행사는 7시에 시작해서 8시 30분까지 진행될 예정이에요. 학부모님들은 저와 다른 선생님들을 만나실 수 있고, 궁금한 점을 물어보거나 여러분이 학교에서 무엇을 하는지 알아가실 수 있어요. 매우 교육적인 행사이니, 꼭 참석하시길 바랍니다.

3 Listen to a principal speaking to the students over the intercom.

W [*intercom sound*] This is an important announcement. Please do not walk on the flowerbeds beside the sidewalk. Ms. Powers planted flowers last week, and they're starting to grow. But some students have been walking in the flowerbeds and killing the flowers. Please stop that. We're trying to make our school beautiful, so we'd like those flowers to grow.

방송을 통해 교장 선생님이 학생들에게 말하는 내용을 들어 보세요.

W [교내 방송 소리] 중요한 안내입니다. 인도 옆 화단 위를 걸어 다니지 마세요. Powers 선생님께서 지난주에 꽃을 심으셨고, 이제 꽃이 자라기 시작했어요. 그런데 일부 학생들이 화단 위를 걸어 다니며 꽃을 죽이고 있습니다. 제발 그만해 주세요. 학교를 아름답게 만들려고 노력하는 중이니, 꽃들이 잘 자라기를 바랍니다.

4 Listen to a librarian making an announcement.

M Sometimes students borrow books and then lose them. If that happens to you, please come and talk to me. We might be able to get a replacement copy easily. But it might be more difficult other times. And you'll have to pay a replacement fee. But you really need to tell me about it if that happens. All right?

사서 선생님이 공지하는 내용을 들어 보세요.

M 가끔 학생들이 책을 빌렸다가 잃어버리는 경우가 있어요. 만약 그런 일이 생기면, 꼭 저한테 와서 말하세요. 경우에 따라 쉽게 대체할 책을 구할 수 있을 수도 있어요. 하지만 때로는 더 어려울 수도 있어요. 그리고 여러분이 교체 비용을 내야 할 겁니다. 그래도 이런 일이 생기면 꼭 저에게 알려야 합니다. 알겠죠?

5 Listen to a social studies teacher talking to a class.

W Before we get started, I believe everyone has homework for me. You all need to turn in your five-page papers. Everyone, please pass your papers to the front of the class. Stacy, would you please collect them and give them to me? I'm really looking forward to reading them.

사회 선생님이 반 학생들에게 말하는 내용을 들어 보세요.

W 수업 시작하기 전에, 여러분 모두 숙제를 가져왔을 거라 믿어요. 5페이지짜리 보고서를 제출해야 합니다. 모두, 보고서를 교실 앞쪽으로 주세요. Stacy, 보고서를 받아서 나한테 전달해 줄래요? 읽어 보는 게 정말 기대되네요.

6 Listen to a school P.E. teacher talking to his students.

M Most of you are not very flexible, so we need to work on stretches today. You should all be able to touch your toes without bending your knees. We're going to practice that today and also do some other stretches. So let's get to it. We have a busy day today.

체육 선생님이 학생들에게 말하는 내용을 들어 보세요.

M 여러분 대부분 유연성이 충분하지 않으니까, 오늘은 스트레칭을 연습해야겠어요. 무릎을 굽히지 않고 발가락을 만질 수 있어야 합니다. 오늘은 그것을 연습하고 다른 스트레칭도 몇 가지 해 볼 거예요. 자, 시작합시다. 오늘은 바쁜 하루가 될 거예요.

7 Listen to a teacher speaking to her class.

W Okay, everybody. The test is now finished. Please put

your pens and pencils on the desk. I'm going to walk around the classroom to collect your test papers. Please give them to me when I pass by. We have about ten minutes left in class, so why don't you do some reading before we finish?

선생님이 반 학생들에게 말하는 내용을 들어 보세요.

W 좋아요, 여러분. 시험은 이제 끝났습니다. 펜과 연필을 책상 위에 놓아 주세요. 제가 교실을 돌아다니면서 시험지를 걷겠습니다. 제가 지나갈 때 시험지를 주세요. 수업 시간은 약 10분 정도 남았으니, 수업이 끝나기 전에 교과서를 읽을까요?

8 Listen to a school coach talking to a group of students.

M We've got a big tournament coming up in two weeks. You guys are playing well these days, but we can do better. Let's try working a bit harder in practice starting today. I've got some new strategies which I believe can help us. We'll learn them today. Two weeks is enough time to master them.

학교 코치 선생님이 학생들에게 말하는 내용을 들어 보세요.

M 2주 후에 큰 토너먼트 대회가 있습니다. 요즘 여러분 잘하고 있긴 한데, 더 잘할 수 있어요. 오늘부터 연습 때 조금 더 열심히 해 봅시다. 내가 도움이 될 수 있다고 생각하는 새로운 전략 몇 가지를 준비했어요. 오늘 그걸 배울 거예요. 2주면 충분히 익힐 수 있는 시간이에요.

PRACTICE 2 Conversation p. 093

1 (C)	2 (D)	3 (B)	4 (C)
5 (D)	6 (C)	7 (A)	8 (B)

1-4 Listen to a conversation between two friends.

G George, did you hear the news about Mr. Kendrick? He's going to be leaving the school at the end of the semester.

B He's retiring? Isn't he a bit too young for that?

G No, he's not giving up teaching. Apparently, he's going to start a new job in his hometown. He wants to move back there to help take care of his parents.

B He's a great teacher. I'm going to miss him, but I'm glad he can be with his parents.

G Yeah, you're right about that.

B Hey. We ought to have a going-away party for him. What do you think?

G That's a wonderful idea. When should we do it?

B We can't have it during the exam period, so how about on the last day of classes? We could do it either during lunch or at the end of school.

G Lunch would be better since some students have to leave school immediately at 3:00.

B Sure. That works. Oh, this needs to be a surprise party. We can't let him find out.

G I'll talk to Jennifer. She's great at planning events and can also keep a secret. I'll let you know what she says later today.

두 친구가 나누는 대화를 들어 보세요.

G George, Kendrick 선생님 소식 들었어? 학기 끝나고 학교를 떠나신대.

B 은퇴하시는 거야? 그러기에 좀 젊으시지 않아?

G 아니, 교직을 그만두시는 건 아니래. 듣자 하니 선생님 고향에서 새 일을 시작하신다나 봐. 부모님을 돌보러 돌아가고 싶으시대.

B 좋은 선생님인데. 선생님이 그리울 거야. 그래도 부모님 곁에 계실 수 있다니 다행이네.

G 응, 맞아.

B 있잖아, 우리 그분 환송회 열자. 어때?

G 좋은 생각이야. 언제 할까?

B 시험 기간 중에는 안 되니까, 마지막 수업 날은 어때? 점심 시간이나 수업 끝나고 할 수 있어.

G 몇몇 학생들은 3시에 바로 가야 하니 점심 시간이 낫겠다.

B 좋아, 괜찮을 것 같아. 아, 서프라이즈 파티가 되어야 해. 선생님께 들키면 안 돼.

G 내가 Jennifer랑 얘기해 볼게. 걔가 이벤트 계획 잘하고 비밀도 잘 지켜. 오늘 이따가 걔가 뭐라고 하는지 알려 줄게.

5-8 Listen to a conversation between a student and a teacher.

B Here's my report, Ms. Campbell. I'm sorry I was late and couldn't turn it in at the beginning of class.

W Thanks for the paper, Eric. I'm looking forward to reading it.

B Great. I need to get to my next class now.

W Hold on a minute.

B Yes?

W Eric, you've been late for school three times this week. What's going on?

B I have to walk to school every morning. It takes me around half an hour to get here. It's kind of a long walk. Sorry.

W Can't your parents take you to school?

B That's not possible. Both of them start their jobs early in the morning, so they have already left home by the time I wake up.

W I see. Then how about riding a bicycle to school? That would be a lot faster, wouldn't it?

B Er . . . I'm not really good at cycling. The last time I was on a bike, I crashed and hurt myself.

W Why don't you let me know your address? I'll see if someone else here lives near you. Then, I'll talk to that student's parents and ask them if they would drive you to school in the morning.

B Thank you, Ms. Campbell. I would appreciate that

very much.

학생과 선생님이 나누는 대화를 들어 보세요.

B Campbell 선생님, 여기 제 보고서예요. 늦어서 수업 시작할 때 제출 못해서 죄송해요.

W 보고서 고마워, Eric. 읽어보는 거 기대하고 있어.

B 좋아요. 저 이제 다음 수업 가야 돼요.

W 잠깐만.

B 네?

W Eric, 이번 주에 세 번이나 지각했더라. 무슨 일이야?

B 매일 아침 학교까지 걸어와야 돼서요. 여기까지 오는 데 한 30분 걸려요. 좀 멀어요. 죄송해요.

W 부모님이 데려다주실 수는 없니?

B 그건 안 돼요. 두 분 다 아침 일찍 출근하셔서, 제가 일어날 때쯤이면 이미 집을 나가셨어요.

W 그렇구나. 그럼 자전거 타고 다니면 어떨까? 훨씬 빠를 텐데, 안 그래?

B 음…. 자전거 타는 건 잘 못해요. 마지막으로 탔을 때 사고 나서 다쳤거든요.

W 주소 알려 줄래? 근처에 사는 다른 학생이 있는지 확인해 보고, 그 학생 부모님께 아침에 데려다주실 수 있는지 물어볼게.

B 감사합니다, Campbell 선생님. 정말 감사해요.

PRACTICE 3 Lecture/Discussion p. 096

1 (C)	2 (D)	3 (B)	4 (C)
5 (A)	6 (A)	7 (D)	8 (B)
9 (C)			

1-5 Listen to a talk in an English class.

M The Elizabethan Era in England lasted from 1558 to 1603. This was when Queen Elizabeth I reigned. It's considered a golden era for England, particularly with regard to literature. William Shakespeare is the best-known writer from this time. Edmund Spenser, whom we talked about in our last class, also wrote during this era. Lesser known is playwright Christopher Marlowe.

Marlowe lived from 1564 to 1593. It's likely that we don't speak of him as Shakespeare's equal—or even his better—because he died so young. He therefore has a much smaller body of work than Shakespeare. But what works he wrote. He penned *Tamburlaine the Great*, a play in two parts. It is a drama about Timur, a warlord from Central Asia. This was Marlowe's first play to be performed regularly in London.

Among his other plays, *Doctor Faustus* is the best known. It tells the tale of a man who makes a deal with the devil and what happens afterward. It features a famous line about Helen of Troy. It goes, "Was this the face that launched a thousand ships and burnt the topless towers of Ilium?" Sadly, Marlowe died in mysterious conditions before turning thirty. Now, uh, let's take a look at *Doctor Faustus* . Open your books to page 194, please.

영어 수업 중 강의 내용을 들어 보세요.

M 영국의 엘리자베스 시대는 1558년부터 1603년까지 지속되었습니다. 이 시기는 엘리자베스 1세 여왕이 통치하던 때로, 특히 문학 분야에서 황금기로 여겨집니다. 이 시대의 가장 잘 알려진 작가는 윌리엄 셰익스피어입니다. 지난 수업에서 이야기한 에드먼드 스펜서도 이 시기에 작품을 썼습니다. 덜 알려진 작가는 극작가 크리스토퍼 말로입니다.

말로는 1564년부터 1593년까지 살았습니다. 그는 아주 젊은 나이에 세상을 떠났기 때문에 셰익스피어와 동등하게 혹은 더 낫게 평가받지 못합니다. 작품 수도 셰익스피어보다 훨씬 적습니다. 그러나 그가 남긴 작품들은 어땠는지요. 그는 두 부분으로 된 희곡 『위대한 탬벌레인』을 썼는데, 이는 중앙아시아의 군주 티무르에 관한 드라마입니다. 이 작품은 런던에서 정기적으로 공연된 말로의 첫 번째 희곡이었습니다.

그의 다른 희곡 작품 중에서는 『파우스터스 박사』가 가장 잘 알려져 있습니다. 이 작품은 악마와 거래를 한 남자와 그 후의 이야기를 다루며, 트로이의 헬렌에 대한 유명한 대사가 나옵니다. "이 얼굴이 천 척의 배를 띄우고 일리온의 지붕 없는 탑들을 불태운 얼굴이었단 말인가?" 안타깝게도 말로는 서른 살이 되기 전에 의문스러운 상황에서 사망했습니다. 이제 『파우스터스 박사』를 살펴보겠습니다. 책 194쪽을 펴세요.

6-9 Listen to part of a discussion in a social studies class.

W Throughout history, there have been countless inventions. These inventions have made work easier for people and enabled us to do all sorts of activities. Most people today would say that computers, the Internet, or smartphones are the most important inventions. But I wonder about you. Excluding those three things, what would you say the most important invention in history is?

B That's easy to answer. It's definitely the wheel. Thanks to the wheel, transportation became easier. People could make pottery by using the potter's wheel. Farming became easier and more productive as well.

W Chad makes a good point, everybody. The wheel was invented around 3500 B.C. in Mesopotamia. It had a tremendous effect not only on ancient times but also on modern times. But what, Chad, do you believe the most important invention in the past 500 years is?

B Hmm . . . I'd go with the microscope. It enabled biologists to see tiny things such as cells, bacteria, and viruses. Thanks to the microscope, humans have made great advances in the fields of biology, botany, and medicine. Pretty much every discovery in those fields has been made thanks to the microscope.

W A very insightful answer. How about you, Hilda? What's your opinion?

사회 수업 중 토론 내용의 일부를 들어 보세요.

W 역사를 통틀어 수많은 발명품이 있었습니다. 이러한 발명품들은 사람들의 일을 더 쉽게 만들어 주었고, 다양한 활동을 할 수 있게 해 주었습니다. 오늘날 대부분의 사람들은 컴퓨터, 인터넷, 또는 스마트폰이 가장 중요한 발명품이라고 말할 것입니다. 그런데 여러분은 어떻게 생각하는지 궁금해요. 이 세 가지를 제외하고, 역사상 가장 중요한 발명품은 무엇이라고 생각하나요?

B 답하기 쉽네요. 당연히 바퀴예요. 바퀴 덕분에 교통이 더 편리해졌어요. 사람들은 물레를 이용해 도자기를 만들 수 있었고, 농사도 더 쉽고 생산적이 되었습니다.

W Chad가 좋은 지적을 했네요, 여러분. 바퀴는 기원전 약 3500년경에 메소포타미아에서 발명되었습니다. 그것은 고대뿐만 아니라 현대에도 엄청난 영향을 끼쳤습니다. 그런데 Chad, 지난 500년 동안 가장 중요한 발명품은 무엇이라고 생각하니?

B 음…. 저는 현미경을 선택하겠어요. 현미경 덕분에 생물학자들은 세포, 박테리아, 바이러스 같은 작은 것들을 볼 수 있게 되었죠. 현미경 덕분에 인간은 생물학, 식물학, 의학 분야에서 큰 발전을 이루었어요. 그 분야들에서 거의 모든 발견이 현미경 덕분에 이루어진 셈이죠.

W 아주 통찰력 있는 답변이네요. Hilda, 너는 어떻게 생각하니? 어떤 의견이야?

PRACTICE TEST

p. 100

1 (C)	2 (A)	3 (D)	4 (C)
5 (D)	6 (A)	7 (D)	8 (C)
9 (D)	10 (C)	11 (D)	12 (A)

1 Listen to a teacher speaking to her students.

W I need to inform you of a rule in my class. I do not allow students to use laptops or any other electronic devices in class. The clicking noise from students taking notes on the laptops bothers others around them. You need to take notes by writing in your notebook with a pen or pencil.

선생님이 학생들에게 말하는 내용을 들어 보세요.

W 제 수업에서의 규칙 하나를 알려 줘야겠어요. 저는 수업에서 노트북이나 다른 전자 기기를 사용하는 것을 허용하지 않습니다. 노트북으로 필기할 때 나는 달각거리는 소리가 주변 학생들에게 방해가 되거든요. 필기는 공책에 펜이나 연필로 해야 합니다.

2 Listen to a school coach talking to a group of students.

M As you all know, Robert got injured in the game tonight. His father just informed me that he has a broken leg and needs an operation. He's going to be in the hospital for a few days. I'm planning to visit him tomorrow after school. If you want to go along with me, please let me know.

학교 코치 선생님이 학생들에게 말하는 내용을 들어 보세요.

M 여러분도 알다시피, 오늘 경기에서 Robert가 다쳤습니다. 그의 아버지께서 방금 연락을 주셨는데, 다리가 부러져 수술을 받아야 한대요. 며칠 동안 병원에 있을 예정입니다. 제가 내일 방과 후에 병문안을 갈 계획인데, 같이 가고 싶은 사람은 저에게 알려 주세요.

3 Listen to an English teacher talking to a class.

W Before you leave, let me tell you your homework. Tonight, everyone needs to write a three-page essay about the short story we just read. You need to focus on two things. First, describe the theme of the essay. Second, write about how the story made you feel. You must submit it during class tomorrow.

영어 선생님이 반 학생들에게 말하는 내용을 들어 보세요.

W 떠나기 전에 숙제를 알려 줄게요. 오늘 저녁에, 여러분은 방금 읽은 단편 소설에 대한 세 페이지 분량의 에세이를 써야 합니다. 두 가지에 집중하세요. 첫째, 에세이의 주제를 설명하세요. 둘째, 그 이야기를 읽고 느낀 점을 적으세요. 숙제는 내일 수업 시간에 제출해야 합니다.

4 Listen to a school principal making an announcement.

M Yesterday, a couple of students purchased some food from the vendors right outside the school's front gate. They got very sick later in the day. One of those students is in the hospital with food poisoning. Please do not buy any food from these vendors since we can't trust the quality of the food.

교장 선생님이 공지하는 내용을 들어 보세요.

M 어제, 몇몇 학생들이 학교 정문 바로 밖의 노점상에서 음식을 샀어요. 그 학생들은 나중에 많이 아팠습니다. 그중 한 명은 식중독으로 병원에 입원했어요. 음식의 질을 믿을 수 없으니, 이런 노점상에서 음식을 사 먹지 마세요.

5-8 Listen to a conversation between a student and a librarian.

G Mr. Waters, can you give me some assistance, please?

M How can I help you, Andrea?

G I'm looking for a book, but I can't find it. It's not on the shelf in its usual place.

M Did you try using the online catalog?

G No. I've borrowed it before, so I know where it should be. I didn't bother looking it up online.

M Let's try finding it on the computer. What's the title of the book?

G It's *Western Art from 900 to 1500*. I need to write an art report, and this book is a great reference.

M Hmm . . . According to the computer, the book was

checked out two days ago.

G Oh, no. That's terrible. Can you tell me who borrowed the book? Maybe I can talk to that person.

M I'm really sorry, but I'm not allowed to do that due to privacy laws.

G What should I do then? My paper is due next Monday, so I've only got a few more days to write it.

M Why don't you visit the public library after school today? I can call the librarian for you now and ask her to set aside the book so that you can borrow it. How does that sound?

G Perfect. Thanks so much, Mr. Waters.

학생과 사서 선생님이 나누는 대화를 들어 보세요.

G Waters 선생님, 도와주실 수 있나요?

M 무슨 일이야, Andrea?

G 책을 찾고 있는데, 찾을 수가 없어요. 서가에 평소 있던 자리에 없어요.

M 온라인 목록은 확인해 봤어?

G 아니요. 전에 빌린 적이 있어서 어디에 있어야 하는지는 알고 있거든요. 온라인으로 찾으려고 하진 않았어요.

M 컴퓨터로 찾아보자. 책 제목이 뭐야?

G 『900년에서 1500년까지의 서양 미술』이에요. 미술 보고서를 써야 하는데, 이 책이 좋은 참고 자료예요.

M 음…. 컴퓨터에 따르면, 그 책은 이틀 전에 내출됐어.

G 아, 안 돼. 큰일이네요. 누가 빌렸는지 알 수 있나요? 그 사람한테 말할 수 있을지도 모르겠어요.

M 정말 미안하지만, 개인정보 보호법 때문에 알려 줄 수 없어.

G 그럼 어떻게 해야 하죠? 보고서 제출일이 다음 주 월요일이라, 쓸 시간이 며칠밖에 안 남았어요.

M 오늘 방과 후에 공공 도서관에 가 보는 건 어때? 내가 지금 사서에게 전화해서 네가 빌릴 수 있도록 책을 따로 빼 놔 달라고 부탁할 수 있어. 어때?

G 완벽해요. 정말 감사합니다, Waters 선생님.

9-12 Listen to part of a talk in a science class.

W Pests are animals harmful to humans or to human concerns such as homes and farmland. Rats, mice, ants, and houseflies are common pests. Another common pest you might not see too often is the cockroach. There are more than 4,600 species of cockroaches. Most live in the wild, so humans rarely see them. Around thirty species live near humans, and four of them are considered pests. One of these species is the American cockroach.

The primary reason cockroaches are considered pests is that they can spread diseases, bacteria, and parasitic worms to humans. Scientists have identified thirty-three types of bacteria that cockroaches spread from their bodies and in their droppings. In addition, they can cause people to suffer from diarrhea, plague, typhoid fever, cholera, and even leprosy. Cockroaches normally come out at night and contaminate surfaces by moving on them. They may consume some food left uncovered on kitchen counters. When people eat that food later, they may suffer health problems.

Cockroaches are hardy animals capable of surviving harsh conditions. They can tolerate extreme heat and cold and can even live in the Arctic. They can survive for up to a month without food. They can even live for a week without their head. This happens because cockroaches breathe by taking in air through holes in their bodies. Fortunately, there are ways to exterminate them.

과학 수업 중 강의 내용을 들어 보세요.

W 해충은 인간이나 인간에게 중요한 것, 예를 들어 집이나 농지에 해를 끼치는 동물을 말합니다. 쥐, 생쥐, 개미, 집파리 등이 흔한 해충입니다. 또 잘 볼 수는 없지만 흔한 해충으로 바퀴벌레가 있습니다. 바퀴벌레는 4,600종 이상이 있습니다. 대부분은 야생에서 살기 때문에 인간이 보는 경우는 드뭅니다. 인간 근처에서 사는 종은 약 30종이며, 그중 4종이 해충으로 간주됩니다. 그중 하나가 이질바퀴입니다.

바퀴벌레가 해충으로 여겨지는 주된 이유는 질병, 세균, 기생충을 인간에게 옮길 수 있기 때문입니다. 과학자들은 바퀴벌레가 몸과 배설물을 통해 퍼뜨리는 33종의 세균을 확인했습니다. 또한 설사, 페스트, 장티푸스, 콜레라, 심지어 나병 등과 같은 질병을 일으킬 수 있습니다. 바퀴벌레는 주로 밤에 활동하며 표면 위를 이동하면서 오염시킵니다. 부엌 조리대 위에 덮지 않고 남겨 둔 음식을 먹기도 합니다. 사람들이 나중에 그 음식을 섭취하면 건강 문제가 생길 수 있습니다.

바퀴벌레는 극한 환경에서도 살아남을 수 있는 강인한 동물입니다. 높은 열과 추위도 견딜 수 있으며, 심지어 북극에서도 살 수 있습니다. 음식 없이 한 달까지 생존할 수 있고, 머리 없이도 일주일이나 살 수 있습니다. 이는 바퀴벌레가 몸의 구멍을 통해 공기를 들이마시며 호흡하기 때문입니다. 다행히 바퀴벌레를 박멸할 방법들이 있습니다.

CHAPTER 06 RHETORICAL DEVICE

PRACTICE 1 Conversation p. 105

1 (D)	2 (A)	3 (C)	4 (A)
5 (A)	6 (C)	7 (B)	8 (D)
9 (B)	10 (D)	11 (A)	12 (B)

1-4 Listen to a conversation between a student and a teacher.

G Mr. Watkins, I need to talk to you about my term paper, please.
M Of course, Cindy. Is there a problem with it?
G Yes, sir. There is. I'm having trouble finding enough sources for it.
M You are writing about the early settlers in this town, aren't you?
G Uh, no. That's not me. I think that's Thomas. I was planning to write about the relationships between the early settlers and the Native Americans living here.
M Ah, that's right. I believe the town library has a lot of original documents. You need to take a look at them.
G That's the problem. I spoke to the librarian, but she wouldn't let me into the archives. She said I'm not old enough. I think I may need a new topic.
M I see. Well, I would rather you not change subjects.
G But how am I supposed to get the information I need to write about it?
M After school today, I'll visit the library and speak with Ms. Reynolds. I've known her for a long time. I can probably convince her to let you into the archives.
G Wow. That's great. Would you mind if I went there with you? I'd like to start doing my research today.
M Of course not. Let's go there as soon as school finishes.

학생과 선생님이 나누는 대화를 들어 보세요.

G Watkins 선생님, 기말 과제 때문에 말씀드릴 게 있어요.
M 물론이지, Cindy. 무슨 문제라도 있니?
G 네, 선생님. 문제가 있어요. 자료를 충분히 찾는 데 어려움을 겪고 있어요.
M 네가 마을 초기 정착민들에 대해 쓰고 있는 거 맞지?
G 아, 아니요. 그건 제가 아니에요. Thomas인 것 같아요. 저는 초기 정착민들과 여기 살던 원주민들과의 관계에 대해 쓰려고 했어요.
M 아, 맞네. 마을 도서관에 원본 문서가 많이 있을 거야. 그걸 확인해 봐야겠지.
G 그게 문제예요. 사서분에게 여쭤봤는데, 서고에 들어가게 해 주지 않으셨어요. 제가 나이가 충분하지 않다고 하더라고요. 주제를 바꿔야 할지도 모르겠어요.
M 알겠네. 근데 주제를 바꾸지 않았으면 좋겠어.
G 하지만 그것에 대해 쓰기 위해 필요한 자료를 어떻게 찾으라고요?
M 오늘 방과 후에 내가 도서관에 가서 Reynolds 씨와 얘기해 볼게. 나랑 오래 알고 지낸 사이라서, 네가 서고에 들어갈 수 있게 해 주시도록 설득할 수 있을 거야.
G 와, 정말 좋네요. 저도 거기 같이 가도 될까요? 오늘 자료 조사를 시작하고 싶어요.
M 물론이지. 학교 끝나자마자 바로 가자.

5-8 Listen to a conversation between a student and his mother.

W How was your day at school today, Martin?
B The same as usual.
W I'm sorry to hear that. What happened today?
B I just don't like this school. It's not anything like my old school. The students aren't particularly friendly either. I've been there for two weeks now and haven't made a single friend yet.
W Are you trying to talk to any of the students?
B Yes, I am. But nobody seems to want to talk to me. Can't I go back to my old school?
W I'm sorry, Martin, but that's just not possible. We had to move to this city for your father's new job. Your old school is too far away for you to go back there to study.
B Yeah, but at least I was happy there.
W I understand how hard it can be to change schools in the middle of the semester. I had to do the same thing once when I was your age.
B Really? How did that go?
W I had a similar experience as you. But I didn't give up and kept trying to make friends. Eventually, I came to like my new school.
B Okay. I get it. I won't give up.

학생과 어머니가 나누는 대화를 들어 보세요.

W 오늘 학교에서 하루 어땠니, Martin?
B 늘 똑같아요.
W 안타깝구나. 오늘 무슨 일이 있었니?
B 그냥 이 학교가 싫어요. 예전 학교랑은 완전히 달라요. 학생들도 별로 친절하지 않아요. 여기 온 지 이제 2주가 됐는데 아직 친구 한 명도 못 사귀었어요.
W 학생들에게 먼저 말을 걸어 보려고는 하니?
B 네, 해요. 근데 아무도 저와 이야기하고 싶어 하는 것 같지 않아요. 예전 학교로 돌아갈 수는 없나요?
W 미안하지만, Martin, 그건 안 돼. 아빠 새 직장 때문에 우리가 이 도시로 이사해야 했잖니. 예전 학교는 너무 멀어서 돌아가서 다닐 수

없어.

B 그래요, 그렇지만 적어도 거기서는 행복했단 말이에요.

W 학기 중간에 학교를 바꾸는 게 얼마나 힘든지 이해해. 나도 네 나이 때 한 번 그래야 했던 적이 있어.

B 정말요? 어떻게 됐어요?

W 나도 너랑 비슷한 경험을 했지만, 포기하지 않고 친구를 사귀려고 계속 노력했어. 결국 새 학교를 좋아하게 됐어.

B 좋아요. 알겠어요. 포기하지 않을게요.

9-12 Listen to a conversation between two friends at school.

G Can you believe how much homework we have?

B I know. It's horrible, and this is only the first week of school. How bad do you think it is going to be a couple of months from now?

G Probably a lot worse.

B You can say that again. What classes do we have homework in again?

G English, history, science, math, and Spanish. At least I already did my math homework, so I don't have to take my book home.

B Lucky you. I've already put that book in my bag.

G Don't worry. If you paid attention in class, you should be able to solve the problems pretty quickly.

B That's good to know. How much of your book report have you written?

G I haven't even started on it. We've got to finish it by tomorrow, don't we?

B That's correct. I'm going to start writing it as soon as I arrive home. I guess we're going to have to study harder than ever before this year.

G You're probably right. Anyway, I imagine we'll get used to the heavier workload in a couple of weeks.

B Yeah. We're older now, so we're expected to work harder. Good luck finishing up your assignments. See you tomorrow.

학교에서 두 친구가 나누는 대화를 들어 보세요.

G 숙제가 얼마나 많은지 믿을 수 있어?

B 알아. 끔찍해. 그런데 이제 학교 첫 주밖에 안 됐잖아. 지금부터 두어 달 뒤에는 얼마나 심해질 것 같아?

G 아마 훨씬 더 심할걸.

B 맞아 우리 어떤 과목에 과제 있다고?

G 영어, 역사, 과학, 수학, 스페인어야. 적어도 나는 이미 수학 숙제 끝냈어. 책 안 가져가도 돼.

B 부럽다. 나는 벌써 책 가방에 넣었는데.

G 걱정 마. 수업 잘 들었으면 문제 금방 풀 수 있을 거야.

B 다행이다. 독후감은 얼마나 썼어?

G 아직 시작도 안 했어. 내일까지 끝내야 하잖아, 그렇지?

B 맞아. 나도 집에 가자마자 바로 쓰기 시작할 거야. 올해는 그 어느 때보다 더 열심히 공부해야 할 것 같아.

G 아마 그럴 거야. 그래도 몇 주 지나면 많은 공부량에도 익숙해질 거야.

B 맞아. 이제 나이도 더 들었으니까 더 열심히 해야겠지. 숙제 마무리 잘해. 내일 봐.

PRACTICE 2 Lecture/Discussion p. 110

1 (C)	2 (A)	3 (D)	4 (C)
5 (B)	6 (A)	7 (B)	8 (D)
9 (C)	10 (B)	11 (A)	12 (D)
13 (B)			

1-4 Listen to part of a talk in a science class.

M A couple of decades ago, acid rain was a huge problem in some places, especially in the Midwest. It's not so bad anymore, but some places still suffer from it. Acid rain, in case you don't know, is rain which is highly acidic. As a general rule, it is created when pollutants such as sulfur and nitrous oxide combine with water in clouds. They then fall to the ground as rain. These pollutants can be released by volcanoes when they erupt. However, most experts believe the burning of fossil fuels accounts for most acid rain. This means that vehicles, factories, and power plants are primarily responsible for acid rain.

Acid rain has a number of negative effects. It can damage lakes and ponds so much that all life in them dies. It's so sad to see beautiful lakes with absolutely no fish in them. It can also harm the soil it falls on. This makes farming the land difficult or even impossible. Acid rain further damages trees and exposes them to harm. It even damages buildings and statues that it falls on by eroding the stone they are made of. That sounds horrible, doesn't it? Fortunately, there are ways to eliminate acid rain and to restore the places that it affects.

과학 수업 중 강의 내용을 들어 보세요.

M 몇 십 년 전, 산성비는 특히 중서부 지역에서 큰 문제였습니다. 요즘은 예전만큼 심하지는 않지만, 아직도 일부 지역은 산성비의 피해를 보고 있습니다. 혹시 산성비가 뭔지 잘 모르는 학생들을 위해, 산성비란 산도가 매우 높은 비를 말합니다. 일반적으로 구름 속에서 황과 아산화질소 같은 오염 물질이 물과 결합하면 만들어지죠. 그리고는 비가 되어 땅으로 떨어지게 됩니다. 화산이 폭발할 때 오염 물질이 방출되지만, 대부분의 전문가들은 화석 연료를 태우는 것이 산성비의 주 원인이라고 보고 있습니다. 즉, 자동차, 공장, 발전소가 주로 산성비를 만들고 있다는 것입니다.

산성비는 여러 가지 부정적인 영향을 줍니다. 호수와 연못을 심하게 오염시켜 그 안의 생물이 모두 죽을 수도 있습니다. 아름다운 호수에 물고기가 한 마리도 없는 것을 보면 참 안타깝습니다. 또한, 산성비는 그것이 떨어진 토양을 오염시킵니다. 그 땅에서 농사를 짓기 어렵거나 아예 불가능해질 수도 있습니다. 산성비는 나무도 손상시키고, 피해에 노출시킵니다. 심지어 건물이나 조각상 같은 것들도 산성비가 내린 돌이 침식되어 훼손될 수 있습니다. 끔찍하지요? 다행히 산성비를 없애고 피해 지역을 복구할 방법들이 있습니다.

5-8 Listen to part of a discussion in a history class.

W The Great Pyramid of Giza was constructed more than 4,500 years ago. It was an enormous undertaking which took approximately twenty years to complete. Here's a picture of it . . . Now, I want you to think for a moment. In your opinion, what kinds of difficulties would the builders of that pyramid have faced?

B I think the biggest problem would have been getting the stones in place. I remember reading that some of those stones weigh around 2.5 tons. How did the Egyptians manage to lift those stones and move them into place?

W Yes, that must have been an enormous problem. Many historians believe they constructed ramps to get the stone blocks up to higher levels. Still, without horses or other pack animals, it must have been a very slow process to move the stones up.

B I just thought of something. How did they move the blocks from the quarries to the pyramid? I mean, uh, I just see sand in that picture. I don't think the rocks came from the local area. So where did they come from, and how did they get there?

W The stones were likely transported by ship down the Nile River. But that also must have been very difficult to do.

역사 수업 중 토론 내용의 일부를 들어 보세요.

W 기자의 대피라미드는 4,500년 이상 전에 지어졌습니다. 완공하는 데 약 20년이 걸린 대규모 공사였죠. 여기 사진을 보세요…. 이제 잠시 생각해 봅시다. 여러분 생각에는 그 피라미드를 건설한 사람들이 어떤 어려움에 직면했을까요?

B 가장 큰 문제는 돌을 제자리에 올리는 것이었을 것 같아요. 어떤 돌은 약 2.5톤이나 된다고 읽은 적이 있어요. 이집트인들은 그 돌들을 어떻게 들어 올리고 제자리에 놓았을까요?

W 맞아요, 정말 큰 문제였을 거예요. 많은 역사학자들은 돌을 높은 층으로 올리기 위해 경사로를 만들었을 것이라고 믿고 있어요. 그래도 말이나 다른 짐승이 없이 돌을 올리는 과정은 매우 느렸을 거예요.

B 방금 생각났는데요. 돌을 채석장에서 피라미드까지 어떻게 옮겼을까요? 사진에는 모래밖에 안 보이는데요. 돌이 근처에서 채석된 게 아닐 것 같아요. 어디서 가져왔고 어떻게 옮겼을까요?

W 돌은 나일강을 따라 배로 운반되었을 가능성이 높아요. 하지만 그것도 매우 어려운 일이었을 테죠.

9-13 Listen to part of a talk in a science class.

W In 1977, NASA, the American space agency, launched two space probes: *Voyager 1* and *Voyager 2*. Their primary mission was to explore the outer planets of the solar system and then to depart the solar system. Both probes exceeded the wildest dreams of their creators.

Voyager 1 launched around two weeks after *Voyager 2*. It passed by both Jupiter and Saturn on its way out of the solar system. NASA then had to choose between doing a flyby of Titan, a moon of Saturn, or Pluto, a dwarf planet. Titan was selected in order to examine its atmosphere. As for *Voyager 2*, it flew by all four outer planets: Jupiter, Saturn, Uranus, and Neptune. It is the only probe to have reached Uranus and Neptune. The two probes explored the rings of the planets, their atmospheres, their moons, and many other aspects of the planets.

The probes then headed out of the solar system. Even today, NASA remains in contact with both probes. Their computer systems are primitive by modern standards. Yet they can still send information back to the Earth. In addition, NASA is still capable of fixing problems with the probes. In 2025, it managed to activate some of *Voyager 1*'s thrusters. They had been inactive since 2004. This will help the probe as it continues its journey into interstellar space.

과학 수업 중 강의 내용의 일부를 들어 보세요.

W 1977년, 미국 항공우주국 NASA는 두 개의 우주 탐사선, 보이저 1호와 보이저 2호를 발사했습니다. 이들의 주 임무는 태양계 외행성을 탐사한 후 태양계를 벗어나는 것이었습니다. 두 탐사선 모두 제작자들의 기대를 훨씬 뛰어넘는 성과를 거두었죠.

보이저 1호는 보이저 2호보다 약 2주 뒤에 발사되었습니다. 태양계를 떠나는 길에 목성과 토성을 지나갔습니다. 이후 NASA는 토성의 위성인 타이탄을 근접 탐사할지, 아니면 왜행성인 명왕성을 근접 탐사할지 결정해야 했습니다. 대기를 조사하기 위해 타이탄이 선택되었습니다. 한편, 보이저 2호는 네 개의 외행성, 즉 목성, 토성, 천왕성, 해왕성을 모두 지나갔습니다. 천왕성과 해왕성에 도달한 유일한 탐사선이기도 합니다. 두 탐사선은 행성의 고리, 대기, 위성, 그리고 행성의 다양한 특성을 탐사했습니다.

탐사선들은 이후 태양계를 벗어나 밖으로 향했습니다. 오늘날에도 NASA는 두 탐사선과 계속 연락을 유지하고 있습니다. 탐사선들의 컴퓨터 시스템은 현대 기준으로 볼 때 원시적이지만, 여전히 지구로 정보를 보낼 수 있습니다. 또한 NASA는 여전히 탐사선의 문제를 해결할 수도 있습니다. 예를 들어 2025년에는 보이저 1호의 추진기 일부를 재가동하는 데 성공했습니다. 이 추진기는 2004년 이후 작동하지 않았었죠. 이로 인해 탐사선이 앞으로 성간 우주 여행을 이어가는 데 도움이 될 것입니다.

PRACTICE TEST p. 116

1 (A)	2 (C)	3 (A)	4 (C)
5 (B)	6 (D)	7 (C)	8 (B)
9 (B)	10 (C)	11 (A)	12 (D)

1-4 Listen to a conversation between a student and a teacher.

G Mr. Foss, I was sick and couldn't come to school yesterday. What did I miss in class?

M I'm really sorry to hear that, Katie. A lot of students have been missing school these days. Are you feeling better now?

G I'm mostly fine. I didn't want to miss more than one day of school since exams are coming up soon. So that's why I'm here.

M That's a good attitude to have. As for yesterday, I lectured for about half of the class. Then, we conducted a lab experiment, so you missed that.

G Oh, no. Lab experiments are my favorite.

M I know. I remember how excited you got when we did the last one.

G Can I come here after school and do the experiment by myself?

M Unfortunately, students aren't permitted to conduct experiments alone. And I've got a staff meeting that's going to last until around 5:00 this evening.

G So . . . when can I do it?

M How about either after school tomorrow or during lunch?

G I've got volleyball practice right after school tomorrow. Coach Moore hates when any of the players are late. How about doing it at lunchtime?

M I'll see you here at noon then.

학생과 선생님이 나누는 대화를 들어 보세요.

G Foss 선생님, 저 어제 아파서 학교에 못 왔어요. 제가 수업에서 뭘 놓쳤나요?

M 그 말을 들으니 안타깝구나, Katie. 요즘 많은 학생들이 결석하고 있어. 지금은 좀 나아졌니?

G 거의 괜찮아요. 시험이 곧 다가와서 하루 이상 결석하고 싶지 않았어요. 그래서 오늘 나온 거예요.

M 좋은 태도야. 어제 수업은 절반 정도 강의를 했고, 나머지 시간에는 실험을 했어. 네가 그 부분을 놓친 거지.

G 아, 저런. 저 실험 제일 좋아하는데.

M 알지. 지난번 실험 때 네가 얼마나 신나했는지 기억나.

G 수업 끝나고 여기 와서 혼자 실험해도 될까요?

M 안타깝게도 학생 혼자 실험하는 건 허락되지 않아. 게다가 나는 오늘 저녁 5시까지 교사 회의가 있어.

G 그러면… 언제 할 수 있나요?

M 내일 방과 후나 점심 시간 중 하나는 어때?

G 내일 방과 후에는 곧바로 배구 연습이 있어요. Moore 코치님은 선수들이 늦는 걸 싫어하세요. 점심 시간에 하면 어떨까요?

M 그럼 정오에 여기서 보자.

5-8 Listen to a conversation between two students at school.

B I'm getting really tired of the food at the cafeteria these days. I mean, uh, look at this food.

G I couldn't agree more. This spaghetti is just awful.

B You're right. And how do you mess up spaghetti? I don't even understand how that's possible.

G We ought to complain to the administration.

B Several students did that earlier in the semester, but the principal said she couldn't do anything about the food.

G That's too bad. So what are you going to do?

B I think I'm going to bring my lunch from home starting tomorrow.

G Really? Does anyone else do that?

B I've seen a few other students do that. If more of us refuse to eat the cafeteria food, the school will have to take action.

G Oh, yeah. That's a really good point. I hadn't considered that. Plus, you'll actually like the food that you're eating.

B Exactly. Half the time, I don't even eat my lunch, so I go hungry until I get home from school and have a snack.

G It's the same with me. I'm going to ask my parents to pack me a lunch from now on. Thanks for the great suggestion.

학교에서 두 학생이 나누는 대화를 들어 보세요.

B 요즘 학교 식당 음식 정말 지겨워. 내 말은, 으, 이 음식 좀 봐.

G 나도 완전히 동의해. 이 스파게티는 정말 형편없어.

B 맞아. 그런데 스파게티를 어떻게 망칠 수 있는 거야? 그게 어떻게 가능한지 도저히 이해가 안 돼.

G 우리 교무처에 항의해야 해.

B 학기 초에 몇몇 학생이 그렇게 했지만, 교장 선생님께서 음식에 대해선 아무것도 할 수 없다고 하셨어.

G 안타깝다. 그럼 넌 어떻게 할 거야?

B 내일부터 집에서 도시락을 가져올 생각이야.

G 정말? 다른 학생들도 그렇게 해?

B 몇몇 학생이 그렇게 하는 걸 본 적 있어. 만약 더 많은 학생이 학교 식당 음식을 거부하면, 학교가 조치를 취할 수밖에 없을 거야.

G 오, 그래. 그거 좋은 생각이네. 나는 그걸 생각 못 했어. 게다가 네가 실제로 먹는 음식이 마음에 들 거야.

B 맞아. 절반 정도는 점심을 안 먹어서 학교 끝나고 집에 가서 간식 먹을 때까지 배고파.

G 나도 똑같아. 앞으로 부모님께 도시락 싸 달라고 해야겠어. 좋은 아이디어 고마워.

9-12 Listen to part of a talk in a science class.

M Everyone knows the highest spot on the Earth is

Mount Everest. But what about the lowest spot on the planet? It's found deep beneath the Pacific Ocean east of the island of Guam. It's called the Mariana Trench. It's so deep that if you could put Mount Everest in there, there would still be more than a mile of water above the mountain.

The Mariana Trench is more than 35,000 feet below sea level. It stretches more than 1,500 miles and has an average width of more than forty miles. It varies in deepness, but the deepest part is called the Challenger Deep. Down that deep, the water is extremely cold, and it is pitch black because no light can penetrate that far beneath the surface. The water pressure is also intense, being around one thousand times as strong as it is on the surface.

Yet even in such harsh conditions, there is life in the Challenger Deep. Four submersibles have dived down to it, and they discovered sea cucumbers, shrimp, and worms. A large number of single-celled organisms were discovered down there as well. Look up here on the screen. You can see some pictures that were taken in the Challenger Deep. Here . . . and here . . . and here . . . Imagine getting to go there in person. It really is beautiful despite being so inhospitable, isn't it?

과학 수업 중 강의 내용의 일부를 들어 보세요.

M 모두 알다시피, 지구에서 가장 높은 곳은 에베레스트산입니다. 그런데 지구에서 가장 낮은 곳은 어디일까요? 그것은 괌섬 동쪽 태평양 아래 깊은 곳에 있습니다. 이곳을 마리아나 해구라고 부릅니다. 깊이가 너무 깊어서 만약 에베레스트산을 거기에 넣는다고 해도 산 위에 여전히 1마일 이상의 물이 남아 있을 정도입니다.

마리아나 해구는 해수면 아래 35,000피트 이상에 위치해 있습니다. 길이는 1,500마일이 넘고 평균 폭은 40마일 이상입니다. 깊이는 지역마다 다르지만, 가장 깊은 곳을 챌린저 해연이라고 합니다. 이곳은 물이 매우 차갑고, 수면 아래 그렇게 깊은 곳에는 빛이 전혀 도달하지 않아 완전히 어둡습니다. 또한 수압이 매우 강한데, 수면에서 수압의 약 1,000배에 달합니다.

그런 극한 환경 속에서도 챌린저 해연에는 생명이 존재합니다. 지금까지 네 척의 잠수정이 이곳을 탐사했고, 해삼, 새우, 벌레들을 발견했습니다. 단세포 생물도 그곳에서 많이 발견되었죠. 여기 위쪽 화면을 보세요. 여기… 여기… 그리고 여기…. 챌린저 해연에서 찍힌 사진들입니다. 직접 그곳에 간다고 상상해 보세요. 매우 극한 환경임에도 불구하고 정말 아름답지 않나요?

CHAPTER 07 PROSODY

PRACTICE 1 Conversation p. 121

1 (B)	2 (A)	3 (A)	4 (B)
5 (C)	6 (B)	7 (C)	8 (D)
9 (C)	10 (D)	11 (A)	12 (B)

1-4 Listen to a conversation between a student and a school counselor.

M Good afternoon, Julie. Thanks for coming to my office. Have a seat, please.

G Thank you, sir.

M I know you're busy, so I won't waste any time with small talk. I'd like to talk about your grades.

G My grades? I . . . I thought I was doing fine this semester.

M You're actually do more than fine. Your teachers showed me your midterm exam grades, and you got all A's on them. Well done.

G Oh, wow. I had no idea. No teachers have given them back yet.

M Expect them tomorrow. You know, two years ago, you were a C and B student. Last year, you mostly got B's. This year, you are continuing to show steady improvement. Congratulations.

G Thanks. My mom and dad have been helping me study after school every night. They deserve the credit.

M Well, I think you have had quite a lot to do with it, too. Now, uh, one more thing . . . Coach Brady talked to me about you. He has seen you in P.E. class and wants you to try out for the basketball team.

G Really? I don't think I'm that good.

M That's not what he said. Why don't you have a talk with him after school today?

G Okay. I suppose I can do that.

학생과 학교 상담 선생님이 나누는 대화를 들어 보세요.

M 안녕, Julie. 내 사무실에 와 줘서 고마워. 앉으렴.

G 감사합니다, 선생님.

M 바쁜 거 아니까 잡담으로 시간 낭비는 하지 않을게. 네 성적에 대해 얘기하고 싶어.

G 제 성적요? 저는… 이번 학기에 괜찮게 하고 있는 줄 알았는데요.

M 사실 괜찮은 정도가 아니라 아주 잘하고 있어. 선생님들이 네 중간고사 성적을 보여 주셨는데, 모두 A를 받았어. 잘했어.

G 오, 우와. 전혀 몰랐어요. 선생님들이 아직 성적을 돌려주지 않으셨어요.

M 내일 받을 거야. 그러고 보니 너 2년 전에는 C랑 B를 받는 학생이었고, 작년에는 대부분 B를 받았지. 올해는 꾸준한 향상을 보여 주고 있어. 축하해.

G 감사합니다. 방과 후에 매일 저녁 부모님께서 공부를 도와주고 계세요. 부모님 덕분이에요.

M 그렇지만 너도 충분히 노력했기 때문에 이만큼 성과를 낸 거야. 이제 한 가지 더…. Brady 코치 선생님이 너에 대해 얘기하셨어. 체육 시간에 너를 보셨는데 네가 농구 팀 선발 테스트를 봤으면 좋겠다고 하시더구나.

G 정말요? 제가 그렇게 잘하는 것 같지 않은데요.

M 그분 말씀은 그렇지 않았어. 오늘 방과 후에 그분과 한번 이야기해 보는 게 어때?

G 네, 그렇게 할 수 있을 것 같아요.

5-8 Listen to a conversation between two friends at school.

G Jason, you're going to the birthday party after school today, right?

B Birthday party?

G Yeah, the surprise party for David. Melissa told us about it in class yesterday. Don't you remember?

B I wasn't at school yesterday. I was at an academic competition all day long, so I had no idea there's a party happening today.

G Well, she invited everyone in the class. So even though you weren't there, you can still go.

B When and where is it?

G It's right after school. Everyone is going to David's house, which is right across the street from school.

B Oh, wait. I don't have a present for him. What should I do?

G David won't show up at his house until around 3:30. Ms. Marsh promised us she would talk to him about his class presentation after school and keep him late for us. So you'll have time to drop by a store really quickly to purchase him something.

B Wow. You all have thought of everything. This sounds like a fun time. You can count me in.

G Wonderful. Just be sure not to say anything to him. We don't want to ruin the surprise.

B I won't say a word. There's no way I would mess this kind of thing up.

학교에서 두 친구가 나누는 대화를 들어 보세요.

G Jason, 오늘 방과 후에 생일 파티 가는 거지?

B 생일 파티?

G 응, David를 위한 깜짝 파티야. Melissa가 어제 수업 시간에 얘기해 줬잖아. 기억 안 나?

B 어제 학교에 없었어. 하루 종일 경시대회에 있어서 오늘 파티가 있는 줄 전혀 몰랐어.
G 음, 그 애가 반 친구들 모두 초대했어. 그러니까 네가 어제 없었어도 갈 수 있어.
B 언제 어디서 하는데?
G 방과 후에 바로. 모두 David네 집에 갈 거야. 학교 바로 맞은편이지.
B 아, 잠깐. 걔한테 줄 선물이 없는데, 어떻게 하지?
G David는 3시 30분쯤 돼야 집에 올 거야. Marsh 선생님이 방과 후에 걔랑 수업 발표에 대해 얘기하면서 조금 늦게 집에 가게 해 주시기로 약속하셨어. 그러니까 잠깐 가게에 들러서 뭔가 살 시간은 있어.
B 와, 모든 걸 생각했구나. 재밌겠다. 나도 끼워 줘.
G 좋아. 그 애한테 절대 말하지 마. 깜짝 파티 망치면 안 되니까.
B 한마디도 안 할게. 이런 걸 망칠 수는 없지.

9-12 Listen to a conversation between a student and a teacher.

M Carrie, I'm going to be taking a small group of students fossil hunting next weekend. I know you're interested in dinosaurs. Would you like to go?
G Totally. When are you going?
M We'll be leaving early on Saturday morning and coming back on Saturday night.
G It's not an overnight trip? I thought you usually did that.
M Everyone who's going said they aren't interested in camping. Plus, it's supposed to rain on Sunday, so we'll just make this a one-day trip.
G That makes sense. Where will you be digging for fossils?
M We're driving out to the river about an hour from school. There's a place where lots of fossils are already exposed, so we won't even need to dig much.
G It sounds like a lot of fun. But I need to ask my parents for permission before I can go.
M That's totally understandable. Can you let me know by tomorrow morning?
G Of course. I'll find out tonight when they get home. I'll email you their response at once.
M Thanks a lot. Oh, you won't need to bring any digging equipment. I have enough for everybody.
G That's good to know. Thanks. I really hope they permit me to go.

학생과 선생님이 나누는 대화를 들어 보세요.

M Carrie, 다음 주말에 학생 몇 명 데리고 화석 채집하러 갈 거야. 네가 공룡에 관심 있는 거 알아. 같이 갈래?
G 정말 가고 싶어요. 언제 가시나요?
M 토요일 아침 일찍 출발해서 토요일 밤에 돌아올 거야.
G 1박 여행이 아닌가요? 보통 그러시는 줄 알았는데.
M 참석자들이 캠핑에 관심 없대. 게다가 일요일은 비가 온대서 당일 일정으로 할 거야.
G 말이 되네요. 어디서 화석을 캐나요?
M 학교에서 차로 한 시간 정도 떨어진 강가로 갈 거야. 이미 화석이 많이 노출된 곳이 있어서 많이 캘 필요도 없어.
G 재밌겠네요. 그런데 가기 전에 부모님께 허락을 받아야 해요.
M 당연하지. 내일 아침까지 알려 줄 수 있겠니?
G 그럼요. 오늘 밤에 부모님이 오시면 여쭤보고 바로 메일로 선생님께 그분들의 대답을 알려 드릴게요.
M 고마워. 아, 굴착 장비는 가져올 필요 없어. 내가 다 준비했거든.
G 좋네요. 감사합니다. 갈 수 있게 부모님이 꼭 허락하셨으면 좋겠어요.

PRACTICE 2 Lecture/Discussion p. 126

1 (A)	2 (C)	3 (D)	4 (C)
5 (D)	6 (D)	7 (B)	8 (B)
9 (B)	10 (B)	11 (C)	12 (A)
13 (D)			

1-5 Listen to a talk in a history class.

W One reason the Roman Empire was so successful was its roads. There were more than 120,000 kilometers of roads throughout the empire. These included the Appian Way, or the Via Appia in Latin. It's arguably the most famous Roman road. Roman roads were as straight as possible. Their roads were constructed to let soldiers, travelers, and merchants get from one point to another as quickly as possible.

Some Roman roads still exist today. It seems impossible, doesn't it? But that's a testament to their building ability. You're probably wondering how they managed to construct roads which have lasted around 2,000 years. Well, let me tell you. Major Roman roads were a standard 4.2 meters wide. This was, in Roman times, wide enough for two wheeled vehicles to pass each other in opposite directions. To make them, first, the Romans dug a trench and then put sand or compacted dry soil above it. The next layer was large stones or pieces of brick around twenty centimeters thick. Above that layer was the *rudus*. It contained gravel and mortar to bind the stones together. The following layer was the *nucleus*. It had fine gravel and crushed stones. Last was the *pavimentum*. It contained a layer of stone slabs closely fitted together. These stones were inclined slightly from the center, which allowed rainwater to run off the sides. Ingenious, wasn't it?

역사 수업 중 강의 내용을 들어 보세요.

W 로마 제국이 그렇게 성공할 수 있었던 이유 중 하나는 도로입니다. 제국 전역에는 12만킬로미터가 넘는 도로가 있었어요. 그중에는 아

피아 가도, 라틴어로는 Via Appia가 포함됩니다. 아마도 가장 유명한 로마 도로일 거예요. 로마의 도로는 가능한 한 직선으로 만들어졌습니다. 병사, 여행자, 상인이 한 지점에서 다른 지점으로 가능한 한 빠르게 이동할 수 있도록 건설된 것이죠.

오늘날에도 일부 로마 도로가 남아 있습니다. 있을 수 없는 일 같죠? 하지만 이것이 그들의 건축 능력을 보여 주는 증거예요. 아마 어떻게 2,000년 가까이 지속된 도로를 만들었는지 궁금할 거예요. 말해 줄게요. 주요 로마 도로는 표준 너비가 4.2미터였습니다. 당시 로마에서 양방향으로 바퀴 달린 차량 두 대가 지나가기 충분한 넓이였죠. 도로를 만들기 위해 먼저 로마인들은 도랑을 파고 그 위에 모래나 다져진 건조된 흙을 깔았습니다. 다음 층은 약 20센티미터 두께의 큰 돌이나 벽돌 조각이었어요. 그 위에는 루두스 층이 있었습니다. 이 층에는 자갈과 모르타르가 들어 있어 돌을 서로 단단히 결합시켰죠. 그 다음 층은 누클레우스였는데, 고운 자갈과 부순 돌로 이루어졌습니다. 마지막으로 파비멘툼 층이 있었는데, 돌판을 촘촘히 맞춰 깔았어요. 이 돌들은 중앙에서 약간 기울어져 있어 빗물이 양쪽으로 흘러가게 했습니다. 정말 기발하지 않나요?

6-9 Listen to part of a discussion in a social studies class.

M The Great Depression started in the United States in 1929. It didn't end until after World War II began in 1941. This was not just an economic depression in the U.S. though. It affected countries around the world. Can anyone tell me what started it?

G In October 1929, the stock market crashed. This is when people traditionally say that it began. However, uh, before that time, there were obvious bad financial conditions which resulted in the Great Depression happening.

M You're right about that. In the 1920s, people in the United States started investing in the stock market. However, the economic situation then wasn't great. Unemployment was high, and people really couldn't afford to be investing in stocks.

G Right. So when the market crashed, plenty of people lost their life savings. Companies went bankrupt, so people also lost their jobs. Then, the federal government began interfering, particularly by introducing the programs in the New Deal. The New Deal itself caused the depression to last much longer than it should have.

M That's a great point. However, you're getting a bit ahead of the discussion. Let's focus on the reasons that the Great Depression started. We can cover how government interference caused economic problems during the depression a bit later.

사회 수업 중 토론 내용의 일부를 들어 보세요.

M 대공황은 1929년에 미국에서 시작됐어요. 1941년 제2차 세계대전이 시작될 때까지 끝나지 않았죠. 근데 이건 미국만의 경제 불황이 아니었어요. 전 세계의 나라들에 영향을 미쳤거든요. 대공황이 어떻게 시작됐는지 누가 말해 줄 수 있나요?

G 1929년 10월에 주식 시장이 폭락했어요. 보통 사람들이 그때를 시작으로 이야기하죠. 하지만 그 이전에도 명백히 안 좋은 금융 상황이 있어서 대공황이 발생하게 되었어요.

M 맞아요. 1920년대 미국 사람들은 주식 시장에 투자하기 시작했죠. 하지만 당시 경제 상황이 좋지는 않았어요. 실업률이 높았고, 사람들은 주식에 투자할 여유가 사실 없었거든요.

G 맞아요. 그래서 시장이 폭락했을 때 많은 사람들이 평생 모은 돈을 잃었어요. 기업들이 파산하면서 사람들도 일자리를 잃었죠. 그 후 연방 정부가 개입하기 시작했는데, 특히 뉴딜 정책을 도입하면서요. 뉴딜 정책 자체가 대공황을 원래 그랬어야 할 것보다 훨씬 오래 지속되게 만들었어요.

M 좋은 지적이에요. 하지만 얘기가 조금 앞서가고 있어요. 대공황이 시작된 이유에 집중해 보죠. 공황 중에 정부 개입이 어떻게 경제 문제를 일으켰는지는 나중에 다루고요.

10-13 Listen to a talk in a science class.

M Nature is violent. There are predators and prey, and predators are always on the hunt for their next meal. We often think of prey animals as being helpless. But that's not actually the case. There are numerous defenses that animals have. Some are pretty standard, such as sharp teeth and claws. Even prey animals such as squirrels, rabbits, and mice have those. They can bite and scratch attackers to protect themselves. Other animals, including deer, zebras, and gazelles, have great speed. They can use it to flee from attacking wolves, lions, and other animals. And some animals use camouflage. They can hide from predators to avoid being killed. Rabbits, chameleons, and turtles use this defense mechanism.

There are, however, other types of defenses which are not standard. These may be unique to a single animal or to a small group of animals. The skunk, for instance, can spray liquid that has a terrible smell at animals. This effectively keeps most predators away from it. The porcupine has extremely sharp quills. These can detach and get stuck in the bodies of animals attacking it. They're quite painful and often convince predators to leave it alone. The armadillo has a very tough exterior that's almost like armor. It can roll itself into a ball when attacked. This protects it from most predators.

과학 수업 중 강의 내용을 들어 보세요.

M 자연은 거칠어요. 포식자와 먹이가 있고, 포식자는 항상 다음 먹잇감을 찾아 다니죠. 우리는 먹이 동물들을 무력하다고 생각하지만, 실제로는 그렇지 않습니다. 동물들은 다양한 방어 수단을 가지고 있거든요. 일부 방어 수단은 꽤 일반적이에요. 날카로운 이빨과 발톱 같은 것들이죠. 다람쥐, 토끼, 쥐 같은 먹이 동물들도 그걸 가지고 있어요. 공격자를 물거나 할퀴어서 자신을 보호할 수 있습니다. 또 다른 동물들은, 예를 들어 사슴, 얼룩말, 가젤 같은 경우, 엄청난 속도

를 가지고 있어서 공격하는 늑대, 사자 및 다른 동물로부터 도망칠 수 있죠. 그리고 일부 동물들은 위장을 사용합니다. 포식자에게 죽임당하지 않도록 몸을 숨기는 거예요. 토끼, 카멜레온, 거북이가 이런 방어 수단을 사용합니다.

그런데 표준적이지 않은 다른 종류의 방어 수단도 있어요. 이런 것들은 특정 동물이나 소수의 동물만 가진 경우가 많습니다. 예를 들어 스컹크는 동물에게 심한 냄새가 나는 액체를 뿌릴 수 있어요. 덕분에 대부분의 포식자가 접근하지 못합니다. 호저는 매우 날카로운 가시를 가지고 있어요. 이것은 몸에서 떨어져 나와 그것을 공격하는 동물의 몸에 박힐 수 있죠. 그건 꽤 아프고, 포식자를 물러나게 만들기도 해요. 아르마딜로는 거의 갑옷 같은 단단한 외피를 가지고 있어요. 공격당하면 몸을 공처럼 말 수 있어서 대부분의 포식자로부터 자신을 보호할 수 있습니다.

PRACTICE TEST p. 132

1 (B)	2 (C)	3 (C)	4 (C)
5 (B)	6 (D)	7 (A)	8 (C)
9 (C)	10 (A)	11 (C)	12 (C)

1-4 Listen to a conversation between two friends at school.

B Hi, Jennifer. Do you mind if I sit here and have lunch with you?

G Not at all, Mark. Go ahead and have a seat.

B Thanks a lot . . . Uh, if you don't mind . . . I have a question.

G Sure.

B How did you do on the math test we got back today?

G I got a ninety-eight on it. I actually got the right answer on the problem I missed, but I wrote it down incorrectly on the answer sheet. It was so frustrating. How did you do?

B Um . . . I got a sixty-seven.

G Oh . . . I'm really sorry to hear that. What happened?

B I don't understand how to solve these problems. Algebra is just too difficult for me. I especially have trouble with word problems.

G Really? Those are so fun to do. I love when the teacher gives us those.

B You understand them? In that case, um . . . would you mind showing me how to solve them? I pay attention in class, but I have trouble understanding Mr. Stigler's explanations. Do you think you could try teaching me what to do?

G I'll do my best. Let me finish eating lunch, and we can go over some problems. I've got my math book right here.

학교에서 두 친구가 나누는 대화를 들어 보세요.

B 안녕, Jennifer. 여기 앉아서 같이 점심 먹어도 돼?

G 당연하지, Mark. 와서 앉아.

B 정말 고마워…. 근데, 괜찮으면… 질문이 하나 있어.

G 말해 봐.

B 오늘 받은 수학 시험 결과 어떻게 나왔어?

G 98점 맞았어. 사실 틀린 문제도 답은 맞았는데, 답안지에 잘못 적었어. 진짜 짜증 났어. 너는 어땠어?

B 음…. 67점 나왔어.

G 아…. 안됐다. 무슨 일이 있었던 거야?

B 문제 푸는 방법을 잘 모르겠어. 대수학이 너무 어려워. 특히 문장제 문제는 더 힘들어.

G 정말? 그거 되게 재미있는데. 선생님이 그 문제 내 주실 때 좋더라.

B 이해가 돼? 그럼, 음… 혹시 나한테 푸는 방법 좀 가르쳐 줄래? 수업 때 집중해서 듣는데, Stigler 선생님 설명을 이해하기 힘들거든. 나한테 어떻게 해야 하는지 가르쳐 줄 수 있을까?

G 최선을 다해 볼게. 점심 다 먹고 나서 몇 문제 같이 풀어 보자. 내 수학책 여기 있어.

5-8 Listen to a conversation between a student and a teacher.

M Brenda, I really liked the poem you wrote in class on Monday. What inspired you to write on that particular topic?

G Thank you for saying that, Mr. Hooper. I was walking in the forest near my house the other day, so there were pictures of the things I saw there in my mind when I wrote the poem.

M Well, the imagery was fantastic. The vocabulary was also well chosen.

G Thank you, sir.

M If you don't mind, I'm going to submit it to the student yearbook committee. Two or three poems written by students are printed in it each year. I believe yours should have that honor.

G Oh, wow. I don't mind at all. I'm glad you think so highly of my work.

M Actually, I'm impressed with your overall writing talent.

G What do you mean?

M You have a knack for putting words together to make phrases and sentences. Have you considered writing for the student magazine? I think you'd be good at it.

G I don't know if I have enough time. I already play a sport, I belong to two clubs, and I work part time on weekends.

M It's not a major commitment. You'd only need to write one article a month. Why don't you think about it?

G Okay. I'll get back to you tomorrow.

학생과 선생님이 나누는 대화를 들어 보세요.

M Brenda, 월요일 수업 시간에 네가 쓴 시 정말 좋았어. 무슨 영감으로 그 주제에 대해 쓴 거야?

G 말씀 감사합니다, Hooper 선생님. 얼마 전에 집 근처 숲속을 산책

했는데, 시를 쓸 때 거기서 본 이미지들이 머릿속에 떠올랐어요.

M 음, 이미지가 정말 환상적이었어. 단어 선택도 좋았고.

G 감사합니다, 선생님.

M 괜찮다면, 이걸 학생 연감 위원회에 제출할 생각이야. 매년 학생이 쓴 시 두세 편이 실리거든. 네 시가 그 영예를 가져야 한다고 생각해.

G 오, 우와. 전혀 문제없어요. 제 작품을 그렇게 높이 평가해 주셔서 기뻐요.

M 사실 네 전체적인 글쓰기 재능이 인상적이야.

G 무슨 말씀이세요?

M 단어를 조합해서 구와 문장을 만드는 감각이 있거든. 혹시 학생 잡지에 글 쓰는 것 고려해 본 적 있어? 잘할 것 같아.

G 시간이 충분할지 모르겠어요. 이미 운동도 하고, 동아리도 두 개 들어가 있고, 주말에는 아르바이트도 하거든요.

M 부담은 크지 않아. 한 달에 기사 하나만 쓰면 돼. 생각 좀 해 보는 게 어때?

G 알겠습니다. 내일 다시 말씀드릴게요.

9-12 Listen to a talk in an art class.

W The Renaissance was a time when some of the greatest works of art ever were created. Artists like Michelangelo, Leonardo da Vinci, Botticelli, and Donatello lived then. They made impressive, timeless works. I, however, am partial to Raphael. I consider him by far the greatest Renaissance artist.

Raphael was born in 1583 and died in 1620. He lived in Urbino, a city in the central part of Italy. His father was an artist and taught Raphael painting as a young boy. Unfortunately, his father died when Raphael was eleven. Nevertheless, he continued to improve his skills as an artist. He later began traveling, going to Perugia, Florence, and Rome. Raphael became a well-known painter and was commissioned to make paintings by rich individuals and the Church.

He was employed by Pope Julius II to make what I consider his greatest work: *The School of Athens*. There's a picture of it on page 128 in your books. Take a look at it . . . It's a fresco painted on a wall in a building in the Vatican. It shows some of the greatest philosophers of ancient Greece. You can see Aristotle here . . . Socrates . . . Plato . . . and many others.

He also painted *The Sistine Madonna*. Here It Is . . . What a gorgeous painting. Let me show you a few things in this painting.

미술 수업 중 강의 내용을 들어 보세요.

W 르네상스는 역사상 가장 위대한 예술 작품들이 탄생한 시기였습니다. 미켈란젤로, 레오나르도 다 빈치, 보티첼리, 도나텔로 같은 예술가들이 살았던 시기죠. 이들은 인상적이고 시대를 초월한 작품들을 남겼습니다. 하지만 저는 개인적으로 라파엘로를 특히 좋아합니다. 저는 그가 르네상스 시대 예술가 중 가장 뛰어나다고 생각합니다.

라파엘로는 1583년에 태어나 1620년에 사망했습니다. 그는 이탈리아 중부의 우르비노라는 도시에서 살았죠. 아버지가 예술가여서 어린 시절부터 라파엘로에게 그림을 가르쳤습니다. 안타깝게도 아버지는 라파엘로가 열한 살 때 돌아가셨지만, 그는 계속해서 예술가로서의 실력을 키워 나갔습니다. 이후 그는 여행을 다니기 시작해 페루자, 피렌체, 로마를 방문했습니다. 라파엘로는 유명한 화가가 되었고, 부유한 개인과 교회로부터 그림 제작 의뢰를 받았습니다.

그는 교황 율리우스 2세의 의뢰를 받아 제가 가장 위대한 작품이라고 생각하는 《아테네 학당》을 제작했습니다. 교과서 128페이지에 그림이 있으니 한번 보세요…. 이것은 바티칸의 한 건물 벽에 그려진 프레스코화로, 고대 그리스의 위대한 철학자들을 보여 주고 있습니다. 여기에서 아리스토텔레스… 소크라테스… 플라톤… 그 외에 많은 철학자들을 볼 수 있습니다.

라파엘로는 또한 《시스티나 마돈나》도 그렸어요. 여기 있네요…. 정말 아름다운 그림이죠. 이 그림에서 몇 가지 주목할 만한 점들을 보여 줄게요.

MEMO

MEMO

MEMO

MEMO

MEMO

MEMO

MEMO

The Best TOEFL Junior®